McCampbell's HEROES

McCampbell's
HEROES

The Story of the U.S. Navy's Most Celebrated Carrier Fighters of the Pacific War

Edwin P. Hoyt

Introduction by Captain David McCampbell

VNR **VAN NOSTRAND REINHOLD COMPANY**
New York Cincinnati Toronto London Melbourne

Copyright © 1983 by Van Nostrand Reinhold Company Inc.

Library of Congress Catalog Card Number 82-17462

ISBN 0-442-26289-2

Printed in the United States of America
Designed by Mort Perry

Published by Van Nostrand Reinhold Company Inc.
135 West 50th Street
New York, New York 10020

Fleet Publishers
1410 Birchmount Road
Scarborough, Ontario M1P 2E7, Canada

Van Nostrand Reinhold
480 Latrobe Street
Melbourne, Victoria 3000, Australia

Van Nostrand Reinhold Company Limited
Molly Millars Lane
Wokingham, Berkshire, England RG11 2PY

16 15 14 13 12 11 10 9 8 7 6 5 4 3 2 1

Library of Congress Cataloging in Publication Data

Hoyt, Edwin Palmer.
    McCampbell's heroes.

    Includes index.
    1. World War, 1939-1945—Aerial operations, American.
2. United States. Navy. Air Group Fifteen—History.
3. World War, 1939-1945—Naval operations, American.
4. World War, 1939-1945—Pacific Ocean. I. Title.
D790.H73   940.54'4973   82-17462
ISBN 0-442-26289-2

CONTENTS

INTRODUCTION

It was my pleasure to meet Edwin Hoyt and his lovely wife, Olga, at Kialua Kona, Hawaii, when I was in the Islands for the Congressional Medal of Honor Society convention in November, 1981. During our interview I found Mr. Hoyt most enlightened on the combat actions of Air Group Fifteen (nicknamed "Fabled Fifteen") of which I was the Commander, and the subject of this book. The decision to focus on the Fabled Fifteen no doubt derived from Hoyt's determined and extensive research and from interviews with some of the actual participants. He is an astute observer and recorder and has pieced together a historical document that will be of interest to other historians and to readers alike who can relate to the people and events described. Personally, I think he has done a remarkable job!

Next, a tribute and vote of thanks to the people who so faithfully supported the operations of the Fabled Fifteen in combat—the plane captains, the mechanics, the flight deck personnel, the combat information directors, the landing signal officers, and the commanding officers of the *Essex* (our base of operations) and their able and considerate Executive Officer. It was an admirable combination of efforts of all the above, in addition to the combat pilots and crewmen who flew the planes that produced the outstanding results of the Fabled Fifteen during our tour of combat.

Although the history of Air Group Fifteen is but a short one (it only had one tour of combat duty of six-and-one-half months during the war), it must have been a relief for the author when he finished his research and decided to complete the work. One might wonder why out of all the valiant, patriotic and dedicated pilots who saw action in the Pacific, the author decided to write about the Fabled Fifteen. Perhaps he was impressed by its outstanding and imposing records established during its tour in combat: it was one of the most highly decorated air groups of the war; most airborne planes shot down (318) by any naval air group; most aircraft destroyed on the ground (348) by any naval air group; never lost a bomber or torpedo aircraft in air-to-air combat; good fighter protection for its ship (U.S.S. *Essex*), which was never attacked while Air Group 15 was embarked; most aircraft destroyed in one day (68); most enemy aircraft destroyed by a section of two planes in one mission (15); most enemy aircraft destroyed by one pilot on a single mission (9), a record unequalled in the annals of aviation history. None of the pilots freaked-out or had to be sent away to recuperate from combat fatigue. Air Group 15 saw action at Marcus and Wake Islands, the Marianas, Palau Islands, the Philippines, Iwo Jima, Formosa, Okinawa, Nansai Shotos, and participated in two major air-sea battles (the battle of the Philippine Sea and the battles of Leyte Gulf). Our combat losses, although high, were more or less average in comparison with other air groups of the time. The preceding statistics are, of course, only a small part of the story; the remainder is covered in the book itself, which I hope you will enjoy reading.

– Captain David McCampbell, U.S.N. (Ret.)

PRELUDE

In Deadly Battle

The time: October 24, 1944.
The place: the waters off the Philippines.
The occasion: the allied invasion of Leyte.

On the morning of October 24, search teams set out from the carrier groups at dawn to find the enemy. All three operating groups of Pacific Fleet Task Force 38 had pulled back toward the Philippine coast so that the planes could cover the west side of Luzon, the Sibuyan Sea, and the Sulu Sea, which lies between Borneo and the Philippines. Activity had been reported in all these areas on October 23. Admiral Gerald F. Bogan's force was near San Bernardino Strait, Admiral Ralph E. Davison's was just off Leyte Gulf, and Admiral Frederick C. Sherman's task group was to the north, off Luzon. Although the *Essex* was involved in the searches, its strength was being saved for a fighter sweep and a quick air strike. Just after 8:00 that morning, planes from the *Intrepid* and the *Cabot* almost simultaneously sighted enemy ships in formation in the Sibuyan Sea. The alert was on.

In Admiral Sherman's task group, the responsibility for combat air patrol that morning lay with the *Princeton*. At 6:10, Lieutenant Commander G.E. Duncan had led a seventeen-plane group on a twenty-degree search over the China Sea approaches and southwest Luzon. If there had been a paucity of Japanese military activity in recent days, such could certainly not be said this day. Almost from the beginning, the *Essex* planes were in action. On the outgoing leg of the search, flying low, Lieutenant (jg) R.P. Fush "tallyhoed" a Lily (Kawasaki 99 light bomber) over Malvar Airfield about a thousand feet below him. He came down like an Arab crossing the desert at night and slid in behind the Lily, firing a few bursts. The plane fell off on a wing, caught fire, and crashed. The pilot had not even known he was in danger until the bullets started coming.

Offshore, the *Essex* pilots found an enemy cruiser travelling alone—or so it seemed. The fighters, which were carrying bombs, attacked, and Lieutenant Commander Duncan scored a hit on the cruiser. Several fighters worked it over with machine guns. The cruiser went off, trailing oil.

On the way back from the search, again over Malvar Airfield, Ensign L.R. Self found two Zero fighters just taking off. Ensign Self selected one of them and fired, hitting the Zero's cockpit. The pilot dropped back to the ground, the plane ground-looped, its port wing struck the field and came off, and the plane burst into flame. The pilot tried to get out, but Self killed him in the cockpit, and he slumped down in the burning plane. Duncan shot the other Zero out of the air at 300 feet. The pilot jumped, but his parachute opened just as he hit the ground, a few moments before his airplane did.

Lieutenant John C.C. Symmes's search team was up closer to the Manila area when Ensign Jerome L. Lathrop discovered a Jill (Nakajima single-engined torpedo bomber). Lathrop jettisoned his 500-pound bomb, attacked, and shot down the torpedo plane. An hour later, Symmes saw two Betties (twin-engined bombers) and one Irving (twin-engined night fighter) between Cabra and Lubang Islands. Symmes still had his bomb, and the Irving was turning in to him. He assigned the two Betties to other pilots, warned his wingman, jettisoned his bomb, and then attacked. The Irving pulled away to the right, but the F6F was faster and Symmes caught the Japanese plane, fired a few bursts, and shot it down.

Lieutenant G.E. Mellon took one of the Betties, made a run, and shot it out of the air. The Betty made a good water landing but sank, and no heads came up.

Lieutenant (jg) R.N. Stime, Jr., shot down the other Betty, which tried a water landing but failed. The plane fell off on one wing, cartwheeled as the wing hit the sea, and broke up. There were no survivors.

By this time they were close to Manila Bay. Most of the fighters had dropped their bombs, one way or another, but Mellon had not. They came across a damaged cruiser (the *Takao*) that was dead in the water. Mellon dropped his bomb and scored a near miss that damaged the ship further. The whole search team strafed the cruiser, giving an already worn-out Japanese crew an even worse time.

The search teams were not halfway out on their journey when the Japanese air threat of the day materialized over Admiral Sherman's task group. Sherman knew that the Japanese had kept track of his ships all night long. Several "snoopers" had been shot down or driven away during the hours of darkness, but had been replaced immediately by others. They made no attempt to attack; it was apparent that they were only keeping track of the ships for future developments.

The developments began at about 7:50. The search radar on several carriers simultaneously picked up a large bunch of blips—planes—coming in from the west. They were virtually uncountable, stacked up from 1,000 feet of altitude to 25,000 feet, and they were only seventy-five miles out. A few moments earlier, the search planes had discovered Admiral Takeo Kurita's main Japanese attack force in the Sibuyan Sea. Aboard the *Essex*, Commander David McCampbell's plane had been spotted on the catapult and was up there being fuelled at the moment. McCampbell was in the ready room when word came that the air strike was for the moment scrubbed and that all fighter pilots must man their planes for immediate interception of an enemy striking group.

"All except Air Group Commander," said the squawk box. "He is not, repeat not, to go."

McCampbell knew the reason. He had once again taken a scolding from the admiral for his last personal fighter sweep three days earlier. "You are not, repeat not, to fly, except as air group commander, with a strike," said Admiral Sherman. "This is a direct order."

Since he was not going, Commander McCampbell sat down in the ready room and relaxed as best he could. Then the squawk box spoke up again.

"Now hear this. . ." it began, "air group commander is to fly, repeat affirmative, air group commander is to go."

So Commander McCampbell put on the parachute and Mae West he had just taken off, and headed for the deck. Meanwhile, on deck, the "airedales" taking care of the air group commander's plane were thoroughly confused. They had been told to gas up. They had been told to stop gassing up. They had been told to gas up again. And to add to the confusion, the gassing of the plane on the catapult had been left to an inexperienced man who did not know much about F6Fs. He had begun by filling the belly tank. It was full and the wing tanks were each about half full. But what the new "airedale" did not know was that the first rule of survival in combat was for a pilot to jettison his belly tank.

Hearing what had happened, Commander McCampbell stalled for a little time so more gas could be put into the wing tanks.

The squawk box came on again. "If the Air Group commander is not off in one minute, send the plane below." McCampbell literally leaped into the cockpit, and in moments was catapulted from the flight deck of the *Essex.*

By this time, every available fighter in Admiral Sherman's air group was getting aloft. But from the *Essex,* only seven planes were fit to fly at that moment, and they were Commander McCampbell's force as he sped up to meet a determined enemy.

The group fighter director was Lieutenant (jg) John Connally (the future governor of Texas, secretary of the treasury, and presidential candidate). Connally then took over, telling the pilots what to do.

They climbed to get altitude and then were vectored out about forty miles. The enemy seemed to be everywhere, up and down.

McCampbell had planned to keep his fighter division together, but in the mad scramble of takeoff, his second division leader did not get a plane. As a result, when McCampbell called for the second combat team to go down and take on the enemy below while he and his team fought those that remained high, five of the seven F6Fs screamed downward in dive, leaving McCampbell and his wingman, Lieutenant Roy W. Rushing, to "handle" everything at high altitude.

They discovered themselves in the midst of a gaggle of fighters that had lost their escort. The fighters had formed themselves into a Lufberry circle, with each plane protecting the tail of the plane ahead of it, and McCampbell and Rushing probed around on all sides, unsuccessfully trying to find an opening to get inside this protective circle and attack. The Japanese were too good at maintaining the formation.

McCampbell then thought for a moment: the Japanese must realize that they had lost their escort and that attack would be sure to bring many casualties. They also must be fairly short of gas, having come from the Manila area out to sea. He would wait and see what happened.

So he and Rushing got above the circle and "sat" on top of it, waiting. They did not have long to wait. As McCampbell had suspected, some of those pilots were going to get itchy and try to act.

McCampbell called Rushing on the radio.

"I told him I thought that they must be running out of gas pretty soon and I knew that we had plenty of gas so they'd have to head somewhere and that's when we would work them over, and they circled for maybe ten or fifteen minutes and headed for Manila. These were the fighters only. The bombers had all scattered and had been pretty well taken care of.

"So Rushing and I followed them back to Manila. We were engaged with them for about an hour and thirty-five minutes. We finally, after much screaming for help, got one other man to help us out there for a little while, and he ran out of ammunition and turned off and went to the ship." [This was Lieutenant (jg) Black, who shot down five planes.]

They were, said McCampbell, like a pair of wolves attacking sheep. They kept on top, and swooped down to attack. A pair of fighters would move out, and Rushing would go right and McCampbell would go left, and two fighters would go down in flames. The Americans would climb immediately and look for stragglers. There was always one, at least, and it would last just long enought to get shot. Occasionally, one fighter would grow furious and turn out at them. They would swoop down on it with the altitude advantage, fire, and the fighter would crash.

"They were scissoring very nicely, keeping good formation and their weave; their tactics were very similar to our own, and perhaps had we not been familiar with those tactics, it wouldn't have been so easy for us. We just bided our time there and I don't think any of them ever got a shot at us.

"There were three kinds of enemy fighters in the formation, Zekes [Zeros] predominated, with a few Oscars [Nakajima army fighters] and Hamps [carrier Zeros]. Most of those fighters carried what appeared to be a 350-pound bomb either on the right stub wing or under the belly."

Finally, McCampbell remembered that his plane had been only half-gassed when he took off, except for the belly tank, which he had dumped when he went into combat. He was getting very low on gas. There were only eighteen aircraft left in the enemy formation when Rushing and he stopped attacking and turned back toward the *Essex*.

"My claim of nine planes destroyed includes only those that were seen by my wingman and myself to flame or explode. Numerous others were seen with engine smoking and diving away, two of which were spinning, apparently out of control, toward the water, and are claimed as probables. Others were hit and undoubtedly damaged. No attempt was made at the time to record types and angle of attack, in fact it was not until we had destroyed five planes and business was beginning to get good that I decided to keep a box score by marking on my instrument panel with a pencil. . . ."

He estimated that the two of them knocked down nine Zeros, three Hamps, and three Oscars.

As they flew back to the carrier, McCampbell began to sweat out the trip. They came into the perimeter of the task group, and their old friend, the *Hornet,* opened fire on them.

"Call off the dogs," McCampbell yelled into his radio. "We're friendlies, trying to get back to the *Essex.*"

Sixty miles out, McCampbell called up the *Essex's* operations office, and identified himself.

"We're coming in. Will you take us?"

"Sure," said the voice on the radio.

But when they arrived, the *Essex's* decks were full of planes from the day's second strike. McCampbell and Rushing were told to go around and wait.

McCampbell took a look at his fuel gauge. It was trembling on the "Empty."

"Can't do it," he said. "Better find a place."

Down on the *Essex,* the landing officers consulted with the captain and the admiral. The air group commander was up there, running out of gas. What should they do?

Admiral Sherman told them. "Send him over to the *Langley.*"

"But her deck is full of TBFs."

"Get them off."

So the TBFs (Torpedo bombers), or enough of them, were cleared off the decks of the *Langley* and *Essex.* Air Group Commander McCampbell landed with lordly ease on the light carrier. After the hook had caught and the plane had stopped rolling, McCampbell gave the engine the gun to take it out of gear so the airedales could take over. The engine quit just then; the plane had to be pushed out of the way when the aircraft was examined, the handlers found its gas tanks completely empty and that Commander McCampbell had six rounds of ammunition left—all jammed in one gun.

The plane was gassed and rearmed, and McCampbell was sent out on "low patrol" at 2000 feet to guard against torpedo planes. It was like sending a knight against a band of sheep. When McCampbell asked why he was being assigned this particular duty he was told: "admiral's orders." Then Commander McCampbell realized that he was in deep trouble with Admiral Sherman.

The patrol was as uneventful as McCampbell had thought it would be, and eventually he made his way back aboard the *Essex.* The engine had scarcely stopped turning when he was told he was wanted in the admiral's cabin. He went up.

The admiral looked up from his desk, saw his air group commander, and frowned.

"I thought I told you not to get involved in these shoot-em-ups."

McCampbell then tried to explain what had happened in those few minutes down in the ready room when he had been put on, taken off, put on, and nearly taken off the flight roster.

"The air officer. . ." McCampbell said. "I presume he asked you. . . ."

"He did not," said the admiral. "Commander McCampbell," he continued, "as far as I am concerned you have deliberately disobeyed my orders. It's all right this time, but don't let it happen again."

After that, McCampbell went off to more friendly quarters where he was congratulated on his remarkable exploit, and by no one more warmly than by Captain Weiber (whom he forever afterward believed to have been the one who told the air officer to get McCampbell into the air).

Then and later, there was always a nagging thought: what would have happened if he had not shot down those nine Japanese planes? He might have been courtmartialed. Instead, he received the Congressional Medal of Honor.

And that is as good a place as any to start on the remarkable story of the airmen of the *Essex,* McCampbell's Heroes.

McCampbell's
HEROES

CHAPTER ONE

Air Group Fifteen

In the summer of 1943, the American carrier air force in the Pacific finally came into its own. After nearly two years of struggle, during which the Japanese held all the cards—in terms of carriers—the results of the building program ordained shortly before Pearl Harbor began to make themselves felt. Instead of one or perhaps two carriers available for assignment to a striking force, Admiral Chester W. Nimitz had half a dozen, with more coming up month after month.

To meet its needs the navy had begun a furious pilot training program. Once that was moving along, the next task was to create new fighting units and to train the men to fly the planes in combat. Late in August, the new fast carrier force of the Pacific went out on its first offensive raid, against Marcus Island. Just then, in Washington, officials in the navy's Bureau of Aeronautics were doing the paperwork to commission a new carrier air group to man the planes of the new carrier *Hornet*.

The group was to be called Carrier Air Group Fifteen. Its commanding officer was to be Lieutenant Commander Irwin L. Dew, a regular naval officer who was also commander of the dive bomber squadron. Besides that squadron the new group consisted of a fighter squadron under Lieutenant Commander David McCampbell, and a torpedo squadron under Ensign Charles G. Hurd (at the time). But this was all temporary, for the purpose of bringing the group into being. Within the month, the three squadrons had been moved to various bases for training.

On September 25, Commander William M. Drane reported to the commander of the Fleet Air Force at Norfolk and took over the group command. By this time his squadrons were far-flung. The torpedo squadron, VT-15, was at Westerly, Rhode Island. The fighter squadron was stationed at Atlantic City. The dive bomber squadron was stationed at Creeds, Virginia.

1

In the next few months came many changes, as the squadrons learned their trades. It was mid-November before they were brought to the Norfolk area, and even then the three squadrons were stationed at different air fields. Their first combined exercise came on November 25, 1943, a week after the fast carrier and the new amphibious force in the Pacific conducted the landings in the Gilbert Islands.

The *Hornet* contingent was only one of twenty such groups getting ready just then. To fight the Japanese, these men would be getting new weapons. The fighter pilots would have the F6F Hellcat, which was in some ways superior to the Japanese Zero fighter. The new Helldiver (SB2C) dive bomber was much faster than the old SBD. The new TBF torpedo bomber was more than 100 miles per hour faster than the old torpedo planes in use at the beginning of the Pacific war.

By Christmas time, 1943, the men of Carrier Air Group Fifteen were in advanced training. The fighter pilots had begun to know the characteristics of their F6F-3 Grumman fighters. They had learned to fly alone and for long distances; they had practiced aerobatics in preparation for combat techniques. They had learned to be at ease flying with oxygen. They had practiced field "carrier" landings for days on end. They had become proficient in formation flying, wingtip to wingtip, in two-plane sections and four-plane divisions—the standard units of the fighter force. They had learned squadron maneuvers.

There were special sessions on dogfighting below 10,000 feet, dogfighting above 10,000 feet, strafing, bombing, and instrument flying. The pilots had to be proficient in flying over water and in navigation. They were even exposed to night flying, although it was not anticipated that the squadron would be called on for that. They learned how to use cameras attached to the fighters, and they practiced attacks coordinated with the torpedo and dive bomber squadrons, and with other fighter squadrons. The one thing they did not learn was minimum altitude bombing.

By the end of September, 1943, the fighter squadron had forty-seven pilots. Two of the original contingent had been killed in training accidents: Ensign J.A. Wakefield crashed on a training flight on September 18, and Ensign D.F. Hoffman crashed two days later. No one ever discovered the causes of these fatal crashes.

Nearly all officers of the squadron were pilots; the exceptions were Lieutenant Joseph J. O'Brien, the administrative officer, Lieutenant Robert McReynolds, the air combat intelligence officer, and Lieutenant John R. Hoffman, the materials officer.

For a while, the fighter squadron at Atlantic City Naval Air Station had an easy time. Atlantic City was in their backyard, and Philadelphia and New York were within reach. The bachelor officers' quarters were comfortable and the officers had the run of Seaview Country Club, where they held dinner dances and cocktail parties.

On November 15 all that changed. Orders came moving them down to the Naval Air Station at Pungo, in Norfolk. This was rugged: the bachelor officers' quarters consisted of long single-story barracks, each heated by a single stove in the center of the room; the stove's heat reached out fifteen feet in all directions and that was all. The navy enlisted men, apparently unhappy at being rousted out of warm beds for the night watch, banged coal shovels and scuttles and furnace doors all night long. The building assigned for ground school was unheated. The chow came from the general mess, and the best the officers of Fighting Fifteen could say for it was that it was un-doubtedly nourishing.

The air station had no recreational facilities; one had to go to Virginia Beach, where a civilian ran a bar he called The Officers' Club and sold liquor at bootleg prices. It was the sort of billet that made a man wonder when he was going to have the privi-lege of going off to war.

The training facilities were not half as good as those at Atlantic City, where the fighter pilots had had an airfield all to themselves. At Pungo they had to share takeoffs and landings with several other air squadrons and with the general air traffic of a large air station.

The fighter pilots of Air Group Fifteen were hard-flying, hard-drinking young men who liked to "party" as well as they liked to be in the air. The most notable event at Pungo, they said, was the squadron party held after the commissioning of the USS *Hornet*, "their" carrier, which began at the navy officers' club in Portsmouth, and ended a number of hours later in the general store in Pungo.

The experience of the dive bomber, or scout, squadron was slightly different. Lieutenant Commander Dew began the training of his men at the naval Air Station at Creeds, Virginia. The pilots began flying the old SBD-5, the Douglas Dauntless, but in November new planes began to arrive: Curtiss Helldivers, or in Navy language, SB2C-1Cs. If the fighter pilots complained about Pungo, the bomber pilots told them they ought to have been at Creeds. The facilities consisted of one frame nose hangar, a handful of frame shops, one big barnlike structure that housed a ready room and offices—separated only by wall-board partitions—and Quonset huts for the officers and men to sleep in and keep their gear. There was only one general mess. There was no "ship's service" and one very bad canteen. The nearest town was Virginia Beach, twenty-three miles away. Since there was nothing else to do, the men of Bombing Fifteen flew. Oh, how they flew! In November they flew more than 2,900 hours, and the Norfolk command ordered an investigation into the enormous amount of gasoline consumed. Never before in the history of the station had so much aviation fuel been required. The investigation proved that Bombing Fifteen was flying, and nothing else.

Bombing Fifteen had its accidents, too. On November 1, Ensign Harry G. Storey and Ensign John P. Walter were killed on an instrument flight when their SNJ trainer shed a wing. Two days later, while flying a cloud-training exercise, two SBDs collided off Kitty Hawk, North Carolina, over the sea. All four men aboard were killed.

There were many non-fatal accidents. One day Ensign Ernest Winters headed out on a flight to Norfolk, and over the East Field discovered that his wheels would not come down. For an hour and a half he tried to operate the hydraulic system to jack them down by hand, but they remained stuck. He made a wheels-up landing and walked away. Three weeks later, he had exactly the same experience and made another belly landing in a Virginia field. Five weeks later, he crash-landed at Manteo Field and again walked away.

Ensign Alfred de Cesaro had difficulties once the squadron started making carrier landings. He crash-landed one plane on the USS *Charger*. Two months later, when he came in hot on the *Hornet* and the arresting hook bounced, he hit the after gun mount, wrecking the plane and the guns.

Ensign David Halland and Ensign Jared Dixon collided on the field one day; neither was hurt, but ARM2c R.S. Stewart, Jr., was critically injured. Ensign John E. Peabody was playing basketball one day on an improvised court on the concrete apron when a gasoline truck ran over one of his feet, breaking several toes. ARM3c Douglas M. Corey was working with a .30 calibre machine gun in the gunnery shack when it suddenly began firing, scattering gunners all over the place. No one was hit. And one day the galley caught fire but did not burn down, which some in the squadron thought was a misfortune.

All the bachelor officers lived on the base, but the married officers found quarters (expensive) in Virginia Beach and commuted. Their vehicles were an old command car that belonged to the base, and an older milk truck. Both came to disastrous ends: the command car demolished a tree one night, and the milk truck had its last gasp in a ditch alongside the road. Only one person was hurt in these mischances, and he was back with the squadron in time to join the *Hornet*.

Like Fighting Fifteen, Bombing Fifteen had its share of parties. The Pine Tree Inn was the officers' favorite watering hole. On weekends, when the bachelor officers could get transportation, they went into Virginia Beach to live it up. The enlisted men had a harder time of it, but at least they had the Chamber Music Society of Lower Hut Seven, which had very little to do with Bach and Beethoven.

One of the problems faced by the pilots of Bombing Fifteen was the late arrival of their new planes—late in terms of the stepped-up schedule to get the *Hornet* out into the Pacific as soon as possible. Consequently, when the pilots left their field and began training aboard the carrier, not one pilot had had more than fifteen hours in the new planes. It was very little flying time to have before stepping into the intricate business of carrier landings.

Following their first coordinated group "strike" on a stationary target on November 24, the group had been operating out of bases around Norfolk and training with the fleet. Two days after Christmas, part of the group reported aboard the newly-commissioned carrier *Hornet* for duty and in January went off with the ship on her shakedown cruise in the Bermuda area.

The scuttlebutt had it that the *Hornet* was to be hurried out to join the fleet, so instead of taking the expected cruise—a month of leisurely workup on the way to and from Jamaica—the *Hornet* moved off Bermuda; the whole cruise lasted just two weeks.

It was a busy time, especially for the bomber pilots, who seemed to be bouncing off all sides of the flight deck. Scarcely had the damage control parties cleaned up the mess made by Ensign de Cesaro, when Ensign Henry Kramer jumped a barrier and crashed. Then Lieutenant Wilfred Saxton did the same thing. Then Ensign Frank Eisenhart jumped two barriers and crashed into Ensign David Hall. It was an expensive learning process.

Captain Miles Browning, the commander of the *Essex,* was not amused. He halted flight operations then and there, and called the senior air group officers to the bridge. Commander Dew did not make a good case for himself, but Lieutenant Commander

McCampbell pointed out that the Helldiver was a new aircraft. How much room was being allowed for takeoff and landing?

Captain Browning replied that he was going "by the curve," which meant by the mathematical calculations of manufacturer about length of deck, load, etc.

That was fine, said McCampbell, if the pilots were all test pilots from Patuxent, but these were green aviators just out of school, and there was no comparison. They simply had to have more room to work in.

Miles Browning was a "tough character," as McCampbell put it, but he was also an officer who knew when another was sure of his ground. McCampbell had already impressed him because, in the very beginning, back before the squadrons ever came aboard, McCampbell had gone down to Newport News where the *Hornet* was out-fitting to get a look at his new ship. Browning had given McCampbell a lecture on what he wanted: none of that worrying about strafing, but get ready to shoot down Japanese planes. Then he had asked McCampbell what sort of an outfit he would be bringing to the *Hornet*. The best in the service, McCampbell had said. And when he brought his fighter pilots aboard, even the old curmudgeon, Miles Browning, was more or less pleased with them.

McCampbell had worked hard already at picking out his men, and would also work hard at their training. One of his pilots was the husband of his niece, Patricia Ann O'Rourke: Ensign B.D. Morris, more popularly known in the late 1930s and early 1940s as Wayne Morris, a Hollywood actor who played heroic roles. At about the time McCampbell was taking command of the squadron, Morris was an instructor in navy primary training at Hutchinson, Kansas. McCampbell stopped by one day and Morris pleaded with him to get him into a fighting squadron.

"Give me a letter," said McCampbell.

Morris gave him a letter of request and soon was transferred, but was assigned to a PBY unit because of his size (he was big). Once again McCampbell came through Jacksonville, Florida, where Morris was training, and once more Morris pleaded with him. "Get me into fighters," he said.

"Give me a letter," said McCampbell, who was on his way to Washington.

Morris gave him another letter, and soon he showed up at Melbourne, Florida, where McCampbell was training fighter pilots. In this way, Ensign Morris got assigned to Fighting Fifteen. McCampbell wanted men who *wanted* to be fighter pilots more than anything else. He was getting them, and it showed. The day of the confrontation over dive bomber mishaps, Miles Browning agreed to give the Helldiver pilots the extra 100 feet of flight deck they needed, and the rate of accidents went down.

The difficulties were not the fault of the new squadron for the most part, but of "bugs" in the new SB2C-1Cs. The landing hooks on the aircraft were not made for the job of landing on a carrier deck. Further, no one knew quite how much deck space and how much wind the new dive bomb demanded for safety, and so all this had to be worked out by trial and error. The shakedown was very nearly a disaster for Bombing Fifteen. Captain Browning felt the need for training was so great that no recreation was allowed, and the training posed so many problems that the squadron came back from it with its morale in tatters.

In part, Captain Browning was swayed by his own frustrations. Browning had been chief of staff to Admiral Halsey during the early days of the war when Halsey was a task force commander. Browning had been the architect of victory at Midway, when Halsey had fallen ill and Admiral Nimitz had had no one to send out in command of Halsey's task force except Admiral Raymond Spruance—who knew nothing about carrier operations. Browning had made the suggestion for the timing of the first strike against the Japanese, knowing that their carrier decks would be filled with planes that had returned from the assault on Midway Island. Browning had then joined Halsey in the South Pacific as chief of staff there, but he had somehow antagonized either Navy Undersecretary James Forrestal or Navy Secretary Frank Knox. Admiral King was annoyed, which usually meant the end of a senior officer's career. Here, early in 1944, Browning had been brought down in prestige to the point of commanding a carrier.

At the moment, Miles Browning was in charge of Carrier Air Group Fifteen, and no one forgot it. There were two ways to run a carrier. One was for the captain to regard the airmen as a group apart, with their own commands and own ways of handling discipline. In that case the air group commander was responsible through the aviation department of the carrier to the captain, and he was let alone for the most part. That form of organization made for a happy air group. The other way was for the captain to assume that the air group was just another part of the ship's complement and that any independence established in the table of organization existed only for the periods when the group was either ashore or in the air. This was Browning's way, and the officers and men of Air Group Fifteen spent a very unhappy time aboard the *Hornet*.

In a sense, Air Group Fifteen's difficulties in getting organized for battle were an indication of the troubles or growing pains of the new navy training.

Air Group Fifteen's experience aboard the *Hornet* had not been a happy one. As soon as the aviators joined the ship, the air group had lost its entity and became the V-5 division of the air department of the carrier. Commander William Drane was assigned to be assistant to the air officer of the carrier and various officers were assigned to intelligence, the daily watch, the ship's medical department, and radar. In all cases the squadron's officers were reduced in function to the level of junior officers of the ship, with no regard for their command function as airmen. The results were a most frustrated group of aviators. Tension between the airmen and the ship's crew never lessened.

The accidents continued. Ensign Emmett Fletcher's dive bomber suffered engine failure on takeoff. He tried to turn into the cross leg to come around and land again, but he did not have the necessary speed or altitude, and the plane spun into the sea. He was killed, although his radioman was saved.

The deck crashes continued, often because the tail hook of the new bomber sometimes refused to hold the barrier cable. Ensign Andrew Peterson and Radioman Leslie W. Gretter were killed while attempting a simulated bombing run on the *Hornet*. An aileron came off as Peterson pulled out of the dive, and the plane crashed into the sea. Was it pilot error or carelessness by the flight deck crew? It might have been either one.

Getting an airplane into the air from the deck of a carrier is a painstaking matter, with no room for carelessness, since the lives of from one to three men depended on the operation. In the fighter squadron (and the same general care, with even more complications, was exercised in the Helldiver and torpedo bomber squadrons) the flight deck chief mustered his flight deck crew forty-five minutes before launch at the after end of "the island." As soon as the planes were spotted, the chief assigned men to inspect each one. The inspectors had a lot to do: they had to check tires, fuel, battery, oil and hydraulic systems for leaks, the oxygen system, the cockpit sliding bubble, the windshield, control surfaces, tail hook, and the belly tank.

If an inspector found something wrong, he would fix it or tell the chief to order up a specialist (electrician), and he would stay with the plane to see that the difficulty was corrected. Sometimes the plane captain could do it—each plane had its own captain and his assistant or assistants. If the condition could not be remedied before launch, then the inspector notified the chief, and the plane would be scratched from the tally board. The pilot would either get another plane or he would not fly.

The planes would then go out on their missions and return. As they came close to the carrier, the call for flight quarters was sounded. That brought the flight deck crews out again. They mustered at the starboard five-inch gun turrets, forward of the island. As the planes came in, directed by the landing signal officer, the flight deck chief assigned them to the men, to inspect after mission. If a pilot came in with a dud or a plane that had been shot up, he could turn thumbs down, or "down" the plane, which meant it would not fly again until a thorough investigation had been made. The inspector could also "down" it himself and then attach a yellow or red flag to the plane's antenna mast: yellow for repairs that could be made on the flight deck, red for all other repairs. All inspectors reported to the chief, who reported to the tally board and the air officer; thus, within minutes after a mission returned, the admiral would know how many planes he had on deck available for the next one.

The pilots' training exercises were long and arduous. The pilots learned sector search, in which planes on a search mission fly out to a specified distance from the carrier, covering wedges of space. They practiced group formation tactics, in which dive bombers, torpedo bombers, and fighters were given specific assignments and altitudes and were taught to make rendezvous at given points and then to find the assigned target. The bombers spent hours practicing bombing dives and torpedo runs, from various angles, on target ships. The fighter and torpedo bomber pilots learned camera techniques, so that records of the actions of the planes could be used by air intelligence officers to correct errors and assess damage. The pilots and crewmen of all aircraft practiced their gunnery, and the fighter pilots spent hours learning the techniques of combat air patrol and how to obey the fighter director's instructions, and the torpedo bombers learned to skim the water in anti-submarine patrol. Carrier war, as the crewmen learned, is a deadly, complex business that began with all the difficulties of getting into the air, and ended with the sometimes unnerving experience of getting back down onto the deck of a carrier that seemed to be going straight up and down.

In February, as Admirals Nimitz and Spruance planned for the Marshalls invasion and as the carrier command changed over into Rear Admiral Marc A. Mitscher's hands, the men of Air Group Fifteen were still training. The shakedown cruise aboard the *Hornet,* the planes lost in operational accidents, and the pilots and aircrewmen killed indicated something unknown to the public: the very nature of carrier flying made for danger, even without any enemy. A slight miscalculation, and a plane headed for the flight deck could become a runaway, smashing into the barrier and going over. A pilot could miss the landing and end up in the sea. Mechanical failure, particularly on takeoff, could cost a plane and lives.

On February 2, the air group moved back to the Naval Air Station at Norfolk for temporary assignment as the *Hornet* went into drydock for correction of difficulties uncovered during the shakedown cruise. Commander Drane was relieved of his command of the air group. Lieutenant Commander Dew was relieved from his post as commander of the dive bomber squadron. The commander of the torpedo squadron was also relieved. On February 9, Lieutenant Commander David McCampbell was made commander of the whole air group and Lieutenant Commander Charles W. Brewer took over the fighter squadron. These assignments were to last.

A week later, the men of Air Group Fifteen were back aboard the carrier and she was heading for the Pacific theatre of operations. For the next two weeks, the ship sailed—down through the Panama Canal and across the Pacific—and the aircrews trained. Two more pilots, two crewmen, and four planes were lost in operational accidents.

During a storm off Cape Hatteras, one SB2C was blown over the side of the ship, five more were so seriously damaged as to require major overhauls and five others were also damaged to a lesser degree. Ensign O.G. Lippincott was killed during a simulated attack on the Panama Canal, when he lost control of his plane and it crashed in the jungle.

After going through the canal, the ship moved north to San Diego, only to have more accidents, most of them caused by mechanical imperfections in the planes—particularly in the new dive bombers.

The ship arrived at San Diego on February 27, but she left again two days later for the Pacific war. A few days later, the *Hornet* pulled into Pearl Harbor, and Air Group Fifteen was replaced by another group.

Apparently the training schedule indicated that the airmen of Air Group Fifteen had not reached the sort of efficiency necessary for survival in the war against a Japanese enemy whose losses had been heavy in the air, but who still packed enormous punch.

One reason for the decision was the emphasis that Captain Browning had placed on shooting down Japanese aircraft. At Pacific Fleet headquarters, the emphasis was the other way; Nimitz and his admirals wanted pilots who were trained in fighter-bomber techniques. As the new F6F aircraft came off the assembly lines they proved admirable in this role, and, since the fighting squadron was not as able as it should have been in such matters and since the bombing squadrons still left a bit to be desired, the decision was made to stop the air group right there for further training.

The group was detached from the *Hornet* and put ashore at Oahu. The fighter squadron and the headquarters of the air group went to Kaneohe Naval Air Station on the north shore of the island, and the two bomber squadrons went to Barber's Point Naval Air Station. But once again they were transferred, this time over to Maui. For six more weeks they trained, while the *Hornet* took on Air Group Two and sailed.

Captain Miles Browning did not last long in his new command. Very soon after bringing the *Hornet* into the Pacific, he ran afoul of "Jocko" Clark, a brand new carrier admiral (who might very well have felt the lash of Browning's tongue in those halcyon days when Browning was Halsey's chief of staff and ran a very taut command). One night in the war zone, when the crew was enjoying movies on the hangar deck, a fire extinguisher somehow went off, and someone pushed the panic button. Many thought the ship was under attack, and the hangar deck became chaotic. Men were climbing out of every aperture, and two of them climbed too far and disappeared. No one noticed it, however, and in the calm after the false alarm, Captain Browning did not order a full muster of the crew, but contented himself with divisional reports. (A full muster would have taken about four hours.) Later, it was discovered that the two men were missing. In the ensuing investigation, Admiral Clark had Captain Browning's head. The next thing anyone in Air Group Fifteen knew, their old captain had been sent to Leavenworth.

"Leavenworth!" said one of the airmen. "I didn't think they would do that to him."

The Leavenworth under discussion was not quite so bad as the federal prison: it was a naval air station; but to Captain Browning, the difference was probably minuscule.

When the squadrons were separated on Oahu, morale went down again. The officers and men had the feeling of being kicked around by the Pacific Fleet. It was not until March 14 that the whole group was reassembled at Puuenene, on Maui Island, and then more confusion was added because the air station was equipped to handle only one air group, and Air Group Eight was still there.

In six weeks at Puuenene, the situation of Air Group Fifteen changed remarkably, largely through the efficient operations of the administrative organization at the base. The bugs in the new aircraft were discovered and corrected. The squadrons trained as a group under their own officers, and their own officers were in charge of administration. But discipline remained a problem because the navy had not yet learned that a fighting unit was no better than its own discipline, and the commander of the air station insisted on handling all disciplinary problems. The squadron commanders and other officers and men resented the system, but could not escape it.

The Maui experience cost the fighter squadron two more pilots and planes. Lieutenant A. Grothaus crashed into the sea following a midair collision, and Ensign G.F. Butler crashed immediately after a predawn takeoff.

The social life was again hectic, ranging from the bars of Wailuku to the estate of the Countess Alexis von Tempsky Abriskie on the slopes of Haleakala, where nearly every pilot in all three squadrons was entertained at one time or another.

On April 28, the air group was ordered back to Pearl Harbor for a new carrier assignment. But when the airmen arrived, although they were told that the unit would be assigned to the *Essex,* no arrangements had been made. The result was more delay, more confusion, and more wondering by the officers and men of Air Group Fifteen about the Pacific command and about the war in general. Finally, over one hundred officers and men and twenty-five tons of baggage were assembled at one place, the *Essex* (CV-9), at about midnight on April 29.

The *Essex* had previously had Air Group Nine aboard, but that group was ready for a rest after combat duty that had begun in the summer of 1943 and had included several strikes on Japanese-held islands, the Gilberts invasion, more air strikes in the Pacific, and the Marshalls invasion which had ended late in February.

Life aboard the new carrier was a vast improvement over life aboard the old. Although by regulation and practice the air group once again became the V-5 Division of the Air Department, Captain Ralph Ofstie, the commander of the *Essex,* had a different approach than Captain Browning of the *Hornet.* Maybe it was because Ofstie had come to his post after a tour as air officer on the staff of Admiral Nimitz. In any case, Commander McCampbell, the commander of the air group, was given charge of the discipline and wellbeing of his officers and men, and all the squadron commanders had an authority denied them in the past.

McCampbell was representative of the new group of young officers who had already seen bloody combat and were now at the senior or "gold braid" level. He was then ten years out of the U.S. Naval Academy; three of those years were spent in sea duty with the cruiser *Portland.* In 1938, he had been sent to Pensacola Naval Air Station for training and then had served aboard the carrier *Ranger* as a fighter pilot until 1940. McCampbell had then been selected as landing signal officer for the new carrier *Wasp* when she was commissioned in 1940, and had served aboard that ship until September, 1942, when the *Wasp* was sunk during the battle for Guadalcanal. The tasks of the landing signal officer of a carrier were extremely exacting, for on him depended the safety and sometimes the lives of the pilots and crewmen. After the *Wasp* was sunk, McCampbell was sent back to Florida as an instructor in the art. He served there until September, 1943, when he was made first commanding officer of the fighter squadron of Air Group Fifteen—Fighting Fifteen.

Commander James Hale Mini was the commanding officer of the dive bomber squadron, VB-15 in navy language, or Bombing Fifteen. He was another Naval Academy graduate, class of 1935, and his experience was significantly different from that of McCampbell. He had served aboard carriers, but became a pilot of float planes and a senior aviator in the battleship fleet. He was senior aviator aboard the USS *Arizona* on December 7, 1941, when that battleship was sunk at her berth off Ford Island in Pearl Harbor by the Japanese sneak attack.

Lieutenant Commander V.G. Lambert, commanding officer of the torpedo squadron (VT-15), had come to the *Essex* via quite a different route, a product of the expansion of the naval aviation program in the late 1930s. He was not a Naval Academy man, but a graduate of Southwestern Louisiana Institute who entered the naval aviation program at Pensacola in 1936. After graduation and commission as an ensign, he became aviation officer aboard the cruiser *Boise,* and then served a tour as an instructor at Pensacola and later as commander of a patrol squadron of flying boats stationed at Floyd Bennet Field in New York. He had become commander of the torpedo squadron in one of the numerous changes that had bedeviled Air Group Fifteen.

Commanding officer of the fighter squadron was Commander Charles Walter Brewer, an Oklahoman who was born in 1911 and graduated from the U.S. Naval Academy in the class of 1934.

These were the men who would lead the airmen of the *Essex* into battle—and very soon.

Their new captain was Ralph Ofstie, one of the "new breed" of pilots. Ofstie had made a name for himself as a racing pilot not long after he took flight training (1924). He had been a fighter squadron commander and most recently was the air officer of Admiral Nimitz's Pacific Fleet staff. For months he had been badgering Nimitz for a combat assignment, and now he had it.

When Commander McCampbell reported aboard the *Essex* to meet his new captain, Ofstie had a few questions.

"Well, commander," he asked, "what kind of an air group are you bringing me?"

"The best in the Pacific Fleet, sir," said Air Group Commander McCampbell.

"I hope so," said the captain. "I've got one word of warning for you. Get your pilots trained to maintain radio silence. The Japanese are listening in, you've got to figure that. And we've had one guy out that you could hear telling where he was all over the Pacific."

That was the beginning of a new relationship between the airmen and their ship captain.

The *Essex* group also took on some specialists: a half-dozen pilots trained for night fighting, with their special night fighter F6Fs. As the *Essex* sailed for the battle zone, the complete group consisted of 122 pilots and 91 aircraft. They sailed in convoy with the *Wasp* and several other ships, for mutual protection against enemy submarine attack. Again the crossing was accompanied by training exercises, but the improved skills of the airmen showed: two aircraft were lost in operational accidents, but there were no casualties.

The destination of the convoy was Majura Lagoon in the Marshalls. There Admiral Spruance was preparing for invasion of the Marianas Islands later in the year. Aviators had already begun to occupy a more important role in the planning and execution of amphibious operations since Admiral John Towers (an aviator himself) had moved up to become Nimitz's deputy, but not solely because of him.

In Washington, two of the principal civilian officials in the navy were fighting hard for naval air. Assistant Secretary of the Navy Artemus Gates was one of them, and the other was Navy Secretary James V. Forrestal, who had been undersecretary and would eventually become secretary of defense. After many lost and drawn battles in the corridors of power they had begun to win.

In May, as the training continued at Majura, Admiral Spruance had a shock: Admirals King and Nimitz decreed that for better understanding of the new naval tactics, every major commander who had come up through the surface fleet must have as chief of staff an airman, and vice versa. Spruance did not like this change at all—he still neither understood nor trusted the carrier force, but there was inexorable demand for change, particularly after the fast carriers struck the big Japanese naval base at Truk and took credit for putting it out of action. In fact, the Truk raid had been enormously effective against enemy aircraft, but the Japanese naval command had already pulled the bulk of its forces back to within the perimeter of what the Japanese regarded as their inner empire.

This next invasion, at the Marianas, would strike for the first time within that perimeter in an attempt to seize a foothold for new air bases. And from those bases the Americans could do something successfully that they were at the moment doing not very well: strike the Japanese homeland from the air. Early in 1944 the only planes capable of reaching Japan from American bases were B-29s stationed far to the west in bases at Xian and elsewhere in Sichuan province, and the big planes had to carry an enormous gas load that cut down their bombing capability. With bases in the Marianas, the B-29s' round trip would be cut sharply from the China distance. More important, the matter of supply would be much easier, since even in the last days of the Pacific war, the supply of China bases was to remain an enormous problem.

In the coming battle, a thousand miles from the closest American base, the new carrier fleet would play an even more important role than in the past.

CHAPTER TWO

Preliminaries

Out of Kikai Channel off Oahu, the *Essex* and her companion ships turned toward the open sea and set course for the Marshall Islands. On May 8, 1944, the convoy arrived at Majuro, and Captain Oftsie reported to Admiral Mitscher. For the next week the ship lay at anchor in the lagoon, as the admirals completed their plans for the invasion of the Marianas. One force was to attack Saipan, and another was scheduled to attack Guam a few days later. But all this was a month in the future. In the interim, Admiral Mitscher was to be occupied with "softening up" the enemy. To that end, and particularly in order to give the untried carrier pilots experience before a battle expected to bring out the Japanese carrier force, Admiral Mitscher sent the *Essex*, the *Wasp*, and the light carrier *San Jacinto* out on a raid of Marcus and Wake Islands. With supporting cruisers and destroyers they sailed on May 15, with Rear Admiral A.E. Montgomery in command.

The two fleet carriers and the light carrier steamed steadily for three days. On May 18, the *San Jacinto* was sent north of Marcus Island to prevent the enemy from bringing in reinforcements to meet the air strike. The pilots and crews of the two big carriers had been training and keeping up combat air patrols to protect the force.

Marcus Island is shaped like a fat triangle, and most of the island was then taken up by two Japanese airfield runaways joined in the shape of a boomerang. Inside the angle were the Japanese hangars, air shops, and revetments. The area bristled with anti-aircraft guns.

The planes of the first strike by Air Group Fifteen got off the carrier at 6:30 on the morning of May 18. The sky was overcast and the wind was strong. Eleven fighters, eight torpedo bombers, and fifteen dive bombers from the *Essex* went to attack

Japanese planes, the air field installations, and shipping. Before the mission began, someone had told the commanding officers of Air Group Fifteen that these air strikes were just another form of training under combat conditions and were not to be regarded as very dangerous. That was comforting, but not quite how it turned out.

At 7:05, the planes began arriving over the south shore of the island. The fighters strafed the gun installations with their .50 calibre machine guns. The torpedo bombers dropped 500-pound bombs from 1,500 feet, destroyed storage dumps, got one hit on a concrete building, and several on frame buildings. The dive bombers bombed from 1,500 feet with 500-pound and 100-pound bombs. The damage really was not very great, but it was a "successful" mission because the group proved its ability to operate smoothly.

Lieutenant Commander McCampbell, the air group commander, was over the target early, and he circled around the area at 8,000 feet while the planes came in. McCampbell and three other fighter pilots remained high, as a combat air patrol, to prevent the planes of the strike from being "bounced" by the Japanese.

At first the Japanese gunners were surprised. Only a third of the anti-aircraft guns fired on the fighters as they swept in. But in a few minutes the Japanese recovered and from that point on the anti-aircraft fire was severe.

The torpedo bombers came in through cloud cover with little time to see their targets; several of the bombs missed entirely.

After the raid, the planes formed up and headed back to the carrier. Four fighters had been hit, two of them hard enough to require engine changes when they landed, and three torpedo bombers and two dive bombers were also damaged. Lieutenant B.L. Stearns of the fighter squadron had been struck in the neck by fragments of a 40mm anti-aircraft shell, just hard enough to make him eligible for a Purple Heart medal, but not enough to keep him from flying.

The planes of the second strike took off from the *Essex* at 10:30. This time there were eleven fighters, eight torpedo bombers, and nine dive bombers. Once again the planes came in without any air opposition. This strike was led by the commander of the *Wasp*'s air group, since McCampbell had led the last one. By this time, the weather had worsened considerably, and the planes missed and overran the target by nine miles and had to double back. Then the dive bombers and the torpedo bombers circled while the fighters went down and strafed the anti-aircraft guns to put them off-balance as the bombers came in. Then the bombers began their assault.

The *Essex*'s eight torpedo bombers were assigned to a wooded dispersal area at the northern tip of the island. They dropped down to 1,500 feet at 300 miles per hour, bombed, and pulled out. Next, the dive bombers came down. They started their dives as a group at 14,000 feet, and then at 8,000 feet the individual planes broke off and headed for the targets. They screamed down to 2,000 feet and then released their bombs. This attack had better—or at least more visible—results.

The American pilots found one patrol craft that had two masts and a diesel engine. It was equipped with three 20mm guns near the bridge. The fighters attacked and strafed the vessel, and the bombers scored two near misses off its stern, and then a bomb hit amidships. The bomb was followed by an explosion, and all hands jumped overboard. The ship went dead in the water and began to list, and was in that condition when the planes left the area and flew back to the carrier.

The Japanese anti-aircraft gunners were thoroughly alert for the second attack. Eleven planes were damaged, and one of the dive bombers crashed into the sea on its way home. Ensign T.A. Woods and his gunner, A. McPherson, were rescued after they jumped out and got into their raft. From the torpedo bomber squadron, Gunner B.K. McNought was hit by a glass marble shot from a 3-inch anti-aircraft shell, but he was not seriously injured.

The third attack of the day was made at 1:25 in the afternoon by ten fighters, seven torpedo bombers, and fourteen dive bombers. This time the flak was fierce.

Air Group Commander McCampbell led the attack. The weather had grown even worse after noon, and by the time the planes reached Marcus Island the cloud cover obscured the approaches. McCampbell went down on the first strafing run to "soften up" the guns below. His plane was hit by anti-aircraft fire and his belly tank and the fuselage caught fire. He jettisoned the belly tank, and the fire in the fuselage went out in a few minutes, but by that time the plane's hydraulic system and electrical system were gone, so he retired to the rendezvous point and waited for the rest of the planes to appear.

As he watched, the other fighters continued to strafe, going in as low as 100 feet above the Japanese guns. Seven fighters were hit by the anti-aircraft gunners, and one plane went down in flames. Two fighters were sent out to help look for a downed bomber; they found a dye marker in the sea, a life raft with two oars hanging in the water, but no airmen.

The bombers came down as low as 800 feet to release their bombs. The Japanese poured anti-aircraft fire at them. The pilots saw black puffs (the 3-inch guns) and white puffs (the 40mm and 20mm guns), and tracers (20mm and 7.6mm) all around them. They began jinking and weaving to avoid the flak.

The torpedo bombers had the worst time. When they came out of the cloud cover they were right over the island and had no time to make their planned approach. They dropped where they could, and the results were not impressive. They had been fitted out with rocket launchers, and after dropping their bombs they made another run. But the anti-aircraft fire and the weather made it impossible to get the sort of straight low level run they needed, so they fired at targets of opportunity.

When the planes landed back on the *Essex,* Commander McCampbell began to count noses. The plane that had gone down in flames over the target was Ensign W.T. Burnham's. He was Commander McCampbell's wingman. The dive bomber that had been hit and was missing was Ensign J.N. Dixon's plane. He and his gunner, Sam Hogue, were put down as missing in action.

At 5:30 that afternoon another *Essex* strike hit the target area. This time there were fighters, six torpedo bombers, and seven dive bombers. The weather over Marcus was solid overcast, with occasional rain. This strike was again led by the commander of the *Wasp* air group. The fighters strafed the anti-aircraft guns, but the real purpose was to hit the runways with something that would cause the Japanese trouble. The half-dozen torpedo bombers were each loaded with a 2,000-pound bomb. The low overcast made it difficult for the Japanese gunners, and only one fighter was damaged. No one was hurt. The photo reconnaissance planes that came in at the end of the strike took pictures. There were thirty-six bomb craters in runway number two.

On May 20, *Essex* planes were over Marcus Island again beginning at 6:30: twelve fighters, seven torpedo bombers, and eight dive bombers. Again the flak was heavy, although the strafing seemed to quiet it down somewhat and apparently damaged some of the guns. The torpedo planes used bombs and rockets, and the dive bombers used 500-pound bombs. The torpedo planes did not do very well because of the cloud cover and their need to come in in a gliding approach. By the time they broke out of the clouds they were usually past the target and had to turn around and try again. Just getting their bombs and rockets onto the island was a chore. The dive bombers went down through the clouds, starting at 14,000 feet, and nosing over into their dives at 12,000 feet, and pulling out at 1,500 feet, just below the cloud cover. Only one plane failed to perform, and its pilot got rattled, pulled out at 2,000 feet above the overcast, and dropped his bombs in the sea.

There was one more strike. After this mission, Captain Ofstie pulled the *Essex* away from the Marcus Island area and headed for Wake Island, the second target of the task group.

On the morning of May 23, the planes of Air Group Fifteen took off at 5:30 and headed for Wake. A dozen fighters, seven torpedo planes, and nine dive bombers set out to attack the former American base that the Japanese had captured early in the war. The first attack was to be made against the air installations around the airstrip. The bombers used 100-, 500-, and 1,000-pound bombs. A second strike force took off at 7:25: eleven fighters, eight torpedo bombers, and eleven dive bombers. Now Peale Island in the Wake Atoll—specifically Hell Point—was the target. This attack was led by Lieutenant Commander Brewer, the commander of Fighting Fifteen, and it included planes from the *San Jacinto*.

The Japanese had done a good job of fortifying Wake against air attack. Most of the installations were at least half underground, and from the air it was difficult for the pilots to tell one white roof from another. Also, the earth around the buildings prevented damage from anything but a direct hit.

The anti-aircraft fire was effective enough to damage one fighter and cause one dive bomber to make a water landing, and then sink. The pilot, Ensign Conrad Crellin, and the gunner, A.T. Graham, were rescued by a destroyer, as the 10:00 strike was approaching Wake Island.

On this strike, Commander McCampbell led twelve F6Fs, six TBFs, and thirteen dive bombers to bomb, fire rockets, and strafe. The cloud cover was heavy, and the results were hard to see; the fighters strafed several barges and small craft in the harbor, but they could not tell how much damage was done. The torpedo bombers took the worst beating from the anti-aircraft because they had to glide to loose their rockets effectively. Three were damaged, and two dive bombers and one fighter, but none of the air crewmen were hurt.

At 12:45 that afternoon, Lieutenant Commander Brewer was back in the air, leading another strike against Wake Island with twnety-eight planes from the *Essex* and twelve from the *San Jacinto*. This time someone scored a direct hit on an oil storage tank, and it burned with thick black smoke. Two torpedo bombers and four dive bombers of the *Essex* group were damaged, but none seriously; strike leader Brewer characterized the anti-aircraft fire as slight and inaccurate.

At 3:00 in the afternoon, Commander McCampbell was again leading a strike of thirty-one planes from the two carriers against the northern half of the island, where the distilling plant for fresh water was located. On this strike, Lieutenant J.J. Collins was wounded in the right thigh when his fighter was hit by shrapnel.

That was the end of the action. The task group turned back toward the base in the Marshall Islands. The planes of the *Essex* had flown 324 missions over the two atolls and had dropped 145 tons of bombs and used 152 rockets to do only limited damage because of the dug-in nature of the buildings, particularly on Wake.

There had been several new developments aboard the *Essex*. For the first time, the carrier had put up six night fighters, although there was no air opposition to them. The planes functioned very well. Also, on this raid, several fighters were equipped with bombs as an experiment. The problem was that the F6Fs loaded with bombs required a greater take-off length, and thus interfered with the spotting of planes on deck and with the speed of getting them into the air. If this technique were to work properly, another catapult would have to be installed.

After the Wake raid, the carriers headed back toward Majura. The men of Air Group Fifteen had been through their baptism of fire and had come off remarkably well. Still, one element was missing: they had yet to encounter their first Zeros or other enemy planes in action.

On May 26, the task group pulled into Majura harbor, and the commanders of the units made their reports to Admiral Mitscher. Admiral Spruance was then assembling his forces from various areas for the invasion of the Marianas. Rear Admiral Richmond Kelly Turner was training the Saipan invasion force at Pearl Harbor and in the outer Hawaiian Islands. The force that would invade Guam was training at Guadalcanal, and at the end of May the ships were beginning to move toward the Marshall Islands, which would be the final staging point before the invasion.

Admiral Mitscher was reorganizing the carrier force, and, in the changes that followed, the *Essex* and Air Group Fifteen became a part of Task Group 58.4, which was a carrier force of three carriers, three cruisers, and twelve destroyers. The *Essex* was accompanied by the light carrier *Langley*, with thirty planes of Air Group Thirty-Two aboard, and light carrier *Cowpens*, with twenty-six planes of Air Group Twenty-Five. Rear Admiral W.K. Harrill was the officer in command.

This fighting group was just one part of Mitscher's large carrier fleet. Three similar groups were each larger by one carrier. This fast-moving attack force, of fifteen carriers, fifteen cruisers, and scores of destroyers, joined the new "battle line" of fast battleships (seven in all), four fast cruisers, and thirteen destroyers, a force that was— theoretically—prepared to engage the Japanese fleet in a surface action if that became feasible.

On May 31, Admiral Mitscher sent Harrill's group to sea for two days of intensive training. The *Essex* was back at Majura from June 1 to June 5, and the next day moved out toward Saipan.

The Imperial Japanese Navy was not loath to give battle. For many months, a theory—espoused first by Admiral Yamamoto, the architect of both the Pearl Harbor attack and the overall Japanese naval war plans—had held that Japan's navy must seek one great battle with the Americans, defeat them, and then turn to the politicians to find a peaceful settlement that would assure Japan of retention of empire. In 1942, the army and the Imperial General Staff in Tokyo had ignored Admiral Yamamoto's warnings that only thus could military Japan survive, but after Yamamoto's death in an American ambush in the spring of 1943, the truth of his contention became clear in Tokyo. By that time, the American navy was on the upsurge and Japan's navy was losing ground in the battle of attrition in the South Pacific.

Admiral Mineichi Koga, who succeeded Yamamoto as commander of the Combined Fleet, brought Yamamoto's argument to Japan, and it was accepted at the highest level. Admiral Koga reorganized the Combined Fleet and moved its main body, called the Mobile Fleet, to a line that ran along the Marianas, the Caroline Islands, and the Philippines.

With this change, Koga hoped to be able to compensate for the serious losses of two years of war. The Japanese carrier fleet had been hard hit at Midway, with the loss or four large carriers, the *Kaga*, the *Akagi*, the *Soryu*, and the *Hiryu*. The light carrier *Ryujo* was lost at Guadalcanal. The Japanese still had the big new carriers *Shokaku* and *Zuikaku* and the light carriers *Junyo, Hiyo,* and *Zuiho*. The giant carrier *Taiho* was under construction, the supercarrier *Shinano*—the largest in the world— was to be completed within two years, and the battleships *Ise* and *Hyuga* were being converted to carriers by the removal of turrets and the installation of flight decks.

All this was happening while the Americans were quickly producing scores of new carriers, fleet carriers, light carriers, and escort carriers. The Kaiser shipbuilding company in northwestern United States was turning out escort carriers in less than three months, from keel laying to commissioning. Faced with this disastrous prospect, the Japanese navy had to find solutions.

Admiral Koga's solution was to make use of the many Pacific islands within the perimeter of the inner empire as air bases. As the Americans came closer, they would be farther from their home bases and supplies, while Japan's navy would be closer. The great naval battle would depend largely on the Japanese naval air force's ability to operate effectively from island bases and from the remaining carriers. This factor was central to the Koga plan. Tinian Island in the Marianas was to be the main base of the land-based naval air force, and Saipan was to be headquarters of the Combined Fleet.

Admiral Koga was killed in an air accident at the end of March, 1944, as the Americans at Pearl Harbor were planning the Marianas invasion. He left behind a major battle plan, known as the Z Plan, which called for a Japanese strike against the Americans with all available power at the moment that they entered the Philippine Sea, either from the south, coming up from New Guinea, or from the east. The major fleet units would come out to attack, but the kernel of the defense would be air power.

Koga planned that 500 planes on the remaining Japanese carriers would shuttle with 500 planes stationed in the Marianas Islands and Palau. Planes from the island bases would attack the Americans, land on the Japanese carriers, refuel, and fly off to attack again, while the carrier planes attacked, landed on the islands, refueled, and flew off to attack again and then return to their carriers. The Koga plan was a wise use of available resources, and on paper it was enormously impressive: effective air power was thus increased by about fifty percent.

It took the Japanese general staff six weeks to choose a successor to Koga for the Combined Fleet post. The new man was Admiral Soemu Toyoda, more of a surface sailor than an airman, and his revision of the Z Plan reflected his views. His major change in Koga's proposal was to make greater use of the surface units of the fleet. By the spring of 1944, these units were separated into two major parts. Much of the fleet was in Japanese waters, where it remained largely immobile because of the shortage of fuel oil caused by the constant sinking of tankers by American submarines.

Part of the fleet was stationed at Tawi Tawi in the Philippines, to be close to the source of supply. Vice Admiral Jisaburo Ozawa was to command both elements and to go forth at the first provocation to seek the "decisive battle" with the Americans. The Koga idea of shuttle air service was retained, but it lost some of its immediacy in the hands of the new commander. It was also severely hampered by the myopia of the Japanese high command in the matter of pilot training. Before the Pacific War moved away from China, Japan's naval air service had been an elite corps. It continued that way. Japanese pilots were among the best in the world, but their ranks were thin. When the war expanded, the Americans launched an immediate mass production drive to create airmen. The Japanese did no such thing, and by 1944 the supply of trained Japanese airmen was vastly diminished, and no proper steps had been taken to replace the fallen. The men who were sent to the front in the early months of 1944 to carry out the expansive Koga air program were barely trained in the art of staying aloft and alive and had no experience in battle. The tables were turned from the days of Pearl Harbor, the Philippines, and Malaya, when the Japanese had the air under their control. Now the Americans were the powerful ones, and many of the American carrier groups (unlike Air Group Fifteen) had seen several battles.

On May 27, as the *Essex* prepared to join Harrill's force at Majura, the Japanese put their war plan into motion. The cause was the allied invasion of Biak in the New Guinea area. Admiral Toyoda reacted to it by ordering a fight that would involve the major elements of the Japanese navy. They would strike the American invasion fleet off New Guinea and destroy it. But even as the ships of the Japanese fleet prepared to move out to attack in the south, a pilot, Lieutenant Takehiko Chihaya, made a flight over the Marshalls on aerial reconnaissance. He managed to move in among the islands without detection, and at Majura he saw the enormous American force assembling for the invasion of the Marianas.

When Chihaya's report was radioed to Tokyo, it created shock and confusion. The naval effort was geared to stopping the Americans at Biak, but from what Chihaya said, an even larger force was assembling at Majura. Where it could be going was a matter for conjecture. One lone staff officer of Toyoda's organization predicted that the invasion would be against Saipan, but he was hooted down by scoffers. There was no way the Americans could take that bastion, they said, and the Americans knew it. Furthermore, it was impossible that the Americans could be launching two invasions simultaneously. (They knew nothing of the major American effort of that month: the invasion of Fortress Europe in Normandy, which would be coming in less than a week.)

The Japanese intelligence system in the Pacific worked marvelously well, and the Japanese were far superior to the Americans in the matter of tactical air reconnaissance, but the Japanese intelligence system failed in its assessment of American capability and American production. The invasion by Admiral Barbey's forces in the Biak area was protected by a fleet of escort carriers. Japanese airmen reporting on them invariably thought that they were the fleet carriers. And since, when Lieutenant Chihaya's remarkable reconnaissance flight was made, the *Essex* and all the other carriers were out on training missions, the lieutenant reported that he saw no carriers in the Majura fleet. That was the decisive factor: the Americans would never try an invasion without a carrier force. The Majura ships must be in support of the Biak operation, said the Toyoda staff.

On June 6, when the *Essex* sailed toward Saipan to begin the softening-up bombing of the island, Admiral Spruance sailed in the *Indianapolis* for Eniwetok. On June 8, while the *Essex* was at sea, still moving northwest, Admiral Spruance met Admiral Turner at Eniwetok and made the last plans for the invasion, and then the *Indianapolis* took him off to join Admiral Mitscher and the airmen. On June 9, Spruance approved Mitscher's request to make the preliminary strikes on the islands of Saipan, Guam, Tinian, and Rota. On June 10, Admiral Toyoda committed the major elements of the Japanese fleet to a fight at Biak, a plan known as Operation Kon. The huge battleships *Musashi* and *Yamato* were ordered to sail from Tawi Tawi to add their 18-inch guns to the power of the fleet.

At dawn on June 11, the airmen of Air Group Fifteen went into action. One fighter-bomber sweep of fifteen planes was launched from the *Essex* to attack Saipan at the same time as planes from other carriers attacked that island and other places in the Marianas.

The Saipan invasion force was rapidly assembling. Admiral Turner's ships had just arrived at Eniwetok from Pearl Harbor. This force would sail in the next few days to reach Saipan on June 15. As the ships refueled at the new bases in the Marshalls, word came that the Japanese seemed to be preparing to meet the invasion with a large naval force. Coastwatchers in the Philippines and American submarines on patrol reported the movement of two separate Japanese naval task forces. It appeared that a major sea and air battle was shaping up.

CHAPTER THREE

First Blood at Saipan

Admiral Harrill's task group was assigned the responsibility for knocking out the air defenses of Saipan and Pagan, another of the Marianas group which consisted of more than a dozen islands ranging from the Farallon de Pajaros (Bird Rock) in the north to Guam in the south. Only five of these islands were important in the military sense: Pagan, Saipan, Tinian, Rota, and Guam (in that geographical order). Pagan housed an airfield, a small runway, and a number of barracks and shops. It was a part of the Japanese shuttle-system, by which they could move land-based aircraft from island to island as far as the South Pacific. Saipan was the center of Japanese activity in the Marianas, with nearby Tinian almost as important. Saipan was Air Group Fifteen's first target, and the task was simple: destroy enemy aircraft.

Just before 1:00 on the afternoon of June 11, the *Essex* was in position to launch planes, and fifteen fighters and two dive bombers were put into the air, along with a dozen fighters from the carrier *Cowpens* and a dozen from the *Langley*. Commander McCampbell led the air strike.

The first American planes reached Saipan at 2:00. The fifteen *Essex* fighters were the carrier's attack force; the two SB2C bombers were rescue planes, which were equipped with extra life rafts and other survival gear to drop to downed pilots and they were to stay around in the air directing rescue. Seven of the F6F fighters carried 350-pound demolition bombs. They dived from 12,000 feet, bombed at 2,500 feet, and then formed a strafing line and strafed the island from east to west as far as the sea. The other eight fighters stayed above them, "flying cover" until the bombing runs ended, and then they went down to strafe. For the next hour and a half they made repeated strafing runs on Saipan, concentrating on the airfields and seaplane installations.

Perhaps the first blood went to the Japanese. On its way down over Tanapag harbor, Lieutenant (jg) L.T. Kenney's fighter was hit by anti-aircraft fire. He continued the dive, straight down into the water, where the plane splashed and disappeared.

Commander Brewer led the fighter down. His point of attack was the harbor seaplane ramp. As he went down he could see three seaplanes parked neatly on the ramp. His bomb struck in the middle of them, destroying all three. Brewer then went on strafing, came around, and headed out to sea. Five miles out at sea, northwest of Marpi Point, Brewer and Ensign R.E. Fowler, Jr., spotted a dark green Kawanishi flying boat with the dull red wing circles denoting the Japanese air force. They attacked.

As they came up, several other fighters were shooting at the Emily, as it was called in U.S. identification parlance. Commander Brewer attacked from above on the side of the plane and saw his bullets hit the Emily's number two engine and the port wing. Ensign Fowler attacked the cockpit and noticed that the plane was smoking as he came in from previous attacks. Twenty seconds later the flying boat turned over on one wing, dropped with engine aflame and smoke coming from the fuselage, and struck the water. It exploded in a geyser of water, smoke, and flame. Three other F6Fs, perhaps from other carriers, participated in this attack, but at the end of the day Commander McCampbell claimed the Emily for Brewer and Fowler.

Brewer then turned west of the town of Garapan, when he saw three Zeros. But by the time he could arrive on the scene, all three had been shot down by other American fighters.

This encounter was the first of the pilots of Air Group Fifteen against enemy aircraft. So much had been said about the Zero that Commander McCampbell was pleased to note that the F6F could stay with the Zero in turns, climbs, and dives, particularly at altitudes above 12,000 feet, where most of the air action took place. He also noted two major deficiencies of the Zero, becoming much more important these days: its lack of armor and its tendency to burn meant unprotected gas tanks. All but one of the Zeros his pilots saw shot down that day went down in flames.

Half an hour after the American attack began, Saipan was wreathed in smoke. The Japanese took advantage of the prevailing wind; they lit smoke-pots on the eastern side of the island, and the easterly wind blew a heavy cloud across to the west, obscuring many installations.

At 2:30, Commander McCampbell was flying at 10,000 feet, southwest of Saipan, flying "mattress," or low air cover, for the attackers and observing the attack as was his responsibility. Suddenly a Zero plummeted down from above the fighters in attack. It pulled up in a high wingover on McCampbell's port beam. McCampbell turned into the Zero immediately and give it a short burst from close up—not more than 250 yards away. The Zero turned over on its left wing to get away, McCampbell followed and got in another short burst, got on the tail and gave the Zero a third brief shelling by machine gun. The Zero pilot frantically made another right wingover, but he was already going down. The plane fell off on that right wing and spiraled toward the sea. Another F6F followed the plane down, firing. McCampbell was too good an air commander to be sucked out of position. The Zero hit the water without burning and sank. No head appeared.

McCampbell had found no difficulty in keeping up with the Zero's highly praised turning ability. He had jettisoned his gasoline belly tank, which was standard procedure when going into action. Then the F6F responded nobly.

During this attack, the American pilots found the Japanese anti-aircraft fire largely inaccurate, except for Lieutenant Kenney's disaster. The real opposition was from Japanese aircraft this time.

The primary targets of the Air Group Fifteen planes were the seaplane base in Tanapag harbor and the port, ships in harbor, and facilities at Marpi Point. The F6Fs secured seven direct hits on the seaplane ramp and the installations next to it, starting one large fire in a building, and they destroyed six seaplanes and damaged five others at the base. Another three seaplanes in the water of Tanapag harbor were destroyed and two more damaged. A small cargo ship in the harbor took an enormous beating from many strafing planes and was left smoking and dead in the water. At Marpi Point, the planes hit the airstrip, and, although they did not find any land-based aircraft on the ground, they did set fire to an oil storage tank that began to burn furiously, and burned as long as the planes' pilots could see it as they retired.

The fighter squadron's lieutenant commander, James F. Rigg, came upon one Japanese seaplane fighter as he was pulling up from the strafing of the harbor, and he shot it down with one burst. He then saw a Zero coming directly at him, head on. Both pilots maintained speed and the collision course until at the last minute the Zero pilot pulled up, presenting the plane's belly for a full deflection shot. Rigg fired, the Zero made a sharp turn to the left, burst into flames, and crashed in the sea.

Lieutenant Morris sighted a Mavis flying boat that had just taken off from Tanapag harbor, and he swooped down on it. The Mavis did not get 200 feet into the air before it turned and crashed onto the reef.

Lieutenant (jg) R.W. Rushing got into a dogfight with a Zero just off the southern tip of Saipan. The planes maneuvered around each other like angry dogs, and the Zero pilot tried a scissors maneuver; Rushing put the F6F into a tight turn and fired his guns. The Zero fell off and burst into flames. The pilot threw back the canopy cover and bailed out just before the Zero exploded. The white parachute unfolded and the pilot swayed gently down toward the water as the fight went on elsewhere.

Rushing learned that day that his F6F could keep up with a Zero at speeds of up to 400 miles per hour and at altitudes from 13,000 to 25,000 feet. This would have surprised most Japanese pilots, who had learned earlier in the war that the Zero outmatched any existing American fighter plane. Suddenly there was an American fighter plane that could do anything the Zero could do.

Ensign K.A. Flinn encountered another Zero in that same area south of Saipan. He saw the Zero, gave chase, and the inexperienced Japanese pilot turned and ran, apparently secure in his belief that the Zero could outfly the American fighter. Flinn kept right up with the enemy plane and got on its tail, then fired a few bursts, and the unarmored Zero burst into flames and crashed.

Ensign D.E. Johnson, Jr., and Ensign G.H. Rader ganged up on one poor Zero pilot off the northern tip of Tinian Island; Ensign Johnson rolled over to make a run from the front; Ensign Rader hit him from the rear, and the Zero began to smoke. The pilot bailed out, and the flaming Zero crashed in the water.

The other fighter pilots of the squadron saw half a dozen Japanese planes, but these were under attack by other American fighters from other carriers, so they left them alone. An hour and a half after the attack began, the fighters and bombers from Air Group Fifteen were on their way back to the *Essex,* leaving smoke wisping up from the island. All planes landed safely on the carrier; only two F6Fs were damaged—both by anti-aircraft fire.

CHAPTER FOUR

The Softening-Up of Saipan

The death of Admiral Yamamoto, and then of Admiral Koga, his successor, had brought about a major change in Japanese fleet and air operations. So many aircraft and pilots had been lost in the attrition battle of the South Pacific and so many destroyers had been sunk that the fleet was sorely hampered. The Japanese had lost their share of carriers, battleships, and cruisers, too. Japanese shipyards were repairing damaged vessels and turning out new ones, but at nowhere near the rate of the Americans. It had become obvious by this summer of 1945 that, in this greater battle of attrition, the American production system must win.

Japan's fleet was still a mighty weapon, but each day's operations made it less so in comparison to the growing American strength. The answer, said the Japanese admirals, was a major single blow, at which they hoped their skill and determination would overcome the odds of numbers and bring about a naval victory that would in turn slow the American advance and force the United States to come to the peace table to make concessions that would let Japan keep the territories she had won.

In September, 1943, the Japanese Combined Fleet came under a new operational policy that demanded all naval force be exerted in that one "final" battle. In the spring of 1944, a new organizational structure had created the Mobile Fleet, which included every ship that could be useful. At the moment of operation, Vice Admiral Jisaburo Ozawa, the commander of the Mobile Fleet, could call on these ships to assemble for the great battle.

When the Americans under General MacArthur landed in Central New Guinea in April, the Japanese figured that the great battle would be fought in that area and began to make their preparations for it. On May 27, the Allied forces landed at Biak, and the Imperial General Staff issued orders that troop reinforcements were to be sent to the area, and the navy was to seek the big battle. Five hundred land-based planes were rushed to various islands in the long chain of defense—most of them in the south.

Operation Kon was begun for relief of the Biak region, and several small naval actions were fought off Biak late in May and early in June. Admiral Thomas Kinkaid, commander of the U.S. naval forces in MacArthur's Southwest Pacific area, was certain by the middle of the first week in June that the Japanese fleet would move into the area to force the issue of the great battle. On June 10 it seemed that this would indeed be the case, for Admiral Toyoda sent the battleships *Yamato* and *Musashi* toward New Guinea, along with several cruisers and destroyers. The carriers were not yet committed because there was no evidence of American carriers in the New Guinea area.

Then, on June 11, came the reports from Saipan that the U.S. carrier planes had attacked all the Marianas Islands in force. This maneuver was the signal in the past for an invasion, so Admiral Toyoda suspended Operation Kon, and ordered Admiral Ozawa to prepare for a major fleet action in the Philippine Sea to stop the invasion of Saipan and to destroy the American carrier force.

The night of June 11, the main Japanese force was anchored at Bajan on the edge of the Molucca Passage and the Ceram Sea, close to the source of petroleum supply for the ships and close to the New Guinea operation of the Americans—too close for Japanese comfort. Admiral Ugaki, former chief of staff to Admiral Yamamoto and now commander of the Biak reinforcement expedition, was prepared to run into Biak and attack the Americans on June 15. But Admiral Toyoda changed his plans that night. The next day, orders came to Ugaki: suspend Operation Kon, head north to join up with Admiral Ozawa, and attack the Americans at Saipan (where Toyoda could see they were heading).

The major portion of the Japanese fleet lay in Lingga Roads, south of Singapore. It included three carriers: the *Taiho* (brand new), the *Shokaku,* and the *Zuikaku.* Six other carriers, the *Junyo,* the *Hiyo,* the *Ryuho,* the *Chitose,* the *Chiyoda,* and the *Zuiho* were in Japanese waters. All began sailing on June 11, accompanied by the battleship *Musashi* and a number of cruisers and destroyers. They were trailed by their support ships. The destination of all these vessels was Tawi Tawi in the Philippines. This island in the Sulu Archipelago provided a point of access to almost any point the Americans might strike. The Japanese fleet was preparing for Operation A-Go, the "decisive battle."

But even as Admiral Ozawa marshaled his forces the airmen of the *Essex* and of the other carriers were destroying half the plan—the aspect that called for maximum impact by the First Air Fleet, the land-based naval aircraft which had been moved to the south to assist the carriers in what was seen as a shuttle operation of carrier to land to carrier, and vice versa.

So Admiral Ugaki moved north with the battleships *Yamato* and *Musashi,* the cruisers *Myoko, Haguro,* and *Noshiro,* and five destroyers. At the same time, Admiral Toyoda ordered all available aircraft to move north from the New Guinea area and reinforce the Marianas. The immediate result of this was to relieve the pressure on

MacArthur's forces, and assure the Japanese defeat at Biak. The Japanese did not regard it thus then; the fleet and the air power were moving "only temporarily." General Anami, commander of the Second Area Army at Davao, ordered his subordinates to string out the defense of Biak, with the implication that the fleet and the air power would return after defeating the Americans at Saipan, and then Operation Kon would be completed.

On June 12, the airmen of the *Essex* were ready to hit the Japanese again at Saipan. This time, the target for the carrier's planes would be the aviation facilities, anti-aircraft guns, and aircraft on the northern part of Saipan. All three squadrons of Air Group Fifteen would be involved.

At four o'clock in the morning, they began taking off: twenty-four fighters, fifteen dive bombers, and eight torpedo bombers, accompanied by sixteen fighters and nine torpedo planes from the *Cowpens*. Again, Commander McCampbell was the officer leading the strike.

The attack began with a night takeoff from the carrier, which was accomplished without incident, much to McCampbell's satisfaction. It was a "first" for the air group. Marpi Point was their destination, but, in the darkness on the way, McCampbell sighted the running lights of a ship which could only be enemy. He sent several fighters down to strafe the ship, and they attacked. The ship's captain tardily turned out his lights, and the attackers then came back since they had no further point of aim.

The American planes arrived over their target before dawn and made their first attack. The anti-aircraft fire was weak and inaccurate. As the wave came in, dawn was breaking, but still the AA fire was not strong. Nor did any fighters come up this day to meet the Americans. The Japanese were saving their air strength for the battle against the fleet, which would be joined with the arrival on the scene of Admiral Ozawa.

After attacking the land targets around the Marpi Point airstrip, the planes found a number of cargo vessels and hit them. They started fires on at least four of these vessels and on the return to the carrier predicted that they would sink—a prediction immediately discounted by the air intelligence officer.

After return to the carrier, the planes were refueled, rearmed, and in half an hour Commander McCampbell was in the air again, leading a second strike of twelve fighters, thirteen dive bombers, eight torpedo bombers, and eight fighters from the *Cowpens*. This strike was against the air installations on the island of Pagan, north of Saipan.

At about 8:15, the forty-one planes were approaching the island, which was surrounded by cumulus clouds and a thin haze, but as they came above Pagan they saw that the targets were clear. The dive bombers "pushed over" at 11,500 feet and began a seventy-degree dive toward the island. The torpedo bombers began a glide approach from 9,000 feet. The planes carried bombs from 100 to 500 pounds, fragmentation and incendiary. Ahead of them went the fighters, strafing the barracks, air strips, and buildings.

Two planes on the airstrip were set afire and burned, and another was strafed but did not burn. Three dummy planes were observed on the edge of the runway.

The bombers hit the runway and put many craters in it. They destroyed three hangars and one building that looked like a factory near the hangars. Three other buildings were bombed, and one exploded with a roar as the ammunition inside blew up. The bombers found an oil storage tank and set it afire, and they left the barracks buildings ablaze. Then, on retirement, they swooped over the harbor and strafed small boats and barges. One lucky Japanese gunner put shells into the wing of a torpedo plane, and Lieutenant (jg) John Chambers had to land in the water about halfway home to the task force. He and his gunner and radio operator were rescued by a destroyer.

The planes were back aboard ship by 9:45, rearming and gassing for another island strike, when word came that a scout plane from the task group had found a Japanese convoy. The plans for the island attack were scrapped, and the planes were hurried into the sky to go after the convoy. Once again, the air strike was led by Commander McCampbell, with sixteen *Essex* fighters, twelve dive bombers and eight torpedo bombers. The *Cowpens* sent off twelve fighters and nine torpedo planes.

At 10:30, the convoy came in sight. It was a large transport convoy, accompanied by a number of patrol craft, a torpedo boat, subchasers, and many fishing boats, headed back to Japan after supplying the Marianas garrisons.

Commander McCampbell kept several fighters with him in the air, high above the target, to protect the attackers from possible Japanese aircraft, but none appeared. As the Japanese captains saw the approaching planes, they first headed in convoy for a cloud bank off to the east, but it was almost immediately apparent that they would not safely reach it, so they began to take individual evasive action, spreading out and making sharp turns to throw off the pilots.

One dive bomber pilot, Lieutenant (jg) Turner, put a bomb into the stern of the largest transport in the middle of the convoy. The gunner of another plane saw the bomb hit and damage the propeller. The ship went dead in the water, a number of fighters strafed, and it began to burn in several places. Later a pilot reported seeing the ship sink.

Lieutenant Sorensen of the torpedo bomber squadron and Ensign Gunter of the dive bomber squadron attacked another cargo ship with bombs (the change in plans had come too quickly for the torpedo planes to rearm with torpedoes). This ship was also reported sunk.

Ensign Otto Bleech of the torpedo squadron attacked another cargo ship with rockets after delivering his bombs. She began to blaze at the stern and on the bridge, and the crew started abandoning ship as fighters came in to strafe.

Ensign Wilfred Bailey of the dive bomber squadron had two near-misses on a single ship. One bomb, a 500-pounder, dropped in the sea fifteen feet from the starboard bow, and the other, a 100-pounder, dropped twenty feet from the port bow. A piece of the bow was blown off, and the ship stopped, to be hit by strafing fighters.

Lieutenant Charles D. Webb of the torpedo squadron made two hits on the side of another transport, blowing two holes in the plating. The ship stopped. Lieutenant Webb's attack on another transport left her stern burning, and Ensign Walter Harper of VT 15 (torpedo squadron) bombed still another transport. By the time the attackers had run out of ammunition and bombs and rockets, escorts, fishing boats, transports, and the torpedo boat were all afire, and several were sinking or sunk. Just before departing for the carriers, Commander McCampbell led his air cover planes down to attack, and as he pulled away from the smoke of the convoy, he counted four ships dead in the water among the furiously evading smaller vessels.

The Japanese attempts to fight back were almost unnoticeable. They had no long-range anti-aircraft guns, and only five planes were damaged—all of them repairable on board the *Essex*. Ensign John Storrs Foote's dive bomber crashed in the sea after a waveoff by the landing signal officer as he came in to land, but he and his gunner were rescued after the water landing. The loss of the plane was put down as operational, not due to combat.

The planes were back on the deck of the *Essex* before 1:00 p.m. Commander McCampbell made his report, and on that basis the decision was made to send another strike against the convoy that afternoon. Commander Brewer, the commanding officer of Fighting Fifteen, was designated to lead the attack.

At 3:00, the second strike took off from the carrier: twelve fighters and fifteen dive bombers. There were no planes from the *Cowpens* this time.

Commander Brewer led the planes back toward the last known position of the convoy, and there passed over five ships dead in the water, the results of the morning's activity. He did not stop to attack, but went on after the vessels that might otherwise get away and soon found them. Commander Brewer led the fighters down, dropping his belly tank on a transport. He made a good shot of it, the tank exploded on the deck and started a fire. Brewer zoomed on, to strafe a ship he identified as a modern destroyer. As he pulled up from his strafing run, Ensign Slack and Ensign Bare came on in on the enemy warship, and as they pulled up it exploded before their eyes and sank. Someone had made a lucky hit on a magazine, but who it was would never be known for virtually every plane was in action just then. Lieutenant (jg) Glass put a five hundred pound bomb into a ship at the stern waterline, and his gunner, George Duncan, saw debris fly up. Ensign Moore dropped a bomb on the starboard side, and his gunner saw fires break out from below deck. Ensign Zanetti saw the ship listing heavily.

It went that way with much of the convoy. Ensign C.W. Plant dropped a bomb from his fighter and saw it hit another transport. Lieutenant Commander Duncan dropped a bomb on yet another cargo ship, and it began to burn. By the time the American planes had completed their attack, the convoy was dispersed, and the sky was full of smoke and flame. Circling, Commander Brewer estimated that there had been a dozen vessels down there: one destroyer, six cargo ships, and five small escort vessels. He believed that the destroyer was sunk, along with two of the transports, and that all the other ships were damaged except for two escorts which were not attacked. The Japanese return fire was minimal; mostly it consisted of small calibre machine gun bullets and none of the *Essex* planes was seriously damaged.

Later that day, an American destroyer moving through the area rescued seven Japanese and Korean survivors from the water and delivered them to the *Essex* for interrogation by Admiral Harrill's staff. The staff tried to identify the ships, and did produce some names—*Inari Maru, Batavia Maru,* etc.—but these were not particularly meaningful to the Americans, since the Japanese did not register all their ships with Lloyd's.

Commander McCampbell and Commander Brewer identified a new type of destroyer in the attack, but the postwar evaluation cut their warships down in size to torpedo boats (roughly the equivalent to destroyer escorts). Altogether, the attack was deemed highly successful, but there seemed to be enough left of the convoy to warrant one more strike.

It was made on the morning of June 13. Commander McCampbell led the strike again, taking off just after 5:00. The force consisted of sixteen fighters, thirteen dive bombers, and eight torpedo bombers. The fighters spread out in a scouting line to find the convoy and an hour and a half out, they did. One fighter had to abort when the plane's belly tank developed an air lock, and the pilot took the F6F back to the carrier. The others attacked; what they attacked was the single remaining merchant ship. The fighters strafed and bombed, the dive bombers bombed, and the torpedo bombers attacked with bombs and rockets. They sank the cargo ship.

Although they searched, the airmen found no other undamaged ships. They passed several hulks in the water on their way back to the carrier, with lifelines hanging over the sides and boats and rafts floating aimlessly in the area. The remainder of the convoy had somehow escaped them in the night.

Returning to the carrier, Ensign W. Fontaine of the dive bomber squadron spotted an enemy bomber below him and made a pass at the plane. He also got on the radio to report.

Flying at 1,000 feet, Commander McCampbell heard the report and looked around.

"I turned left and saw the plane, a Helen [Nakajima army bomber], 200 feet above the water. He turned right, poured on coal, and I chased him from astern. He was about two miles away. I caught up in two and a half minutes. My entire division [four planes] engaged him. I made first and last runs, in addition to one in the middle. The division overtook him at high speed, pulling out to the side. I pulled up above him to get positive identification and kill speed, then made two rear runs before losing enough speed to get on the third time and sit there until he blew up. . . . He blew up fifty feet off the water, no survivors. No visible fire from the Helen, possibly no rear gunner; looked like a brand new plane, very bright paint, possibly being ferried south. Saw gun in turret."

Quite probably Commander McCampbell was right in his assessment. With the realization that the battle for the Marianas was about to be joined, the Japanese navy had been furiously ferrying planes into the island pipeline that led south.

McCampbell's planes did not get back to the *Essex* that day until 9:30 a.m. By the time they returned, Commander Brewer had already taken off with another strike against Saipan and little Maniagassa Island nearby. Forty planes from the *Essex* and the light carrier *Langley* approached the enemy territory, looking for anti-aircraft and coastal defense guns. They bombed and strafed gun positions and several cargo craft just off the islands, and they left a barracks burning at Mutcho Point. There they encountered their only opposition, highly inaccurate fire from heavy and light anti-aircraft guns. Before noon, Commander Brewer's planes were back on the deck of the *Essex*.

The airmen of the *Essex* were making shuttle runs that day in their effort to knock out the air defenses of Saipan before the invasion.

At 11:30 in the morning, twenty bombers and eleven fighters set out for the west side of Saipan to make another attack. They were led by Lieutenant Commander J.F. Rigg of the dive bomber squadron.

There was something different about today's performance at Saipan: the invasion date was very near and the American fleet lay on the water offshore, beginning a three-day bombardment of the island. The new element was the presence of an entirely modern battleship fleet of seven ships under command of Rear Admiral W.A. Lee. This new force was called the "battle line"; it had been developed as the last gasp of the battleship admirals, in the belief that at some point the Pacific war would be settled by an old-fashioned slugging match between capital ships. So far, the closest action to that had been the battles around Guadalcanal; but the Japanese possessed a number of battleships, including the *Yamato* and *Musashi,* the largest in the world, and as long as they existed the possibility of a major surface engagement remained. To that date, the most important effort of any battleship of the American fleet had been the work of the *Washington* at Guadalcanal and in the Bismarck Sea.

The battleships under Admiral Lee were assigned to the Fifth Fleet, Admiral Spruance's invasion force. If a fleet action developed, they would go with the carriers to fight. At the moment, they were given a task for which they had no preparation, the bombardment of Saipan in the softening-up process.

Until the Marianas invasion, the bombardments had been led by the old battleships (those that survived the Pearl Harbor attack). They would do most of the job here at Saipan, too, but they had not yet arrived; and since the fast battleships *were* on the scene with the carriers, they started the task on June 13.

The bombardment began early in the morning, but as the Rigg detachment arrived for the air attack on the Mutcho Point area at 12:45 in the afternoon the big ships were supposed to suspend activity for six minutes, to give the dive bombers, torpedo bombers, and strafing fighters their chance to attack. The battleships had been banging away at nothing in particular for a long time. When Commander Rigg's planes got into position at 13,000 feet above the target, he ordered them to attack, and they nosed down. They bombed from 2,500 feet. Several of the battleships did not receive the word, or perhaps their clocks were off. As the *Essex* attack planes came down, the 5-inch and 16-inch shells were bursting below them and seemed to the pilots to be more of a threat than the weak anti-aircraft fire thrown up by the Japanese gunners. But all planes escaped serious damage, and all returned to the *Essex,* while the battleship gunners went back to what one sailor called a "farm project."

The shells plowed into the fields, knocked down trees, smashed sugar cane and rice in the open, and did virtually no damage to Japanese defenses. Indeed, at Charan Kanoa the Japanese had erected a tall smokestack to serve the sugar mill there, and it went untouched in this and later bombardments. For days it remained as a most important Japanese spotting position. Some high ranking officer had decided that the smokestack would make a fine radio aerial for the occupation force, so the gunners and pilots were forbidden to knock it down.

This softening-up process proved excellent for the squadrons of the *Essex*, as a training device, with just enough enemy activity to make the pilots stay on their toes, but no real opposition. The next strike on the 13th of June, was led by Lieutenant Commander Lambert, commanding officer of the torpedo squadron. He took seven bombers, accompanied by a dozen fighters from the *Essex* and the *Langley*, to attack anti-aircraft guns on the south shore of Saipan, at Magicienne Bay. They found two gun positions and bombed and strafed both. The anti-aircraft fire stopped, but not before one torpedo bomber was damaged by hits in the wings, the bomb bay, and the tunnel to the gunner's position.

While the torpedo planes went after the guns, Lieutenant Commander G.C. Duncan of the fighter squadron took six fighters and six dive bombers to strike Japanese shipping at Pagan. They found two small cargo ships there and bombed and strafed them both, setting fires.

On his return to the *Essex* in mid-afternoon, Ensign K.B. West spotted a Betty above and behind the American planes. Lieutenant J.E. Barry, Jr., and his wingman, Ensign J.M. Power, Jr., reversed course and went after the Japanese airplane.

Four minutes later the two fighters approached the Japanese plane. Ensign Power, overeager, began firing from below before he was in range, and the Japanese pilot suddenly discovered he was under attack. He turned sharply to the right, and dropped into a dive, putting his rear gunner in position to fire at the attackers. Lieutenant Barry was just closing in as the Japanese gunner began shooting. Barry's F6F was struck in the leading edge of the left wing. The shells tore up the wing, damaged the hydraulic system, and weakened the main spar. Lieutenant Barry kept on with his attack, moving up behind the Betty, firing all the time. The Japanese gunner was hit and the gun stopped firing. The two planes were speeding down toward the sea. The attack had begun at 8,000 feet. At 5,000 feet, the Japanese plane began to flame and then plunged straight down into the sea. There were no survivors.

The American planes then turned and headed back to the carrier. When they arrived over the *Essex*, Lieutenant Barry discovered that only one of his wheels would go down. He made a one wheel landing on the deck, but the plane dropped over on its left wing and skidded, and the wing was torn up so badly that the F6F had to be pushed over the side.

Aboard the *Essex* the airmen had been running all day long. As the other strikes took off, just after 1:00 p.m., so did six two-plane search sections, out looking for targets. Three sections found shipping around Saipan and attacked, leaving a number of small vessels burning or sinking.

On June 14, Admiral Harrill's task group moved out so there were no attacks. The admiral's move was toward the Volcano Islands, where the *Essex* airmen would strike at Japanese air installations on Iwo Jima. This island and nearby Chichi Jima were important staging points on the Japanese air route south. Admiral Spruance was not very pleased to have the carriers moving out that far from Saipan (about 700 miles to the northwest) and he told Rear Admiral J.J. Clark to bring his three carriers and Harrill's task group back after a single day of attack on June 16. But the carriers arrived within striking distance on the afternoon of June 15, and the first *Essex* attack was launched at 1:30 on the afternoon of the 15th.

Commander McCampbell led this "air sweep," which involved twenty-two fighters from the *Essex*, sixteen from the *Yorktown*, and eight from the *Bataan*. The plan called for the fighters to come in at low level, to avoid radar (if the Japanese had it) and visual observation from afar in any event, but an extensive weather front forced the planes to climb to 8,000 feet and they overshot the island of Iwo Jima and had to come back to it. On this turn, the Japanese managed to get several planes into the air to meet the Americans.

Commander McCampbell was at 8,000 feet when a Zero approached from his left side.

"I turned into him and gave him a burst, head-on, he continued straight and level until dangerously close and I pulled out above and to the right before he did. He pulled left and head for...a hole in the mattress [cloud cover], doing a Split-S. I followed astern and gave him a long burst at 2,500 feet. Then, through the hole I saw him dead ahead. He had pulled half through a wingover to the right. In order to get back on his tail I made a vertical "flipper" turn to the right, and "grayed out" but was able to get in a short burst from 1,000 feet. He made another wingover to the right, ending up on my tail. Lieutenant (jg) Rushing, my wingman, followed the action down and saw me pull back up through the cloud with the Zeke on my tail. Rushing was getting ready to make a run when the Zeke pulled back into the cloud. I kicked rudder to see astern and determine whether I had enough distance to turn back in again. He was not on my tail but at the same instant I saw a big splash in the water below. I believe it was the Zeke although two other pilots saw the same splash and thought it might have been a belly tank. My excess speed in the dive prohibited my turning sharp enough to get on his tail. The Zeke pressed home his head-on attack, forcing me to pull out. I didn't see any fire from his wing guns although he may have been firing from his synchronized guns, which I was unable to observe because of my own tracer."

Then they were over the airfields, diving down in neat four-plane formations to strafe. The anti-aircraft fire was severe: three fighters were hit hard. But the damage to the Japanese was enormous; they had been caught virtually flatfooted, with dozens of planes on the parking strips near the runways. The pilots counted a hundred planes on the two airfields. They were grouped by types—twin-engined Betty bombers, Zero fighters, stub-winged Zeros for carrier use (called Hamps), various sorts of torpedo bombers and observation planes, and several transports that looked much like the DC-3 transport in general use in the American forces. The pilots estimated that they burned or destroyed at least half these planes. In fact, they must have done far more damage because many strafed planes did not burn, which meant that they were not filled with fuel. Other parts were hit with explosives, tracers, and bombs. Commander McCampbell's division made a total of six strafing runs on the airfields.

Southwest of the airfields, Commander Brewer encountered a Zero. He was flying at 6,000 feet when he saw the Japanese fighter below. He turned into a dive and went down to 1,500 feet and opened fire. From a thousand feet away, he began shooting in three-second bursts, and closed to within 100 feet before the Zero began to burn. The pilot bailed out, his parachute opened, and he dropped into the sea, as the plane rolled over on its back, flew for a few moments, and then nosed down and splashed.

Lieutenant Commander Duncan was leading his four-plane division in the strafing. They pulled up from one run and went around to start another. Three miles east of Iwo Jima they encountered a flight of four Zeros at 5,000 feet. The Zeros turned and fled. Duncan led the chase and pulled up on them after he turned on the water injection system, a sort of supercharger on the F6F that increased its speed noticeably.

Finally he caught up with the "tail-end Charlie," the last pilot in the Zero formation. The pilot tried to evade, going into turns, skids, and roll-overs to get away from the pursuing F6Fs, but Commander Duncan caught up, opened fire, and apparently killed or wounded the Japanese flier. The Zero nosed over and went down into the sea, while the other three Japanese planes escaped into a cloud bank.

Lieutenant (jg) A.A. Jones and his wingman were strafing across the south airfield, from east to west. They came in and leveled off at 800 feet above the field and went straight down the runway, firing. Below, the Japanese anti-aircraft gunners fired back, and caught Jones's plane in a crossfire. Jones was hit, he pulled up into a tight wingover, rolled completely over, and the plane crashed into the sea. It was the only loss of the mission.

Lieutenant J.R. Crittenden was hit in the leg by anti-aircraft fire, but managed to bring his F6F back to the carrier and land safely. Six other fighters were also damaged, mostly in the fuselages, by anti-aircraft shells. It was a long mission, nearly six hours, which represented a calculated risk on the part of Admiral Clark. Those fighters were very nearly out of gas by the time they returned to the carrier.

Commander McCampbell did not return with his strike wave. Instead he waited at the target, supervising the second strike, which came almost on the heels of the first. This second strike was led out by Lieutenant Commander James Mini, the commanding officer of the bombing and scouting squadron. This strike depended heavily on the planes of the light carrier *Langley;* only eight fighters from the *Essex* could be mounted for the strike, in addition to eighteen dive bombers and twelve torpedo bombers. The *Langley* provided sixteen fighters and nine torpedo bombers. The bombers carried 500-, 250-, and 100-pound bombs to use against the runways, aircraft, and buildings.

The second strike got a hot reception from the Japanese. The surprise on the ground had evaporated; it was now replaced with a grim determination. The bombers of both carrier groups got the worst of it, but they did their job, which was to work over the aircraft on the ground and destroy the air facilities. The dive bombers concentrated on the runways with their 500-pound bombs and destroyed two buildings. The torpedo bombers dropped their fragmentation bombs among the parked aircraft and blew many of them apart. But Ensign Theodore Clement and his gunner, Kenneth

Jackson, were last seen over the target. Their plane was one of those hit by anti-aircraft fire that were seen to crash on the island.

Ensign Conrad W. Crellin's dive bomber made it away from the target after being hit, but crashed in the water on the way back to the carrier. Crellin and his gunner, Alfred T. Graham, Jr., were rescued by a destroyer.

Two of the torpedo bombers were hit hard. One TBF, piloted by Ensign A.D. McRae, crashed; McRae and his crewmen, L.C. Lifset and H.R. Dudley, were killed. Ensign T.W. Sterling's TBF was seen to make a water landing off the coast of Iwo Jima. The pilot and his crewmen, J.R. Cooper and S.B. Gitelson, clambered out of the floating plane into a life raft. They were still floating when the air strike planes had to turn and go back to the carrier because of fuel shortage.

There were other losses that day. One fighter's wings were neatly stitched by bullets from anti-aircraft guns and another was hit in the tail, but both made safe carrier landings. Ensign Arthur Singer, Jr., was assigned to photo reconnaissance and flew over the island in the middle of the strike, taking pictures. When his mission was complete, he turned and encountered a Zero; Singer opened fire and shot it down. The Japanese pilot bailed out safely, but his parachute opened just before he hit the water. When last seen, the Japanese pilot was being dragged along the surface of the sea by the wind.

One dive bomber crashed on takeoff, and the crewmen were rescued. Two others were damaged but returned, and so did two damaged torpedo bombers. It was the toughest mission the airmen of the *Essex* had yet faced.

CHAPTER FIVE

The Softening-Up of Saipan—Part 2

That first day's strike at Iwo Jima proved the contention of Admiral "Jocko" Clark and the other "firebrands" of the naval air service, who had argued since the opening days of the war that the carriers must be used daringly and that thus they could deal devastating blows against the Japanese. In this one day's strike by planes from two carriers the enemy potential for supply of the Marianas air forces had been lowered enormously.

That night of June 15, the weather worsened seriously. Aboard the *Essex* the torpedo pilots gave a thought to Ensign Sterling and his crewmen, floating around somewhere out at sea in the storm. Even as he made his water landing the waves had been high and the white caps scudding along the surface as the three men climbed into their raft. Lieutenant Sorensen, who had seen the plane go in, radioed for the life-guard submarine that was supposed to be standing off Iwo Jima to pick up downed fliers. He repeated the call, but apparently did not make contact. The next day the crew had to be reported as missing in action.

The morning strike against Chichi Jima and Iwo Jima had to be cancelled, but by afternoon the weather had cleared enough so that Admiral Clark authorized take-off, and the *Essex* put up forty planes and the *Cowpens* sent sixteen planes to attack Iwo Jima once again. Commander McCampbell was the leader of the wave.

On this second day, the planes were much closer to target from the start, and it took them only forty-five minutes to reach Iwo Jima. By the time the first fighters arrived it was apparent that the first day's strike had been most effective. The Japanese knew they were in the area and might have been expected to launch an attack against the carriers, but the combat air patrol reported no such activity. Over the

36

target Commander McCampbell observed that fires started the previous day were still burning.

The fighters went in first, starting their dives from 8,000 feet above the island. The anti-aircraft fire was heavy and accurate. Lieutenant J.R. Ivey was hit as he went down, blinded in the left eye, with blood streaming into his right eye, which virtually destroyed all vision. Still, he completed his dive, pulled out, jettisoned his plotting board, and flew back to the carrier.

Lieutenant (jg) George R. Carr and Ensign Glenn E. Mellon, Jr., flew alongside, guiding Ivey home; Ivey was unconscious about half the time and flying apparently by reflex. Carr flew on his wing, so skillfully that he was able to nudge Ivey's plane into proper attitude whenever it faltered, by putting his wing against the other's. Ivey's radio was shot out, but his friends tried to attract his attention and persuade him to bail out. Ivey was either too weak to do so, or too nearly unconscious. He remained with the plane.

They got him back to the *Essex*, but there Carr and Mellon were ordered to land, and the combat air patrol took over the task of trying to bring Ivey in. He was last seen flying into a cloud. A little later, a dye marker (as carried by the fighters) was seen on the surface of the water, but no F6F nor any sign of Lieutenant Ivey.

The dive bombers and torpedo bombers again concentrated on the buildings and facilities. The pilots noted all the signs of the previous day's damage, but also saw that an enormous effort was being made to clean up and rebuild—not twenty-four hours later. More planes were lined up on the runway aprons—more new planes, Commander McCampbell observed. The Japanese pipeline was still operating, but once again Admiral Clark had outguessed the enemy. The weather was so rough that the Japanese obviously had not expected a strike and the claim of the Americans for this one was sixty-three planes destroyed. (Later the Japanese records denied this account, but the photos taken by the American planes showed undeniable damage of major proportions, and events would confirm this view.)

On June 13, as the airmen of the *Essex* were making those early strikes on Saipan and Pagan, the American submarine *Redfin* reported that Admiral Ozawa's Mobile Fleet had moved out of Tawi Tawi and was headed somewhere, but Admiral Spruance was not quite sure where. He asked General MacArthur to put more aircraft on the search routes from the Southwest Pacific to try to find the Japanese fleet. General MacArthur did so, but the land-based aircraft looked too far south and west and did not find the enemy.

Admiral Ozawa was largely responsible for this: he had chosen a route to reach Saipan that took him outside the normal range of American land-based aircraft from the south. So Spruance's major source of information was the reporting of American submarines through their bases at Australia and Pearl Harbor. The process was slow and reports sometimes seemed to conflict. On the 14th, Spruance was still in the dark, and also again on the morning of June 15. It was not until the evening of June 15 that the reports began to add up: the *Flying Fish* reported a number of heavy Japanese fleet units moving through San Bernardino Strait in the Philippines, toward the

Marianas. The *Seahorse* reported more heavy ships moving through Surigao Strait, heading northeast. These two reports indicated that the Japanese were coming. Spruance had to decide what he was going to do about it.

One of his first actions was to radio his carrier commands. He had already recalled them to the Saipan area to arrive by the 17th. Now he prepared a battle plan that would really allow Admiral Mitscher's carrier task force to go into battle. Indeed, he indicated that Admiral Mitscher had full discretion to act. So, as Admiral Clark brought the two task groups under his command back to rendezvous with the main elements of the task force, it seemed likely that a battle was in the offing.

On the morning of June 15, the American troops began streaming ashore on Saipan. Several transports steamed up to Mutcho Point and put landing craft over the side, indicating they were going to move right into Tanapag Harbor. But it was all a diversion, the real landings were on the coast south of Garapan, almost as far down as Agingan Point. The Japanese manned their coastal defenses, and the fighting on the beaches was fierce, but by the end of the day the marines had a firm foothold, and they were determined to stay. They had not achieved more than one of their D-Day objectives, but that was understandable: at Saipan, the Japanese had tanks, heavy guns, and an extremely powerful and well-planned defense.

By nightfall on the 15th it was apparent that the invasion of Saipan would be harder than anticipated, but 20,000 American troops had been landed. The serious problem was that 2,000 of them had become casualties in those first hours of desperate fighting, and that gave General Holland M. Smith a lot to think about! He might have to commit his reserves sooner than he expected. Smith's concern over the progress of the land battle and reports from the submarines about the movement of the Japanese that night caused Admiral Spruance to postpone the invasion of Guam, which was scheduled to take place within hours, and to move the reserves closer to Saipan. What upset Spruance was the indication that the Japanese were coming in two separate groups. He could envisage one group attacking the American fleet with its carriers and battleships, while another group came around from another direction and attacked the invasion force that was protecting the beaches. Spruance's native caution made him decide to stop all other activity in order to defend his invasion force.

On the morning of June 16, Admiral Spruance went aboard Admiral Turner's invasion flagship, the *Rocky Mount*, for a conference. He heard the sobering news about the heavy fighting on Saipan, but also that Admiral Ozawa was obviously coming for a fleet engagement. Still, there was no accurate word from any air searchers as to the movement of the Japanese fleet. The submarine reports were tardy and difficult to interpret.

Admiral Clark and Admiral Harrill were moving their task groups toward the rendezvous. The *Essex* paused on June 17 for another swipe at Pagan's airfield; Lieutenant Commander James F. Rigg led the attack.

When the planes reached Pagan, at a few minutes before 4:00 in the afternoon, they found no enemy fighters in the air, nor any visible on the ground except those wrecked in the previous raids.

Ensign Singer and his wingman, Lieutenant James L. Bruce, strafed several small craft in the harbor, and the other fighters strafed targets they found here and there. The torpedo bombers were loaded with bombs and rockets, and they burned up the Pagan radio station building and most of the other structures on the island. The dive bombers carried delayed-action 500-pound bombs, some of them set to go off in twelve hours. These were dropped on the runway to keep the Japanese from clearing it, repairing it, and again bringing in and sending out planes for that shuttle to the Marianas.

Two of the divebombers were damaged on this mission, one of them seriously enough to occasion a major overhaul, but no pilots were lost or wounded.

That night, the *Essex* steamed rapidly toward the rendezvous point. Admiral Spruance was now a worried man. He had issued his brave battle orders, but he was having second thoughts. The submarine *Cavalla* that night reported a number of enemy warships at a point (12 degrees north, 132 degrees east) off Guam, which indicated the Japanese were indeed coming to attack in two sections. Admiral Ozawa was known to the Americans to be a driving officer (just as Spruance was known to the Japanese as overcautious). The idea that Ozawa was splitting his force to break up the Saipan invasion nagged Spruance. What was wanted desperately was an aerial sighting of the Japanese units, and a count. Why were they so invisible?

The reason was Admiral Ozawa's canny approach to the Marianas, taking advantage of his resources and of the known American deficiencies. Most important of these deficiencies was the relatively short range of American carrier aircraft. The American planes were superior to the Japanese in the matter of protective armor, but their range was only about 350 miles from the carriers. The Japanese planes were not armored and were much more vulnerable because of it, as seen in the fighting of the *Essex* airmen, but the Zeros and the bombers were also able to search out more than 200 miles further than the Americans. So Ozawa kept away from American bases in the Southwest Pacific and a good 400 to 500 miles off the American carrier tracks and moved in undetected.

That night of June 17, Admiral Ozawa knew of the recent attacks on Iwo Jima and Chichi Jima and of that day's strike on Pagan. He learned of the state of fighting on Saipan and realized that a large American fleet must be lying off the island. He knew that small carriers were supporting the landings, and that at least one carrier group was off Guam (or had been twenty-four hours earlier).

Admiral Ozawa also had some faulty information, or, really, lack of information. The A-Go Operation's plan for the great naval victory depended heavily on the interchange between carriers and land bases. Land-based naval aircraft at Yap, Guam, Tinian, Pagan, and the Palaus were all scheduled to participate in the shuttle attacks on the American fleet. Vice Admiral Kakuji Kakuta, the commander of the First Air Fleet, had recently moved down to Tinian to direct this assault from the island side.

Kakuta had been promised (wildly) that he would have 2,000 aircraft for the bases in the inner South Sea region. The planning had been knocked askew by the MacArthur landings at Hollandia, and Admiral Kakuta had been shifting planes around from Biak to Palau to Tinian as though he were in the transport business. The American carriers and land-based aircraft in the Southwest Pacific had taken a heavy toll of his aircraft; those promised from the Japan pipeline were slow in coming, and many of them were destroyed in just such raids as that of the *Essex* at Iwo Jima.

Ozawa, at sea, had no way of knowing what was happening to Kakuta's air force unless the latter chose to tell him. But it was not the Japanese way to indicate difficulties that might lead to failure. Kakuta's way was to conceal the unpleasant truth, and to rely on the spirit of bushido for his diminishing air force to do more than a man-sized job.

So Admiral Ozawa steamed on with the pleasant belief that his 450 carrier planes, plus the hundreds that Kakuta could supply, would raise havoc with the Americans when the battle was joined. The failure of the Japanese to find the American fleet at Midway and to make the first strike was very much on Admiral Ozawa's mind, and his efforts were now concentrated on discovering the specific whereabouts of his enemy.

Admiral Spruance was concerned about finding Ozawa, and that concern showed in his orders to the carriers on the night of June 17. On the morning of the 18th, the *Essex* was back in touch with the fleet and the mission, launched early in the morning, was to locate the Japanese fleet.

Admiral Mitscher had already suffered his first major disappointment of the battle. That night before, when the carriers had been coming back from the Volcano Islands (Mitscher was riding in the *Lexington,* one of Admiral Clark's ships), Admiral Mitscher had been informed of the *Cavalla's* report of Japanese ships off Guam, steaming east. His look at the map indicated that his own force and that of the enemy were about 800 miles apart. But at twenty-five knots or so it would not take long to get into position to launch planes, figuring that the enemy was coming their way at about the same speed. In five or six hours, a battle might be joined.

So Admiral Mitscher, armed with the brave battle orders of Admiral Spruance which gave him authority to seek out the enemy and destroy him, asked Admiral Lee, the commander of the "battle line" (or fast battleships and cruisers), if he wanted to go ahead, with the possibility of a night engagement. Admiral Lee had seen night engagements before. He had commanded the *Washington* and other ships in the South Pacific, where the Japanese had consistently cleaned up on the Americans in night actions. The Americans had radar, but the Japanese had been practicing and perfecting their night-fighting naval techniques for years, and the Americans were really not very good at this sort of warfare. To complicate matters further, as indicated by the miserable showing the of the new battleships in that first day's bombardment of Saipan, the crews of these battleships left a great deal to be desired. The crews of the Japanese heavy ships were all highly trained and experienced. Admiral Lee was suffering from the problem that plagued the Americans throughout the first years of the war: inexperience. The enormous military build-up by the United States hid many real deficiencies, one of which was the inferior training of the Americans. There simply had not been enough time to get those new battleships assembled and to train the crews into "battle crews." So, with this knowledge, Admiral Lee objected when Admiral Mitscher suggested that a night engagement might be in the offing for the surface ships.

"Do not, repeat NOT, believe we should seek night engagement," he replied by radio the Mitscher's question. "Possible advantages of radar more than offset by difficulties of communications and lack of training in fleet tactics at night. . . ."

There, for history to see, Admiral Lee was calling a spade a spade. He did not have much confidence in the ability of his new fast battleships to beat the Japanese under such conditions. It must have been a wrench for Admiral Lee to make that admission, but it was cold truth, nonetheless. Admiral Ozawa would have liked nothing better than to engage the Americans under conditions where skill and training could turn the balance.

At 5:30 a.m. the planes of the *Essex* (and of other carriers) began the search for the enemy fleet somewhere southwest of the American force. The planes went out in teams of one F6F fighter and one SB2c dive bomber.

The search region was cut into pie-shaped sectors; each team went out on one leg, crossed over at the end of the line and came back on the other leg. The first team out was that of bomber pilot Lieutenant (jg) R.L. Turner and fighter pilot Ensign James E. Duffy. At the end of their search radius Lieutenant Turner turned to make the cross-leg and then saw a single-engined plane. It was a Japanese Nakajima B6N torpedo bomber, engaged in precisely the same mission as the Americans: trying to find the enemy.

The Japanese plane was about five miles away when Turner first saw it. He zoomed up to attract Duffy's attention and when Duffy came up Turner pointed to the enemy plane off the right side of his bomber. Duffy saw it too and closed up on Turner's left wing. They headed toward the Japanese plane in a climbing turn to get above it: all three had been flying at about 1,000 feet when the contact was made.

The American pilots got within a quarter mile of the Japanese bomber before they were seen. Ensign Duffy made an attack against the side of the bomber, and Turner came up from below, firing his 20mm cannon. He fired a hundred rounds, many of them striking the Japanese plane, and part of its left wing came off and very nearly hit Turner's dive bomber. He could see the pilot of the Japanese bomber trying to get out of his cockpit, and the gunner half out but hanging there, apparently dead. Both enemy fliers were surrounded by flames, and their clothing was burning. The Japanese plane then winged over and fell into the sea.

The second search team also encountered a Japanese search plane, a twin-engined Betty bomber, almost at the end of the primary search leg. Lieutenant (jg) William S. Rising saw it first from his dive bomber. He pointed out the enemy plane to his fighter pilot companion, Ensign Kenneth A. Flinn. Flinn poured on the gas and ducked into a cloud bank above the Japanese plane, then came down out of it at 300 knots on a beam attack. This Japanese pilot, like the other, was taken by surprise. Before he could evade, his plane was badly hit in the port side. It began to lose altitude. Ensign Flinn kept after the Japanese bomber, making another firing run, then zooming off and coming in again like an angry bee. After the fourth attack, the Betty's port wing tank caught fire and began to blaze. The plane lost more altitude, came down almost on the water, the port wing dipped, caught a wave, and the plane cartwheeled and exploded in the sea. There were no survivors.

Lieutenant Rising had been taking photos of the attack, but when the American planes returned to the *Essex* he discovered that his camera magazine had jammed and none of them came out.

Shortly after this first set of search planes moved out, a second set was sent out in a slightly different direction. Once again, the Americans encountered enemy aircraft almost at the end of their search patterns—indicating that the Japanese were closing. But the American carrier pilots did not find Admiral Ozawa's Japanese fleet that day.

Nor did the land-based American search planes from the southern islands find Ozawa that day. The Japanese admiral was in an admirable position; he could attack the Americans, and his planes could return to their carriers. The Americans did not know where he was, nor could they attack and return from their present distance.

Ozawa had several contact reports from his search aircraft by 3:30 on the afternoon of June 18. Independently, Rear Admiral Sueo Obayashi, commander of Carrier Division Three, received a report of the sighting of the American fleet, and began launching an air strike at about 4:30 that afternoon. But as his planes got into the air, Obayashi received a radio message from Admiral Ozawa (who did not know about the launch) ordering the fleet to retire for the night and prepare for the next day's joint attack on the Americans in combination with Admiral Kakuta's island-based air force. Then Ozawa did something that negated his major advantage of surprise: he broke radio silence to call up Admiral Kakuta for assistance in the next day's attacks.

Admiral Spruance had some knowledge of the proposed Japanese battle scheme, via Pacific Fleet intelligence. Admiral Koga, the successor to Admiral Yamamoto, had developed the Z Plan before he was killed in a plane crash in the Philippines. Apparently, Filipino guerillas got to the site of the crash before the Japanese, and found in one of the planes a number of secret documents, including a copy of the Z Plan. This made its way to General MacArthur in Australia, and to Nimitz's headquarters at Pearl Harbor. It was not "authoritative" by the spring of 1944 because Koga was dead, Admiral Toyoda was in command of the Japanese fleet, and no one knew exactly how much credence to give a plan devised by his predecessor. It discussed the concept of concentration of land-based aircraft in the islands and the shuttle system of operating planes between islands and carriers if the Americans attacked the Palaus, the Marianas, or the Philippines. It also suggested that the Japanese might send a diversionary force of carriers to draw off the American carrier fleet while the Japanese surface ships attacked the American expeditionary forces landing on one island or an other.

Aboard Admiral Spruance's flagship, the cruiser *Indianapolis,* Commander Gilven Slonim (radio-intelligence and Japanese-language officer) had Ozawa's call signs and information about the Japanese fleet's communications. But in all these days that the Japanese fleet had been moving toward the Marianas, Admiral Ozawa had kept strict radio silence so the information was of little use. Then, on the night of June 18 when Ozawa made his brief transmission to Kakuta on Saipan, back at Pearl Harbor and at the other points where the Americans maintained their delicate radio direction finders, the Americans were able to get a "fix," and Pearl Harbor radioed Admiral Spruance the position of the Japanese fleet.

But Spruance could not be told precisely how many ships were in the fleet on the basis of that brief radio fix. And, with his copy of the old Z Plan, Spruance worried even more lest Admiral Ozawa be luring his carriers off on a goose chase, so another Japanese force could strike Saipan.

That night, after the message from Pearl Harbor had come in, Admiral Mitscher urged Admiral Spruance to let him speed west toward the Japanese position so that at dawn he would be in a position to launch a strike against the Japanese fleet. Following Spruance's orders, he was just then sailing in directly the opposite direction, back toward Saipan, away from the Japanese.

Spruance did not reply immediately. He spent an hour agonizing over the decision. Then he seized upon one new element: the submarine *Stingray,* which had been in contact with the Japanese ships earlier, had made a new report, but the atmospheric conditions were so bad that the report was garbled, and Pacific Fleet Submarine Headquarters could not make out its contents. What if it meant the Japanese had another fleet element coming from another direction? That unanswered question made up Spruance's mind. No, he told Mitscher, he could not attack the Japanese. He must stand back to the Saipan area and keep the fleet to protect the beachhead.

Whether or not this was necessary has not truly been explored. Admiral Turner did not think it was because earlier he had advised Spruance to let Mitscher go; with his old battleships and his cruisers, destroyers, and the escort carriers (six of them), Turner felt he could protect the beachhead against any section of ships that Ozawa might send. Mitscher felt that the best defense was a good offense, and he wanted to wipe out the Japanese carriers as quickly as possible. But both Turner and Mitscher were good naval officers, and when Spruance, who had the responsibility, made the decision that the American fleet was to adopt a defensive posture, they complied with out plaint.

Mitscher made his dispositions for the morning of June 19 accordingly. The fighter-bomber teams were sent out again that morning to try to find the enemy.

CHAPTER SIX

The Marianas Turkey Shoot

Admiral Spruance was more than mildly upset when his search planes failed time and again to come to grips with the Japanese. He had no way of knowing that Admiral Ozawa relished the importance of surprise, that Ozawa had absolutely no intention of splitting his force to draw off the American carriers and then attack the landing place at Saipan, or that Ozawa was determined to force the "decisive battle" about which the Japanese had long talked.

The pilots of the first search team, Lieutenant (jg) D. McCutcheon and Lieutenant John R. Strane, found a Japanese float plane, and Strane shot it down. A little later, Strane sighted a Nakajima torpedo bomber and attacked. This attack was made in and out of the clouds. The Japanese pilot made as good a use of cloud cover as he could, but Strane kept finding him and making brief runs. Finally Strane's fighter guns set fire to the Nakajima's left wing. The plane nosed over and plunged straight down from 3,000 feet into the sea. The rear gunner had gotten in one burst before Strane killed him. After the crash, wreckage came floating up, but there were no survivors.

The second search team of this mission sighted another float plane, just after 8:30 that morning. This one was first seen by Gunner Stanley Whitey of Lieutenant (jg) Clifford Jordan's dive bomber. Ensign James D. Bare, the fighter pilot who was with the bomber, then climbed above the enemy plane and attacked. The Japanese plane turned, and the American fighter was on its tail. Ensign Bare fired twenty rounds from his guns, and the Japanese plane exploded. Again there were no survivors.

Half an hour later, Lieutenant Jordan spotted another Japanese search plane, this one a Kate, or Nakajima 97 torpedo bomber. This time, Ensign Bare did not see the enemy, so Lieutenant Jordan attacked. The Japanese plane was flying at 1,500 feet and the Americans at about 700 feet, so it meant climbing into the enemy. Jordan climbed and Bare followed. Jordan got within range and began firing his cannon. The Japanese plane dropped, trying to get down "on the deck" to escape. Jordan made another attack and the shells struck home in the cockpit. The plane burst into flames. As the dive bomber came by, Gunner Whitey began firing on it. The plane crashed, and Ensign Bare confirmed the "kill."

This search team found still another Japanese torpedo bomber not long afterward. Ensign Bare attacked; one of his guns did not fire, but he got some hits with the others. The Japanese plane tried to escape, but Jordan attacked, and Gunner Whitey made more hits on the plane. Then Ensign Bare recharged his guns and attacked once more with full fire power. The torpedo bomber blazed, and the pilot tried to escape. He got out of the cockpit and jumped. The parachute had just opened when the pilot struck the water as the plane crashed nearby. The American planes flew over and saw the parachute floating but no sign of life near it or in it.

But with all this action, the pilots of the *Essex* air group did not find the enemy fleet that day. Nor did any of the other Americans, flying out as far as they could from their carriers. There was a good reason for it: Admiral Ozawa's search planes had pinpointed the American carrier force, and Ozawa turned and turned again to keep four hundred miles between his force and the Americans. That way he could keep track of them until he was ready to attack, but with their shorter range the American planes could not find him.

At 4:15 on the morning of June 19, Admiral Ozawa was ready to strike. All he had to do at this point was find out where the Americans had gone during the night and, knowing Admiral Spruance, he estimated that they would move back to Saipan, which is precisely what they had done. Mitscher had placed his three strongest carrier groups ahead (each of them consisted of two big carriers and one small one). Admiral Harrill's task group, which consisted of the *Essex* and two light carriers, was held back by the battleships to furnish protection to the fleet.

The activity on the morning of June 19 began at Guam, where the Japanese air command had orders from Admiral Kakuta to carry out their part of the victory plan. They were to attack the American force (once it was found) and then fly to the carriers, refuel, reload, and come back and attack again, and fly home to Guam. Theoretically, they could continue this from dawn until dark.

Before dawn, a number of scout planes were sent out from Guam to find the American fleet somewhere off Saipan. At 5:50 in the morning, a Zero did find the fleet. The pilot came down out of a cloud and dropped a bomb aimed at the destroyer *Stockham,* one of the thirteen pickets and escorts assigned to the battleship line. The bomb missed, and anti-aircraft gunners aboard the destroyers shot down the Zero. Apparently the pilot managed to get off a message before he was killed because less than an hour later, when planes from the carrier *Belleau Wood* arrived to check out the Guam airfields, they found them in full operation. The enemy was sending off dozens of planes from Orote Airfield. The fighters sent back the message, and immediately other American fighters were ordered to head for Guam and help the *Belleau Wood* planes.

Admiral Kakuta was in action. Other planes were coming from Yap and Palau. The Japanese on Guam saw the American planes coming over at 6:30 that morning and began firing. But the American fighters were at 15,000 feet and the bursts exploded 2,000 feet below them. It was a surprise then when the F6Fs were "jumped" by Zeros that were even higher. Lieutenant G.I. Oveland of the *Belleau Wood* was leading the six-fighter division, and he shot down one Zero on the first pass when the Japanese pilot overran the American fighters. Lieutenant (jg) R.G. Tabler shot down another. But more kept coming, so Oveland formed his Hellcats into a tight echelon, went into a dive that took them down to 8,000 feet, and lost the pursuing Japanese fighters. Oveland called for help and then went into a furious defensive battle, the Americans totally outnumbered. It was not long, however, before planes from the *Hornet,* the *Yorktown,* and the *Cabot* arrived at Guam to improve the odds.

These Japanese planes in the Guam area were all part of Kakuta's land-based air force. Admiral Ozawa's carrier planes were preparing to attack the American carriers, too. From 4:00 on, they waited for word from the scouts as to the position of the Americans. Nine carriers were all ready to launch planes.

That morning the *Langley* took much of the responsibility for the dawn search from Harrill's protective carrier formation in the battle line area. The *Langley*'s planes shot down half a dozen Japanese searchers, but at about 7:00 a.m. one plane radioed back to Ozawa that elements of the American fleet—carriers and battleships—had been sighted and gave the position. So the first Japanese strike force from Admiral Obayashi's *Chiyoda, Chitose,* and *Zuiho,* was launched to find the Americans. The first effort was to be to take out the American air defenses around the carriers, so the strike consisted of sixty-one Zeros, forty-five of them carrying bombs, and eight torpedo planes.

At 10:00 that morning, the Americans' great advantage over the Japanese came into play: radar. Admiral Lee's battleships picked up a large number of "bogies" on the radar screens, estimated distance out from the force: 150 miles. That gave the Americans plenty of time; the Japanese planes were still a good half hour away from the ships, and planes could be launched and intercept them well out ahead.

At that point, eleven of the *Essex*'s fighters and eight from the *Cowpens* were already in the air. They had taken off at 9:10 to take over the duty as combat air patrol above the carriers and battleships. Commander Brewer led the fighters. For an hour they were occupied with routine checks, including a chase after one "bogey" that turned out to be a TBF with his IFF (Identification Friend or Foe) turned off. But at 10:13 the fighter director announced that a raid was coming in: bearing, 250 degrees; distance, 118 miles.

Commander Brewer was ordered to take his planes up to 24,000 feet. At 10:15, all available fighters on the *Essex* were told to "be prepared to scramble." At 10:24, Commander Brewer headed toward the enemy planes. A minute later, four fighters were catapulted off the deck of the *Essex* to replace Brewer's planes as combat air patrol over the ships.

The deck of the *Essex* was crowded with planes preparing for a strike. The fighters were out front, and behind them were a dozen dive bombers. At 10:35, Commander

Brewer shouted "tallyho" over the radio: he had sighted the first Japanese raiding force, thirty-five miles away. "Twenty four rats, sixteen hawks, no fish at 18,000." (Fighters and dive bombers, but no torpedo bombers, according to Brewer.) He moved out with eight planes following him.

Two minutes later, Commander McCampbell's fighter was launched, and after it came eleven more *Essex* fighters to join Brewer and repel the raiders.

Then a problem had to be solved on the deck of the *Essex*. Those twelve dive bombers were now in the way, and more fighters had to be brought up and launched, and the decks cleared for landing planes. Lieutenant John Brodhead of the dive bomber squadron was instructed to take off with his bombers and strike the airfields at Guam. But it was pure afterthought by Captain Ofstie—the real reason to get the bombers off that deck was to keep it clear in case of attack. When they were airborne, Brodhead was told to go to Orote Air field and bomb. That had been the mission scheduled, but McCampbell's fighters were supposed to go along for protection and when they could not, the mission had been cancelled. Captain Ofstie knew the air over Guam was alive with American fighters from other carriers, so he sent the bombers out without protection.

Commander Brewer saw sixteen bomb-carrying Zeros and correctly identified them as Judies (Aichi dive bombers). They were flying at 18,000 feet in tight formation, with a division of four Zero fighters on each flank. A thousand feet or so above and behind the formation came another sixteen planes, Zero fighters.

Commander Brewer chose the leading dive bomber as his first target. He sped along until he was 800 feet from the enemy plane, then opened fire. The Zero exploded so quickly it was unbelievable! He actually flew through the debris of this plane as he moved to attack a second one. This, too, blazed up; half the wing fell off, and the plane cartwheeled into the sea.

Moving out to the edge of the Japanese formation, Brewer then fired on another Zero and kept firing until he was 400 feet away, when that plane began to come apart and dived into the water. A Zero came in to get on Brewer's tail, and the turning capacity of the F6F saved him. Brewer rolled, and turned, and was on the Zero's tail in a moment. The Zero pilot maneuvered forcefully to escape, doing half-rolls, barrel-rolls, and wingovers, but Brewer stayed right with this Japanese fighter that had until recently been called the most maneuverable plane in the Pacific. He got in many bursts, and finally the Zero turned downward in a tight spiral and crashed in the sea. By this time the first raid had been dispersed, and Brewer and the others flew back over the carrier where they remained above the ship formation, as combat air patrol.

Ensign Richard E. Fowler, Jr., who was Commander Brewer's wingman, was flying in position on Brewer's right and stayed there during the first two passes at those planes Brewer downed. On the third encounter, the wingman of the Zero Brewer was attacking either stalled out or made a diving turn that brought him directly in front of Fowler's F6F. Fowler fired, got on the tail of the Japanese fighter, and shot it down. It began smoking, fell off on a wing, and spiraled tightly down into the water.

Fowler was then at about 10,000 feet. He saw two Zeros flying in a tight Lufberry circle. He made a pass at one, but missed, and both got on his tail and began firing at him. He dived to 6,000 feet, and tried to break away. Another F6F joined the fracas, and the Zeros turned to attack it; Fowler whipped around and fired at one of them, shot off part of its left wing, and the plane spun in toward the sea. The pilot jumped, but no parachute opened.

Fowler saw another Zero out of the corner of his eye off to starboard, and turned to attack. He got on its tail and began firing. The Zero yawed wildly, and in a moment Fowler saw that part of its vertical stabilizer had been shot off. He kept firing until the plane began to smoke, and flame burst out aft of the engine. It smoked its way down to the sea.

Fowler then saw two F6Fs and went to "join up" on them. They were chasing a Hamp (the carrier version of the Zero, with stubby wings). The Hamp flew into a cloud and Fowler saw it come out the other side and got into position and attacked. His guns stopped firing suddenly but by this time the Japanese plane was smoking and fell off into the sea. Fowler saw two other planes that he identified as Judies and attacked from overhead. He fired on one of them; only one of his guns worked, and that quit soon enough. The enemy plane shuddered and pieces came off, but it remained in formation with the other plane, and Fowler, out of ammunition, headed back to the carrier.

Lieutenant Edward W. Overton, Jr., was a section leader in Brewer's group. For some reason his F6F was too slow to keep up with the others after the first pass, and he fell back. He saw one plane carrying bombs and identified it as a Judy. He shot it down. He saw a Zero, and attacked; he put several shots into its wing roots, and saw smoke coming out. The plane fell off on one wing, but Overton did not see it crash because he was just then attacked by another Zero and was flying hard to save himself. He joined up on several other F6Fs, but by this time they had run out of enemy planes.

Ensign Mellon, who was Overton's wingman, fired on one Judy and it burned; he lost track of Overton and joined up on another F6F and covered the other pilot's tail while he attacked several Judies. Mellon fired too, but made no effort to go off on his own.

Lieutenant Carr went in behind Commander Brewer as leader of the second division of four F6Fs. He too set fire to a bomb-carrying plane, and it exploded in his face. He flew through debris, ducked under the formation to get his bearings back, climbed, and saw another enemy plane sitting, just waiting to be fired on. He fired, and the enemy plane "went into a graveyard spiral" and spun into the sea.

Carr found an enemy fighter on his tail and went into a steep ninety-degree dive, getting a log of more than 430 knots, and then made an aileron roll to the right. His windshield fogged up, although the defroster was on, and he could hardly see. An enemy Zero was coming at him, and both fired. The enemy plane began to blaze. Carr's F6F was hit in the bullet-proof windshield, which snowed up, but he could still see well enough to make out two Zeros ahead.

He got on the tail of one and set it afire. Something went whizzing by and it may have been the pilot of the plane, but he could not tell because he was concentrating on shooting at the second one. It began to smoke, and dropped off. Carr made a split-S move to get down and back at the plane, but it exploded before he could fire again; he followed the plane down, looking for others, but saw no more. He began to count splashes and oil slicks in the water and had counted seventeen when he saw a pair of F6Fs come by. He decided it was time to go home and joined them. They returned to the carrier area, seeing no more enemy planes.

Ensign Norman Berree, Carr's wingman, selected one of the Zeros (Hamps) on the edge of the bomber formation for that first pass. He did not believe the Japanese pilot ever saw him; he began firing and kept the button depressed, until the Hamp exploded. Then he found that plane's wingman on his tail, in turn, so he dove, turned sharp right, and lost the enemy. He was at 10,000 feet. He saw another enemy fighter on a parallel course. They turned to each other and opened fire. The enemy plane almost immediately began to blaze. It rolled over but kept coming, firing, until almost the collision point, when the pilot veered off smoking badly. Berree's plane was hit and its water injection system was knocked out. He saw the enemy plane explode and then he saw no more enemy, so he joined up on several F6Fs and went back to the carrier to fly above in combat air patrol.

Lieutenant (jg) Walter A. Lundin, who was the leader of Carr's second section, came in to fire from overhead on the Japanese formation. An F6F loomed in his sights, so he held the trigger. He had dropped below the formation, so he climbed back up and made another run. He began firing on a Zero and stitched it from tail to cockpit. It exploded. Lundin and his wingman then found another plane carrying bombs and attacked it. The enemy plane began to fishtail, but broke off on one wing, went down in a ninety-degree dive, and crashed. Lundin looked around and saw seven enemy planes flaming and heading down toward the sea. "It was a real sight," he said.

Lieutenant J.L. Bruce, Lundin's wingman, got separated from Lundin on the second pass, and then could not find anyone to join up on. He saw at least six F6Fs making passes at enemy planes from different directions. He did see one Judy going by, fired on it, and scored some hits, but then it was gone and the sky seemed empty. He flew back, found some other F6Fs, and went home.

Commander McCampbell had set out with twelve planes to join the fighting, but by the time he got the group organized, the fighter controller announced that Japanese air raid number two was on its way in, apparently consisting of fifty planes, traveling at 150 knots, and about forty-five miles from the carrier. McCampbell was to intercept.

The American planes already up had done a good job on the first Japanese raid. Commander Brewer and his men had knocked down many, but so had planes from the *Cowpens,* the *Bunker Hill,* the *Princeton,* the *Lexington,* and the *Enterprise.* About forty Japanese planes made their way past the first group of American fighters, but, as they closed on the ships, other planes came to attack them, and soon there were only about twenty attackers. They crossed the picket line of destroyers and attacked both the *Yarnall* and the *Stockham,* the blossoms of anti-aircraft fire filled the air and several more Japanese planes went down. Some came through to the battleship line, which Admiral Lee had formed into a circle, with the *Indiana* in the center and six battleships and four cruisers around, with destroyers interspersed in the circle. They were moving at twenty-two knots.

One bomber got through to the *South Dakota* and dropped; the explosion killed twenty-seven men and wounded twenty-three others, but the battleship kept right on going. No enemy plane got really close to the carriers, although some men on the flight deck of the *Essex* saw a few shapes in the sky.

Ozawa's second strike, which consisted of fifty-three dive bombers (Judies), twenty-seven torpedo bombers (Jills), and forty-eight Zeros, was launched from the big carriers just before 9:00 o'clock that morning. Even as the launch began, the Japanese carrier force was in deadly peril from a source that had not really been anticipated.

In order to achieve maximum protection for the big carriers, Admiral Ozawa had put his three small carriers up front, where the sea literally bristled with Japanese destroyers. The idea was to stop any American air attack up there before it could get back to harry the six big flight decks. But to do this, Admiral Ozawa had virtually stripped his capital ships at the rear of destroyer protection against submarines. And it was just his bad luck that the American submarines were out in force in the area that day—something Ozawa did not expect because, in previous fleet actions, American submarines had played minor roles.

In May, while Admiral Nimitz was assembling the forces that would participate in the battle for the Marianas, Vice Admiral Charles Lockwood, the commander of Pacific Fleet Submarines, had sent more boats out to the Central Pacific than had ever before gone at one time. The *Silversides*, the *Sand Lance*, the *Pilotfish*, the *Tunny*, the *Shark II*, and the *Pintado* all patrolled the Marianas waters in the month of May. They were exceedingly effective.

On May 10, the *Silversides* sank three ships of a convoy bringing supplies to Saipan. On May 29, she sank two ships of a convoy bringing aviation gas. The *Shark* arrived, and so did the *Pilotfish* and the *Pintado*, just as another convoy came up. The waters around Saipan were soon ringed with oil from sunken tankers and floating with debris from sunken transports. One of the convoys was bringing troop reinforcements to Saipan; the submarines sank five of the seven ships.

The submarines moved around then: to Palau, to Truk, to the waters off Japan, and, most important, to the Philippines area where the Japanese fleet would have to stage any counterattack on the Marianas invasion.

When Admiral Ozawa ordered the fleet out of Tawi Tawi on June 13, the *Redfin* was watching, and the alert had begun. Two days later, the *Flying Fish* had seen the capital ships readying to move through San Bernardino Strait; that course would take them east of the islands. The *Seahorse* spotted them coming out on the east side.

That day, June 15, Admiral Lockwood ordered the submarines *Cavalla* and *Pipefish* to scout between the Philippines and the Marianas to try to keep an eye on Admiral Ozawa—not an easy task since the fast Japanese ships could easily outdistance a submarine, particularly a submerged submarine.

The *Cavalla* ran afoul of several of Ozawa's destroyers off the Philippines. They were escorting the tankers that would fuel the carriers and battleships on the eve of the battle. When Lockwood learned of the encounter, he grew excited and gave orders to the *Cavalla*, the *Muskellunge*, the *Seahorse*, and the *Pipefish* to try to get those tankers. The submarine force was getting deeply involved in this particular fleet action. Lockwood also shifted the *Albacore, Bang, Finback,* and *Stingray* out of Japanese waters west of Saipan, back to the south and east.

At 8:00 on the morning of June 19, the *Albacore* raised her periscope, and Captain James Blanchard found himself squarely in the middle of Ozawa's main carrier force. Nobody aboard the carriers was paying too much attention to the surface of the sea around the force; concentration was on the launch of the second air strike against the American carriers.

Blanchard let one carrier go by, then a destroyer, took aim at another carrier and fired six torpedoes from his bow tubes, then went deep, as three destroyers came charging after the submarine. There were destroyers around—but they had not been doing their anti-submarine patrol job the night before and that morning.

The carrier at which Blanchard fired was the *Taiho*, Japan's newest, and Admiral Ozawa's flagship. She was a 31,000 ton ship, the pride of the imperial fleet. She was just launching planes for air raid number two. One of the torpedoes hit the carrier, but she only shuddered and went on. She might have been hit by another (Blanchard heared a second explosion), but she was saved by the bravery of Warrant Officer Sakio Komatsu, who had just taken off from the deck of the carrier to go on the raid. Leveling off, he saw the torpedo track heading for his ship and without a second's hesitation dived his plane into the torpedo; it exploded, the plane disintegrated, and the carrier was saved.

The strike was launched without further excitement, and no one on the bridge of the carrier worried much about that single torpedo hit. The Japanese carriers, like the American, were built in compartments, so that damage in one area could be isolated and controlled without losing the fighting power of the ship.

The launching continued until in all 128 planes were in the air. The strike leader made the error of flying over the three forward carriers and their escorting cruisers and destroyers, and the anti-aircraft gunners opened fire on their own planes. They shot down two Japanese planes and damaged eight more such that they had to give up the mission and return to their carriers. But more than 100 planes were coming as Commander McCampbell had the order to head out at 245 degrees to meet the enemy.

McCampbell took his planes to 25,000 feet. Two were affected by the altitude and their engines cut out intermittently; he ordered them to go down and orbit over the *Essex* for protection. He began converting the high altitude to speed and nosed over. By the time the *Essex* group reached the Japanese, they were able to make a high-speed run on top of the enemy formation, leaving four planes above for protection. Then McCampbell was down in the thick of the fight:

"My first target was a Judy [dive bomber] on the left flank and approximately half way back on the formation. It was my... intention after completing the run on this plane, to pass under it, retire across the formation and take under fire a plane on the right flank with a low side attack. These plans became upset when the first plane fired at blew up, practically in my face, and caused a pullout above the entire formation. I remember being unable to get to the other side fast enough, feeling as though every rear gunner had his fire directed at me. My second attack was made on a Judy on the right flank of the formation, which burned favorably on one pass and fell away from the formation out of control. (A rather long burst from above rear to tail position.) Retirement was made below and ahead, my efforts were directed to retaining as much speed as possible and working myself ahead and into position for an attack on the leader. A third pass was made from below rear on a Judy which was hit and smoking as he pulled out and down from the formation. Retirement was made by pulling up and to the side, which shortly placed me in position for a run on the leader, closely formed with his port wingman, the other wingman trailing somewhat to right rear. While reaching a favorable position on the leader, it was noted that the formation really consisted of two groups. . . .

"After my first pass on the leader with no visible damage observed, pullout was made below and to the left. Deciding it would be easier to concentrate on the port wingman than on the leader, my next pass was an above-rear from seven o'clock, causing the wingman to explode in an envelope of flames. Breaking away down and to the left placed me in position for a below rear run on the leader from six o'clock, after which I worked on his tail and continued to fire until he burned furiously and spiraled down out of control. During the last bursts on the leader, gun stoppages occurred. Both port and starboard guns were charged in an attempt to clear before firing again."

At this point McCampbell looked around. He saw that the enemy formation had been decimated and the attack more or less broken up. The leader of the lower formation was still going, however, and McCampbell attacked him.

"Only my starboard guns fired on this run, which threw me into a violent skid and an early pullout was made after a short burst. Guns were charged again—twice—and since my target had pushed over and gained high speed, a stern chase ensued."

McCampbell chased, firing, but only the starboard guns responded. Then they quit too, but not before the Japanese plane pulled up in a high wingover and then dropped into the sea.

McCampbell tried to clear his guns but nothing happened. As he worked on them, he watched the Japanese plane go down; neither the pilot nor the gunner tried to get out as it sped for the blue water. As the plane crashed McCampbell decided he must be out of ammunition and started back for the carrier. It was not far: as he shot down that last plane, he found himself within easy sight of the battleship line. In fact, he was too close and had to circle around to the north to avoid anti-aircraft fire from the American ships, whose gunners were "trigger-happy." While he was moving, he looked down and saw that at least one Japanese plane had gotten through: a bomb exploded on the battleship *South Dakota*. That bomb killed or wounded fifty men.

When Commander McCampbell led the attack in against the Japanese air strike, Lieutenant (jg) John C.C. Symmes stayed above with his third division until his radio cut out. He then turned the leadership over to Lieutenant (jg) Charles B. Milton, who waited until he was sure there were no Japanese planes anywhere above 18,000 feet and then this division too went down into the air battle. Symmes first made a run on a Judy, swung in from the high side, left, and put shells into its wing root. The whole plane caught fire immediately and crashed so quickly it was surprising. Symmes then saw three F6Fs chasing three Zeros. He joined that chase, but then saw two other Zeros at ten o'clock below him and rolled over and made an overhead pass at one. That plane exploded, the entire port wing came off. He saw another Zero off to the right and turned and fired, just as another F6F came in on the Zero's tail, firing. The Zero exploded. They were all so close that cartridge cases from the other F6Fs smashed into Symme's windshield but did no damage. Symmes continued to attack other planes until he ran out of ammunition.

Lieutenant Milton lost track of his wingman on his first pass, and he joined up on Symmes. His second pass was as ill-timed as the first; he managed to damage the plane, he could see, but he was too far away. Cursing himself, he determined to get in close before firing, and when he saw a Zero at ten o'clock, he climbed up and fired at close range. The Zero responded satisfactorily: the entire empennage came off and it crashed into the sea without burning. Milton was the pilot on the tail of the Zero that Symmes was also shooting up, and it was Milton's cartridge cases that hit Symmes's plane. The sky was nearly empty of enemy planes at this time, and when Milton heard the air controller vectoring planes out to intercept low bogies at 230 degrees, he took off, but got there too late for the action.

Ensign Ralph E. Foltz was flying wing on Commander McCampbell and went down with him on that first fast pass. Foltz burned one Zero on that run, but then a Zero got on his tail, and he was in a dogfight. He gave the plane full throttle and water injection and pulled away from the Zero. He climbed then to join two other F6Fs, but as he did, oil began spurting onto his windshield. The Japanese fighter had put some bullets into his engine and damaged an oil line. Through the blur, he saw that he was coming up on a Judy, he began firing, and the plane exploded. The debris flew all around Foltz's plane. As he got clear, his oil pressure began kiting—up and down—and he decided it was time to head for the carrier.

Ensign Claude W. Plant was another member of McCampbell's leading division. He chose one of the covering enemy Zeros as his target for that first high-speed pass. The Zero burst into flames. Almost immediately Plant was firing on another Zero, and it too flamed and fell off into the sea. Below, Plant saw a Zero on the tail of an F6F, and he went down to help; he came up behind the Zero and fired a long burst all the way up the back of the enemy plane, from tail to cockpit, and then at the engine. Parts of the Zero's stabilizer broke off, the engine began to flame, and the pilot slumped over his stick. The Zero fell off on one wing, burning, and spun into the water out of control.

Plant then found two more Zeros and attacked the nearest, about 500 feet below him, making a high side run. The Zero pilot turned left sharply, but Plant managed to stay with him, and fired until the enemy plane fell off. This plane did not flame, but went down in a crazy falling-leaf pattern, until it pancaked into the water.

Ensign Plant was watching, when a Zero got on his tail. ("It was not so pleasant.")

This Japanese pilot was extremely skillful. Plant used every trick he had learned to shake off the attacking Zero, but he could not get away. He saw another plane ahead and fired on it and felt he had damaged it, but the enemy behind him was still coming. The F6F was shuddering from the impact of 20mm shells and 7.7mm shells in the empennage, fuselage, wings, cockpit, engine, propeller, and water injection tank. He could hear the bullets splattering off the armor plate behind his seat (which undoubtedly saved his life).

He was a very lucky young man, because another F6F came to his rescue and shot the Zero off his tail. Shakily, he went up to join the other fighter, and they headed home. When Plant landed on the *Essex* the "airedales" (handlers) counted 150 holes in the plane, including one in each propeller blade. The performance of that particular F6F was proof positive of the new advantage the Americans had over the Japanese. Zeros subjected to that sort of punishment were invariably destroyed.

Ensign George W. Pigman was in Lieutenant Milton's division. He stayed up flying high cover for a few moments longer than the others, then came down to join the fight. He made a pass at one Judy, fired a long burst, and destroyed the enemy bomber, which broke into pieces and crashed. Then Pigman nearly collided with a Judy that passed directly in front of him and above, showing its belly. He let go a burst, the Judy started a wing over and exploded. There was no armor there, obviously.

Pigman then saw another Judy below him, attacked, and after what seemed to be a very long time, the Japanese plane began to burn. It made violent skids and burst into flames, then turned lazily, and gracefully landed in the sea, to splash and sink.

The odd thing (Pigman noted) was that none of the Japanese Zeros seemed to make any effort to defend their bombers. Also it was impressive that so few Japanese planes recovered from that original surprise, and that so few of them made effective attacks on the American airmen. (What the American aviators did not then know was that the Japanese naval air force had never recovered from the Midway disaster—where they lost nearly all the aircrews of four fleet carriers—and from the battle of attrition in the Solomon Islands, which was carried almost entirely by the Japanese naval air force. By the time of the Saipan invasion, Japan was woefully short of trained pilots, and virtually none of these pilots had much experience.)

Ensign Power was one of the few F6F pilots that day to have a really narrow escape. He exploded one Zero and turned into another. The Japanese pilot came straight at him, firing. Both planes were hit in the wing roots, but the difference was that the Zero exploded and the American plane kept flying. Ensign Power was hit in the leg by shrapnel from a 20mm shell that exploded inside the plane. He dove down to the water, pulled out at 1,500 feet, and returned to the carrier.

Ensign Albert C. Slack came out of the high cover division to attack a Judy and sent it crashing to the sea, but then a Zero got on his tail and gave the F6F a serious working over before another American fighter shot the Japanese pilot down from behind. Slack then joined up with the other plane and returned to the carrier.

The single loss that day was Ensign George H. Rader, who reached the point of attack with the others, and went in to hit the Japanese. But in the excitement no one saw what he was doing, or what happened to him. He must have been shot down by one of the Japanese planes, and that day, he was put down as "missing in action."

By 12:30 that afternoon it was all over, and the *Essex* planes, except Rader's, were back aboard the carrier. A few Japanese had gotten through to attack the battleship force: besides the hit on the *South Dakota,* the *Indiana* was struck by a torpedo bomber that was badly shot up; its pilot tried to crash his torpedo into the ship. He succeeded, but the torpedo did not arm and so the damage was limited. The *Alabama* was near- missed by two bombs, and the *Iowa* narrowly missed torpedoing.

Six dive bombers managed to make an attack on the American carriers. One bomb exploded above the *Wasp*'s flight deck and killed one man and wounded a dozen. The *Bunker Hill* was lucky and got away with two near misses which killed three men and wounded seventy-three, and did a considerable volume of damage to the ship and to the planes aboard.

The *Enterprise,* north of the other carriers, was nearly torpedoed, and the *Princeton* was attacked by two torpedo bombers, but the anti-aircraft gunners splashed both.

Ozawa's third wave of forty-seven planes arrived around the carriers at 1:00 in the afternoon, but were intercepted by planes from the *Hornet* and the *Yorktown,* and the raid was broken up without doing any damage. A number of those Japanese planes then landed on Guam or Tinian, trying to carry out the shuttle program.

Lieutenant Brodhead's *Essex* dive bombers were helping make that shuttle program very difficult for Admiral Kakuta and the Japanese carrier pilots. They put a number of holes into the runway at Orote Airfield in Guam, and then came home. Some of the planes jettisoned their bombs to be sure they had enough gas to make the long flight back, and two crashed on deck on landing. But there were no casualties among the bomber air crews.

When Admiral Mitscher found that the carrier planes from the first three waves of Ozawa's attack were landing at various island airfields, he doubled his efforts to knock out the "pipeline." At 2:25 on the afternoon of June 19, Commander McCampbell was back in the air again, this time leading a twelve-plane mission to Guam to destroy planes on the ground and in the air.

McCampbell took his fighters up to 24,000 feet again, to be sure that he would have the edge on any enemy formations they might encounter. On the way in, they saw many Japanese aircraft, in ones and twos, heading for Orote.

McCampbell led the attack, as he always did. He exploded his first plane, then noticed that his wingman, who had come right in with him, was in trouble, and that his plane was smoking. This time, McCampbell was encountering experienced pilots; on his second pass, the two Japanese planes up ahead turned into him and his wingman, Ensign R.L. Nall, and fired with accuracy. His plane was holed by 20mm and 7.7mm shells (six of the latter) and his wingman's elevator was shot away. Ensign Nall's plane was obviously badly damaged. McCampbell broke off and tried to elude the Japanese, but they came after the pair, and wingman Nall was unable to maintain speed with his damaged plane. The two Zeros began to stalk him.

McCampbell wasn't having any of that; he scissored his plane, moved across, and shot down the leading Zero, then turned after the second, which immediately broke off and ran for Orote Airfield. McCampbell got on his tail and began firing. The Japanese pilot then executed what McCampbell called "the most beautiful slow roll I had ever seen; it was so perfect there was no need even for changing point of aim or discontinuance of fire." After making that mistake, the Japanese pilot miraculously still survived, and dived for Orote Airfield to make an emergency landing. McCampbell did not follow him down: he had lost track of Nall and was alone in the air in this area, surrounded by scores of Zeros, and the best thing he could do was get out of there and join some other F6Fs.

While looking around for more F6Fs, Commander McCampbell saw two American seaplanes on the water, picking up downed fliers. A pair of F4U fighters were circling above them, but in spite of this protection there were so many Japanese planes in the air that they were able to slip under the cover, and Zeros were moving around, strafing the Americans on the water. Commander McCampbell began making runs on the Zeros, threatening, keeping them off.

At this time, he was joined by Lieutenant Commander Duncan of the *Essex*, who helped keep the Japanese away. It was not the sort of activity that made for dogfighting, and no planes were shot down. After half an hour, a number of American fighters had formed up on Commander McCampbell, and he led them back to the carriers. He landed and counted noses; everyone had gotten home safely to the *Essex*, and the others told their stories to the combat intelligence officer.

Lieutenant Commander James F. Rigg had move out over Apra Harbor on Guam and made a pass at two Japanese dive bombers. He noticed that these (like almost all the planes they saw on this mission) were brand new aircraft, just off the manufacturer's assembly line, with bright gray paint and new belly tanks.

When Rigg attacked, he suddenly found himself in a nest of Japanese dive bombers. Apparently he had disturbed an incoming flight of reinforcements in its landing pattern.

The Japanese planes were flying in tight three-plane sections. As he came in, he saw that he was making hits, but he also could feel his plane shudder from hits being made by the Japanese gunners. Rigg's guns were badly burned by the morning's action, and he found that he had to get up close to any target to be sure of hitting it.

At 500 feet, going over the harbor, he attacked one dive bomber. Then he came in low over the airfield at Orote, and shot up a landing dive bomber. He did not see any hits, but the plane groundlooped. He saw another with its nose down, tail high, and burning on the runway. He went across the harbor at 300 feet, firing on several planes, and was surprised that no one seemed to fire back. Nor did most of them take evasive action.

But then all he had said about lack of resistance was contradicted when a Val (Aichi 99 dive bomber) gunner began firing and hit him good and hard in the belly tank and fuselage. Feeling very lonely, Rigg saw two F6Fs at 1,500 feet, with another flight circling above them. He went to join up, and then saw that the circling flight was not F6Fs but Zeros. He went into full low pitch, full throttle, and water injection as the Zeros came down to get him. He went right through the formation, making a head-on run against one Zero. One Zero came after him on the left side, making a full deflection shot and hitting the F6F squarely. That Zero pilot, Rigg said to himself, was good! He took some hits in the engine and propeller, and the prop began to vibrate dreadfully. He had to ease back on the power, but he could because the two F6Fs above him took the pressure off. He slowed down, cutting his rpm, and headed for the *Enterprise,* the nearest carrier, not sure he could make it back to the *Essex.* He landed safely on the *Enterprise,* but had to stay aboard for several days while his plane was repaired.

Ensign Wallace E. Johnson, Rigg's wingman, went in with his leader and got one Val right away; pieces began flying off the plane. But the plane did not crash—these Aichi 99s seemed to be tougher than some of the other Japanese planes. Johnson had to pull up because another Val appeared right in front of him, but he managed to get into position and make a firing run that caused the Val to crash. Then Johnson was busy, trying to shoot down another Val, with the interference of a good pilot in a Zero who distracted him and then escaped his guns.

Lieutenant John Collins's four-plane division was flying top cover at the beginning, but it soon became apparent that all the action around Guam was down on the deck, so the division split into two sections and went down. Collins lost no time. He saw one Zero and went after it in one long pass; the Zero rolled, went into a split-S, and then dove into the water. Collins did not see it—he was too busy—but his wingman, Ensign Frank R. West, saw the plane splash. Collins then went after five different Zeros, getting hits on all of them, and perhaps downing one—he could not be sure. He could not turn his F6F as tightly as the Zeros turned, which was probably a compliment to the particular pilots of those Zeros, since under the best of conditions the F6F could go with the Japanese fighter.

Ensign West contented himself with covering Lieutenant Collins; he was having trouble with his fuel pressure during the whole flight and never knew when the engine would cut out on him—it could be fatal in a dogfight, so he kept to "snap shots", and made no claims as to planes shot down.

Ensign Duffy was leader of the second section of the high cover team, and, by the time he got into the action area, everything seemed to be over. But he and his wingman got into a sparring match with several Zeros, and he shot one of them down.

Ensign Len S. Hammelin was Duffy's wingman. He went with Duffy through the dogfight with the Zeros. One Zero passed directly in front of him, trying to evade another F6F, and Hammelin shot the Japanese plane down. Then another Zero closed on Hammelin from behind and put 7.7mm shells into his engine and a 20mm shell into one wing. The plane began to quiver, and Hammelin broke off and joined up with another F6F, which led him back to the task group.

Lieutenant Commander Duncan led a four-plane division into this fight. He intercepted a call from the two American seaplanes that were picking up downed fliers on the water off Cabras Island, and when he went over there, he saw two parachutes floating in the water and a number of Zeros strafing the area and the two Navy Seagull planes. Duncan went after the Zeros and shot one down, hitting it in the engine and cockpit, and probably killing the pilot.

After that, events moved so quickly it was hard for Duncan to remember them. He was in a whirl of enemy aircraft, Zeros, dive bombers, and seaplanes. He shot down one plane, a Japanese Zero got on his tail, he lost it, he took a snap shot at another plane and it fell into the sea. Another crashed on the beach and burned. Lieutenant Commander Duncan came home trying to sort out his activity; he had destroyed three Zeros, and damaged two more and a bomber.

Ensign Wendell V. Twelves, who as Duncan's wingman, caught one of the Japanese Zeros just as it was strafing the first of the Navy Seagull rescue planes on the water. It did many hearts good to see the Zero start to flame at 200 feet, then cartwheel and skip along the surface, and then go in, leaving what Twelves called "a beautiful trail of fire" on the water behind it.

Twelves then got another sidelong shot at a Zero, and it spouted a long plume of black smoke and crashed. Then he got into a dogfight and tried to match turns with a Zero—which he could not quite do. Luckily, another F6F got him out of trouble by shooting down the Zero.

Lieutenant (jg) William V. Henning was the leader of Duncan's second fighter section. He and Lt. (jg) Carleton White caught a Zero as they went in. They fired simultaneously, and the Zero blew up in their faces. Henning then caught another Zero from behind and chased him. The Zero pilot tried to get down on the deck, and the F6F responded nobly—Henning caught up and began firing. He was close—too close, he said later—because the Zero blew up just off the surface and pelted the F6F with pieces, which he could hear bouncing off wings and fuselage.

Ensign Nall was flying wing on Commander McCampbell when his plane was hit on that first pass. McCampbell went on, but Nall managed to shoot down one of the nine Zeros that jumped them, and then to make his way home with his limping engine.

They came home, then, in the bright afternoon sun of the Central Pacific, and made their reports of the day's fighting as the sun began to lower. But they were not the last men from the *Essex* to be out that day. At 5:00 that afternoon, as McCampbell and company were returning from a very successful mission (like shooting fish in a barrel, as one pilot put it), another group of *Essex* fighter pilots was heading out to get into the clean-up over Guam. They were seven, led by Commander Brewer, who was on his second long mission of the day.

The late afternoon weather was beginning to change, and a front was developing between the carriers and Guam. As Brewer led his F6Fs out, he climbed to get above the overcast at 15,000 feet. By the time they reached Guam, the shadows had grown long, and they saw no aircraft in the sky over Orote or any other part of Guam. Finally, in the twilight at 6:20, they spotted a lone dive bomber (Judy) circling low, apparently getting ready to land at Orote. The whole division attacked and shot down the Judy in its landing pattern.

But that dive bomber must have been a decoy, because as they moved, so did four divisions (sixteen planes) of Zeros, which had been lurking in the cloud cover at 6,000 feet. The F6Fs were in the worst possible position, down on the deck, with the Zeros coming at them from above and behind, and strung out. Only Commander Brewer and his wingman, Ensign Thomas Tarr, and Lieutenant N.W. Overton and his wingman, Ensign G.E. Mellon, were in a position to turn and meet the attack, and they were down too low, with no reserve altitude to convert to speed, and had to climb up to meet the Zeros.

The Zero pilots had spent part of that afternoon on the ground planning this counterattack against the Americans, and they were aiming for the kill. Four Zeros went after each of the leading planes in coordinated attack. Commander Brewer turned up and shot down the leading plane that was attacking him. It sped past him and went straight in to crash. At almost that moment, Ensign Tarr shot down the second one and it followed its leader into the ground off Orote.

At that point the melee became general, with the Japanese zooming down to attack and the F6Fs trying to elude and get into position for countermeasures. No one could tell which plane was which. But at one point during the head of the encounter, an F6F was seen to pull up above the fracas, start a wingover, then to shudder and fall off, and crash. It did not burn on the way down, indicating that the pilot was either dead or mortally wounded. That pilot was Commander Brewer or Ensign Tarr.

Only as they were going home did the Americans of the *Essex* realize that they had been sucked into a trap. It had been an expensive maneuver for the Japanese: they traded eleven for two, but to the men of the *Essex* the loss of Commander Brewer, the commanding officer of the fighter squadron, was a severe blow and one they would not forget.

The Zeros outnumbered the *Essex* fighters—the only American planes over Guam that late evening—by about four to one as they began the fight. Lieutenant Overton shot down two, got one more probable, and got hits on several others. After about a half an hour, suddenly the Zeros all disappeared; there simply were no more to be seen, and they were not on the runways and not parked on the ground. No one then knew that Commander Brewer had crashed, so they began calling him, but there was no answer. Overton called for a rendezvous and managed to collect a number of planes, some of them from carriers other than the *Essex* who were appearing on the scene. They circled, looking for Brewer, but they found nothing, and when it was dark and they were low on gas, they started back to the *Essex*.

Ensign Mellon shot down one Zero and possibly another. His plane was hit hard by that first attack and he had some trouble with it on the way home.

Lieutenant Strane shot down one Judy, but was very nearly done in by a pair of Zeros who came at him in the failing light, when their dark camouflage worked almost perfectly. He saw them just in time, pulled away, and joined up on another F6F and went home in the dark.

Lieutenant (jg) Thorolf Thompson and Ensign David Johnson spent most of their evening chasing Zeros off the tails of other F6Fs, and Thompson shot down one of them. Johnson shot down one Zero and probably another, then headed back. The darkness was growing thicker as they neared the carrier; it was after 7:00 p.m. when they landed.

During the evening, the various carriers reported in to Admiral Mitscher, and it was not long before the admiral's staff knew that a major victory had been scored against the Japanese that day. There was no major damage to *any* American ship. The returning air commanders reported finally that of the hundreds of aircraft engaged in fighting and bombing the Japanese in the air and at Guam, only twenty-three planes were shot down from all carriers, and that six more were lost in operational accidents (which did not involve enemy action). The total casualties among the airmen were twenty pilots and seven enlisted men killed. The Japanese carriers had launched 373 planes that day, and several hundred more had flown out from Admiral Kakuta's island air forces, and only 130 planes had returned to the carriers. No one at that moment knew precisely how many Japanese planes had been shot down, or how many had been wrecked on the airfields. The final American figure on Japanese losses was 315, according to Samuel Eliot Morison's official account.

Someone that night summed it all up for the airmen when he compared it to an ancient and honorable American sport that went back to colonial days. It was just like a turkey shoot, he said, and that is how the one-sided battle of June 19, 1944, came to be known in American naval history as "The Great Marianas Turkey Shoot."

CHAPTER SEVEN

The Twilight of the A-Go Operation

The single torpedo that had struck the Japanese flagship *Taiho* did not cause Admiral Ozawa much concern at noon on June 19. In fact, he was elated: he had found the enemy and had launched two strikes against him, and the enemy had not found him. Furthermore, Admiral Kakuta's land-based airplanes should be showing up at any time, having attacked the Americans from Guam, Rota, and other bases, to be refueled on the carriers before attacking again.

But at noon, the American submarine *Cavalla* found Ozawa's fleet, about sixty miles south of the point where the *Albacore* was still dodging Japanese destroyers. Lieutenant Commander H.J. Kossler raised the periscope, and there in the sights was the famous Japanese carrier *Shokaku*, although he did not then know its identity. He did know he had run across a Japanese carrier because the rising sun battle flag was flying in the breeze. The *Shokaku* was just then recovering planes that had returned from her combat air patrol. Kossler fired six torpedoes, and three of them hit the big carrier.

Smoke and flames billowed up from the nether decks of the carrier and made the flight deck untenable. Shortly, this was a matter of concern to Admiral Ozawa. He kept looking at the smoke and flame coming from the *Shokaku*. As for the *Taiho*, damage control parties below deck were having a difficult time of it. The forward elevator was jammed, and recovery of the second strike would be hampered accordingly. But no one told the admiral that yet; perhaps it could be worked loose in time. Repair crews forced their way into the compartment below the jammed elevator. There they found gasoline sloshing around in the pit: one of the gasoline storage tanks next to the elevator had been ruptured by the concussion of the torpedo. The damage control officer decided that the best way to clear the air down there, as they pumped out the gasoline, was to turn on all the air conditioning units and blow the fumes away. This was done, and because it was done, gasoline vapor spread throughout the ship. The admiral on his bridge did not notice, as a good breeze was blowing and he was too high in the air to smell the aviation gasoline.

Just after noon, the admiral's bridge was tense. It was time that the admiral had some word for that second strike.

The first strike had not reported, but those were Obayashi's planes and they might not be heard from until the admiral had his affairs in order. But the second strike was Ozawa's own, and it should be coming back.

A little more time went by and then specks began to appear in the air, coming from the east. But there were so few of them.

When the pilots had landed and come up to the bridge to report, they told a story of difficulty. They had been set upon by dozens of Hellcats, they said, and the raid had been most difficult. But they had gotten through, and they had shot down many American planes, and they had attacked battleships and carriers, and several of these must now be sinking. Why were there so few of the returnees? That was because many of the planes must have chosen to land at Rota, or Guam, or Tinian, said the pilots. Since radio silence was still in effect between fleet and Admiral Kakuta's headquarters, there was no way Admiral Ozawa could be sure, but he and his staff were beginning to have some grave doubts. The one comforting fact was still that the Americans had been hit, and they had not yet found the Japanese fleet to hit back.

One o'clock came and a few more stragglers returned. None could land on the fiery decks of the *Shokaku*, but the *Taiho* and the *Zuikaku* could recover planes and did. The Second carrier Division (the *Junyo*, the *Ryuho*, and the *Hiyo*) had sent off the third strike in mid-morning, and the fourth strike just before noon. The *Zuikaku* had contributed her reserves to that last strike, too.

Two o'clock came and more stragglers limped in, many of them badly shot up. But there was no despair among the pilots; their story was that they had hit the enemy and had scored a decisive victory. The fourth strike did not find the enemy, and the pilots reported that they were heading for Guam to stay overnight and attack again the next day. (These were many of the planes that the men of the *Essex* encountered over Guam.)

By 2:30, the fires aboard the *Shokaku* were growing much worse and the flight deck was spouting flame. Destroyers were still moving about, dropping depth charges, and the *Cavalla* was down deep, waiting for the hunters to go away.

At 3:00 that afternoon, the *Shokaku* grumbled deep down inside, and then the ship was shaken by an enormous explosion and the carrier began to come apart, bombs went off, they triggered torpedoes, and finally the magazines and fuel supply went and the famous ship became a funeral pyre for hundreds of her crewmen before she sank.

The American naval air force still had not found the Japanese carrier fleet, but one of that fleet's biggest and best carriers was already destroyed.

It was not long after the explosions that wrecked the *Shokaku* that the damage control officer of the *Taiho* had to warn the bridge that his efforts had not been successful; a few minutes later an enormous explosion shook the flagship—a combination of gases throughout the ship went up and simply blew the top off; the flight deck buckled up, and the sides of the ship buckled out; the bottom was holed by internal explosion and the engineering gang died immediately.

A destroyer came by, Admiral Ozawa and his staff were transferred to the cruiser *Haguro,* and not long afterward the *Taiho* sank. Admiral Mitscher still knew nothing about it, but the submarines had given him two Japanese carriers, or twenty-two percent of the carriers committed to battle in terms of numbers. In terms of importance, the *Taiho* and the *Shokaku* represented much more, perhaps thirty-five or forty percent of the striking power of the force.

As for the Japanese air losses, in one way the inability of the Americans to find the Japanese fleet worked in Admiral Mitscher's favor. Had he found the fleet in striking range, he would have launched many of his own fighters and bombers to strike the enemy, and not so many would have been available to defend the American ships against the Japanese planes. So Admiral Ozawa's highly successful effort to conceal his presence from the Americans while he attacked rebounded against him, and June 19 ended with his knowledge that something had gone amiss. But he was as determined as ever to press the battle. That night, the Japanese force moved north, to stay out of range of the Americans yet be in position the next day to make another air strike. Admiral Ozawa decided to fuel. Meanwhile the offensive could be renewed by those planes he had sent off (which had presumably landed on friendly islands).

That evening, the American fleet was off Guam. Since the *Essex* and the other ships of Admiral Harrill's task group were short of fuel, they were assigned the use of the oilers on June 20. They were also assigned the tasks of watching Guam and Rota and of preventing the Japanese from bringing up new air forces during the night and/or launching an attack before dawn from the Guam airfields.

Just after 2:00 on the morning of June 20, four F6F night fighters were launched by catapult. Lieutenant (jg) J.C. Hogue and Ensign E. Roycraft were assigned to cover Rota, while Lieutenant Commander R.M. Freeman and Ensign G.L. Tarleton were to fly over Agana and Orote Airfields in Guam.

It was a clear, moonless night. Since Guam was 144 miles away at the time of launch, Freeman and Tarleton went off first. They climbed to 6,000 feet and circled the carrier. Below they could see a blue exhaust light—the only light on the ship— which came from some mechanic on the flight deck testing magnetos on a plane. They took off for Guam, while the other two pilots headed for Rota.

These night fighters were something relatively new for the American navy; the F6Fs were equipped with exhaust flame dampeners which kept the flames down so the planes could be seen at no farther than 200 feet, a distance at which their silhouette would be clear anyhow. The inboard guns of each plane were fitted with flash hiders. The outboard guns could not be so fitted, so the pilots were cautioned not to use those guns unless they were out after daybreak.

The night seemed very peaceful, until they caught a glimpse of Saipan, where starshells were rocketing through the air, and occasionally a yellow, red, or green flare burst high and lighted up the ground.

All four planes used their radar to keep track of the American ships (and stay away from them) and to search for enemy shipping in the waters around the islands. Rota's field was lighted, which indicated Japanese activity there, probably in preparation for the next day. The Americans saw no enemy aircraft. Orote Airfield was dark, but Guam's Agana Airfield was also lighted, and it was apparent that the Japanese down there were expecting friendly planes because, as the two night fighters came in, flashing lights went on at the end of the runway, some sort of signal to guide Japanese pilots.

The two pilots over Guam swung around to the downwind side of the field and began a strafing run, aiming at the blinkers. After the third burst, the anti-aircraft guns opened up on the two planes, and they broke off. It was 3:35 in the morning. The lights on the field went out; the pilots moved off and orbited the field about five miles east, waiting to see if the lights would come on again. In five minutes, they did come on. At 3:50, Freeman and Tarleton were west of the Agana airfield, preparing to make another strafing run. Suddenly, one of them saw a white light passing below at 5,000 feet. Freeman made a pass at the light, which he presumed to be a Japanese plane's tail light. The light went out, but he could see no more. Tarleton got separated from Freeman on this run, and they ended up on opposite sides of the airfield. Then the action began, as recalled by Lieutenant Commander Freeman:

"I noticed a light moving in the traffic circle around the field. About that time Ensign Tarleton called that he saw a plane and was going to make a run. I told him to go ahead, that I was clear.

"About ten seconds later I spotted two blinking lights traveling around the traffic circle, apparently effecting a rendezvous. I crossed to the east side of the field to join up on the rear light. Just before I got into visual range of the plane silhouette, another plane behind my original target turned on wing lights and an amber tail light. I therefore joined up on this plane. It was a single-engined plane with fixed landing gear. I had him on my radar one mile search scale but there was considerable land signal interference and I didn't need the radar anyway since he had his lights on. He was circling the field in a slow left turn (about 130 mph) at 2,000 feet. I joined up on his port quarter and opened fire at about 100 feet with my four inboard guns, aiming just ahead of his cowling. The display of incendiaries striking his fuselage at that range was so surprising that I involuntarily chopped my throttle. It looked as if an electric arc welder had run from his nose to his tail, completely blanking him out in blue flame. A long orange flame appeared on the starboard side and persisted from four to six seconds, then disappeared. I was by this time directly astern. He accelerated rapidly as if his engine had quit and I had to drop my flaps to stay behind. He continued in the same slow turn to port, nosing over into a glide of about 85 knots. Even with my throttle slowed and my flaps down I slid directly underneath him. From this position I could see the elliptical wing typical of a Val. I slowly dropped back to shooting position again and opened fire from directly astern at about fifty yards, moving my point of aim around the fuselage to get guns to bear at that close range.

"I could see incendiary flashes on the wing roots, tail, and fuselage. After about six three-second bursts from this position the Val nosed down sharply into a steep dive toward the water. As we had glided to 500 feet at this time I did not care to follow the maneuver so I broke off the action.

"I did not see him crash because it was too dark, but I am certain that he could not have survived. . . ."

This action came at 4:10 a.m. Freeman made another circle of the field, but found no more targets and the field lights were out again. He climbed to 8,000 feet and hung around west of the field, keeping it in sight, until 4:45, when he joined up with Ensign Tarleton and started back to the carrier.

Ensign Tarleton had this to report:

After he had seen the lights in the landing pattern and announced that he was going down, he climbed, and then:

"I went in fast (mistake no. 1) and had to make a complete circle of the field before I slowed down. I was on the south side of the field when I saw some running lights on the northern end. I do not know if it was the same plane I saw when I was high. I was doing about 120 knots and was closing on him rapidly. I dropped my flaps and was about 200 feet astern of the target when I fired from below. I fired a short burst and didn't observe any hits. I felt my lead was too great for the range (mistake no. 2) so I pulled my nose up and fired a five-second burst. I observed several hits on the wings and belly. He leveled his wings and then he nosed over and crashed into the water. From the time I dropped my flaps I was very close to 100 feet altitude by my altimeter. I then circled the field again two or three times. I was at the northern end of the strip when I saw more lights at the southern end. . . .I closed on the lights much too fast and before I knew it was I was on top of him (mistake no. 3). I was afraid to chop my throttle because it makes too much flame from the exhaust. Just as I was underneath this plane I saw another plane (lights out) about 300 feet ahead. . . . I fired a burst and again felt I had too much deflection (mistake no. 2 again). I pulled up sharply and fired again. He rolled over on his back and his nose dropped. He did not have enough altitude to recover. I saw several hits. . . . just as I went under him there was a big orange flash on my port wing. . . . I do not know what it was. . . .

"I observed my altimeter once during this run and it read 50 feet. I circled the field three or four times, but the lights were out and there was no activity. I climbed. . . ."

Freeman and Tarleton then went home. In his report of this first action of the *Essex* night fighters Freeman observed that the enemy planes appeared to have been completely unaware of their presence until fired upon. A pair of night fighters over any field all night could effectively cancel out enemy night flying operations. So the night fighters should be able to keep land-based air strikes down until morning when a dawn group of day fighters could hit the field.

Freeman also noted that the night fighter technique seemed to be superior to the old way of trying to keep airfields immobilized—by using delayed action bombs. (The next night, when day planes had left delayed action bombs on the Guam runways, the night fighters did not observe any explosions, which meant that the Japanese demolition squads had made themselves familiar with American bomb fusing.)

Thus, by the summer of 1944, the night fighter had come into its own in the Pacific Fleet. It would not be too long before the fleet would have a night carrier, most of whose planes were geared to just this sort of action. But just now, at Saipan, the major concern was to find the Japanese fleet, and for some reason no one made the decision to use the night fighters on the night of June 19 for that purpose, and so once more the fleet was not discovered before dawn.

Once again the responsibility was Spruance's. He was more interested in detaching a task group to protect the Saipan force than in hitting the enemy, so Harrill's three carriers would largely waste their time for the next twenty-four hours.

The *Essex* did not participate in the air strikes against the Japanese fleet on June 20. Her assignment continued to be to control the Marianas airfields and prevent the shuttle bombing that Admiral Kakuta had promised. In fact the mission proved much simpler than anyone had expected. Just after 4:00 on the morning of June 20, Commander McCampbell led a fighter sweep over Rota and the Guam airfields. Off the west coast of Guam, the high (25,000 feet) American fighters saw four Japanese planes "down on the deck," but they were too far away to go after unless McCampbell wanted to break up his formation and sacrifice the altitude-speed factor before reaching his objective.

In fact, there was little other activity at either Guam or Rota, but on the return trip the fighters saw four planes again, possibly the same four. Two fighter divisions peeled off to "bounce" them, and went screaming down from 18,000 feet. Two of the Japanese Zeros ducked into cloud cover. The other two turned to fight. One then escaped into cloud cover, while the second was hit by passes made by several pilots, and when last seen was spinning into a cloud.

So that was all, except for sighting a lone cargo ship in the water between Guam and the task group. The fighters dropped down and strafed the ship, which was left burning. They also strafed the ground and hit perhaps twenty parked planes at Guam.

Shortly after 2:00 that afternoon, the *Essex* sent another twenty fighters on a Guam sweep, led by Lieutenant Collins. The fighters also carried bombs (some 500-pounders) to crater the runways and thus make it even more difficult for the Japanese to fight back in the air.

But this second sweep found that the Japanese were not quite "finished off" as the pilots of Task Force 58 had been bragging overnight. One division, led by Lieutenant J.E. Barry, Jr., started down off Orote Point to bomb the airfield. As they nosed over they were jumped by four Hamps—the carrier Zeros—and they bracketed the last plane in the formation, that of Ensign J.W. Power. When last seen, Ensign Power was heading desperately for a cloud, with a Japanese fighter close on his tail. And as the fighters tried to recover, they were jumped by another four Zeros.

The Japanese apparently believed that the four F6Fs of that division represented the whole strike, so they were surprised when eight covering aircraft swooped down on them from above. The Zeros ran for cloud cover. Ensign A.C. Black started after one of them, got him into gun range, and began firing. The Japanese fighter pulled up into a stall, fell off, and spun into the water. A large oil slick formed on the surface, and that was the end of one Japanese airman.

The American fighters looked around for the Japanese but did not hang around the area, even though they knew there were a number of planes somewhere in the clouds. They were back aboard the carrier before dusk.

Most of the planes of the other three carrier groups on the morning of June 20 had experienced one frustration after another. Admiral Ozawa was still skillful in concealing his presence from the Americans, and, not very privately, a number of Admiral Mitscher's staff officers were observing (with some bitterness) that the Japanese had turned around and gone home already. But that was not at all how Admiral Ozawa had reacted. He still believed that most of his missing planes had landed on some friendly base and would eventually come home to his carriers to roost. He still had 100 planes on the carriers and if Admiral Kakuta had 300 or 400 on the islands, then the Americans were in for a hard time.

It still did not occur to Admiral Ozawa that the shuttle strategy might have failed, and no one enlightened him. He kept radio silence and so did Kakuta. They were not "reading the American mail". In fact, Admiral Ozawa was having a most difficult time with his fleet communications; the cruiser *Haguro* was not equipped as a command ship and the radio facilities were inadequate. Further, Ozawa had no way of getting "the feel" of what the returned Japanese pilots were saying. The fleet intelligence officers who interviewed the returning fliers aboard the four remaining Japanese carriers were less than critical, and the reports that reached Ozawa indicated victory, victory, victory—and gave only a few hints of the debacle that had overcome the air fleet.

In Tokyo, Admiral Toyoda had a much clearer picture of the disaster. He had reports from Saipan, from Tinian, from Rota, from Guam, and from other places, and they did not indicate victory, but, to the contrary, enormous destruction of the Japanese facilities. When Ozawa had to report the loss of the carriers *Shokaku* and *Taiho*, Admiral Toyoda made the decision to break off the action and he ordered Admiral Ozawa to head for the protection of Okinawa. Ozawa said he had to fuel first, but actually he was delaying, for to lose this battle would cost him his reputation.

Early in the afternoon of June 20, quite beside himself because of the communications failures of the *Haguro*, he transferred his flag and his staff to the carrier *Zuikaku*, the sister ship of the sunken *Shokaku*. From early morning, he had ordered out a constant stream of search planes, trying to find the American fleet again. The planes kept encountering American carrier aircraft in the skies, so Ozawa knew the U.S. fleet was still in the area and apparently still searching for him.

But Ozawa was unlucky again; his planes did not find the American carriers. [The Japanese official war history indicates that the carrier pilots of the Japanese fleet and Admiral Kakuta's search planes from the Marianas made many serious errors of calculation on June 19 and 20. Several times Japanese planes found the American fleet, only to misinform their bases as to location. Inexperience was the answer.] Had they done so, particularly early in the day, he would have learned that, contrary to the reports his airmen gave, the American fleet was undamaged and he was badly outnumbered, twelve American carriers to his four, with about 650 planes left to fight against his 100 or so (and that did not count the planes of Admiral Harrill's three carriers, which could be thrown into the battle if necessary).

The Americans almost missed the Japanese entirely. Admiral Ozawa's ships were steaming about on a fuel pattern, but not actually fueling. At 1:30 p.m., the *Enterprise* launched another search. Lieutenant R.S. Nelson was part of it. He went out on his line and had reached a point 325 miles from his carrier; in a moment he would have to turn back if he was to make it at all. Just as he was ready to turn he saw them, the Japanese carriers, battleships, cruisers, and destroyers, milling about with some oilers in the area. He was so near the end of his run that he felt he had not time even to stop for a count, but turned and got on the radio.

This was just the sort of situation in which breaking radio silence was welcomed. Excitedly he called up his carrier and reported that he saw the Japanese; he gave the position and said they were moving northwest at twenty knots. That news was immediately passed through the American fleet by voice radio—no time to encode—and so the Japanese got it too. The intelligence officer of the carrier *Atago,* an English-speaking officer, listened to the American chatter. At 4:15 p.m., he reported to Admiral Ozawa that the Americans were launching an air strike. Thus warned, Ozawa stopped all attempts at fueling and ordered the fleet to increase its speed and head in earnest for Okinawa, off to the northwest.

Unfortunately, the report by Lieutenant Nelson was garbled, and it was nearly 6:00 p.m. before Admiral Mitscher actually knew where the Japanese fleet was. In the meantime, all twelve of the striking carriers had been put on the alert, and some had launched planes, but the planes had to head out blindly, in what they thought was the right general direction, to be corrected later. When the Japanese were finally pinpointed on the chart, they were found to be 300 miles away, which was at the absolute outer limit of American striking power. If Admiral Spruance had been making the decision, the Japanese fleet would have gotten clean away that day; the risk was enormous to send aircraft out to fight at their fuel limit; a plane's fuel consumption in battle was vastly greater than that at cruising speed. It was a foregone conclusion by any trained aviator that if Mitscher ordered the strike, a large number of people were going to end up in the drink. Mitscher did not hesitate. The strike was on.

"Give 'em hell, boys," said Admiral Mitscher. "I wish I were with you."

CHAPTER EIGHT

Death Knell for an Air Force

The airmen of those twelve American carriers did themselves proud on the afternoon of June 20, 1944. Nearly all of them understood how slender the chances of survival—as far as landing back on the carriers—but there was no hesitation. They took off and they flew into the teeth of the enemy, knowing that their real enemies were two: the Japanese and the sea.

It was 6:40 that evening before the first American planes were in position to attack: eleven dive bombers from the *Enterprise*. About seventy-five Japanese planes were coming up to meet the Americans. The dive bombers ignored the Japanese fighters that swarmed about them and went through, and the other bombers, torpedo bombers, and fighters of their carrier and the others came in after them. Even the *Langley*, one of Admiral Harrill's carriers, got into the act, but not the *Essex* this day. The *Essex* had to bask in the reflected glory of the others, who sank the carrier *Hiyo* and damaged the *Chiyoda*, the *Junyo*, and the *Ryuho*. They also damaged one battleship and a cruiser and sank two of Japan's precious oilers.

When it was all over and the Japanese fleet escaped to the north, Admiral Ozawa had less than half the hundred planes that had graced the decks of his carriers in the morning. Long after the war, when the Japanese defense establishment finally wrote a 102-volume history of the Pacific conflict, the official historians of the Self Defense Agency assessed the A-Go Operation:

"From the 18th to the 20th [of June] our Number One Mobile Fleet set out to crush the enemy invasion of Saipan. However, our pre-emptive strike did not have success, and resulted in the loss of three aircraft carriers and enormous damage to the rest. The result was clearly nothing. The A-Go Operation has to be called a total failure."

To the Americans, the sea proved a greater enemy than the Japanese. The carriers were too far away, and many of the American pilots could not make it home, particularly those whose planes had been shot up in the attack. Admiral Mitscher did all he could, including turning on the lights of the carriers so the pilots could see the flight decks in the dark. But of the 216 planes that went out to attack the Japanese fleet, 100 had been lost. Some of the pilots and air crews were recovered; the next day Admiral Spruance agreed to Mitscher's taking the ships away from Saipan to try to rescue downed fliers (and pick off any crippled Japanese ships). The battle of the Philippine Sea was over, however; the Japanese were going straight back to Japan, having been recalled that night by Admiral Toyoda. But the vestiges of the A-Go Operation still existed, and Admiral Kakuta was still committed, even if the day was lost, to sacrifice of his land-based aircraft to stop the American invasion of the Marianas.

On June 21, the airmen of the *Essex* were again assigned to hit the air installations and aircraft at Agana Airfield on Guam. Commander McCampbell took fourteen fighters, fourteen dive bombers, and seven torpedo bombers to the target. There were no Japanese planes in the air, and McCampbell radioed back to the commander of support aircraft (Rear Admiral G.F. Bogan, commander of the auxiliary carriers that were supporting the Saipan invasion) to see if the wanted the strike diverted. The implication was clear that it was a waste of time and ammunition to hit Guam again, but the base said to go on with the strike, so McCampbell did. The fighters went in to strafe, and the bombers cratered the runway at Agana Airfield.

But whatever the Japanese were doing down on Guam, they were in no position (or perhaps no condition) to strike back. The anti-aircraft fire was slight and ineffective, and no planes were seen except those wrecked on the airfield on previous days. As Commander McCampbell had indicated in his query to higher authority, the raid was really an unnecessary bit of icing on the cake.

But the next *Essex* air operation that day, in support of American forces landed on Saipan, was quite a different matter. Twelve fighters, fifteen dive bombers, and seven torpedo bombers set out to bomb and strafe the Japanese airstrip and installations at Marpi Point on Saipan.

The dive bombers reached 11,000 feet over the target, and then approached at 200 knots, and pushed over into their dives at 9,000 feet. All went well until it was Ensign William Nolte's turn. He may have been hit by the anti-aircraft fire, which was heavy, or he may have blacked out on his dive. Whatever the cause, his shipmates saw the plane go into a spin. It seemed intact, but the spin continued until the plane was at 1,500 feet, then came out; the recovery stopped abruptly, the spin continued; the plane, bearing its pilot and Gunner William Lowe, went into the water at high speed.

Seven torpedo bombers, six of them loaded with rockets and ten 100-pound general-purpose bombs, and the last loaded with fragmentation bombs, attacked the anti-aircraft positions near Marpi Airstrip. Lieutenant Commander V.G. Lambert led them in.

Earlier, the Japanese had mounted several three-inch anti-aircraft guns on the bluff there, but the reports had it that the guns had been knocked out much earlier. Not this day, they weren't. The gunners opened up on the bombers and gave them so much trouble that Lambert diverted several of his planes with rockets to attack the three-inch guns, and they did, with bombs and rockets. Once more the guns fell silent, but that may have meant only that the gunners had been killed or wounded and that in a matter of hours they would be replaced.

That day Admiral Mitscher chased the Japanese fleet but never caught up. There was one salutary effect of this waste of diesel fuel: Admiral Lee's battleship force moved out to the area where the Japanese carriers had been operating at the time of the American attack, and they—or the float planes of their cruisers—picked up nine fliers who were sitting in their rubber rafts waiting for a rescue they were not at all sure would come. Admiral Mitscher's destroyers and Catalina flying boats from Saipan were also brought into the search and they rescued another fifty-nine airmen.

Admiral Ozawa tried to resign as commander of the Mobile Fleet, but Admiral Toyoda refused to accept his resignation. The fleet stopped at Okinawa, at Nakagasuku Bay, and there Admiral Ozawa took stock of the damage. Several of his ships had to be sent back to Japan for overhaul. He had the unpleasant duty of reporting he had only thirty-five serviceable planes for his carriers. Yes, the battle of the Philippines Sea had been a disaster for Japan.

On June 22, the major portion of the American invasion fleet's task force fueled at sea. There were a few encounters between Japanese and American planes from the major section of the task force, but not many. The *Essex* did not have an official mission of any consequence that day, but conducted a search of the whole area, which was divided into six sectors. No enemy planes were encountered, but Lieutenant (jg) John P. Van Altena and his radioman, R.E. Kataja, located some American survivors of one air strike, who were floating around in a raft on the sea below, and stuck with them in site of heavy cloud cover and roughening seas, until a rescue plane arrived.

The Japanese were not in evidence in the air over any of the Marianas during those two days, June 21 and June 22, but that did not mean that Imperial Headquarters had abandoned the Saipan air defense. Not at all. Planes were already in the pipeline to begin the attack on the American forces, and Admiral Kakuta was marshaling whatever aircraft he had left in the south and west that could be spared for the effort. The weather was rough around Tinian, Saipan, and Guam, but it was even worse near Japan, and at Iwo Jima and Chichi Jima, the major staging bases for the Marianas. Scores of aircraft had reached those two islands and the pilots were waiting for word that the Guam and Tinian bases were ready to receive them. By June 22, Admiral Kakuta had given positive word: the runways were repaired and the fields were operational. The movement began.

On June 23, at 5:30 in the morning, Commander McCampbell took his fighters (a dozen) on a sweep of Orote Airfield at Guam. It was a simple, routine mission, and most of the pilots did not expect much action, since the Japanese seemed to have been knocked out so well that a night fighter sweep two nights earlier had found no action at all.

McCampbell, however, was a careful man. The fighters went in at 22,000 feet and circled to approach Guam from down-sun, which would put the light in the enemy's faces. As they circled above the island, the glint of the sun on metal below indicated that seven or eight planes were turning over their engines on the airfield. Several other planes were hidden in revetments around the runways and would not have been noticed, so effective was their green and brown camouflage, except that the sun glinted on their moving propellers, too.

McCampbell decided that he would make a strafing run on the field to knock out the planes, but as he got into position he saw that some of them were taking off, so he held back and continued the sweep around the area to see just what air opposition might develop. He hoped to be able to follow the movements of the Japanese planes on the ground, but the camouflage was too good, and although a number of planes took off the airmen of the *Essex* quickly lost track of them. Below, the Japanese were making every effort to help their aviators. Smoke pots were lighted, and they obscured the lower half of the runway so that very little could be seen from above.

McCampbell took his planes over Agana Airfield, where they saw no activity. So whatever would develop was going to come from Orote.

The Japanese were using every trick they knew. When Commander McCampbell turned his planes back toward Orote, he saw a formation of four fighters in the usual American divisional pattern, but as he came closer he saw that they were not F6Fs but Zeros. Just in time, he recognized them and turned into them.

The Americans were then at 15,000 feet, and so were the Japanese. As McCampbell turned toward the Japanese planes, their leader took them down 2,000 feet, where they formed into a tight Lufberry circle. It was an effective defensive maneuver; the American planes had too much speed and were too widely scattered to make an effective attack, so McCampbell circled the enemy formation, waiting for an opening and looking around for other enemy aircraft.

Finally, eight F6Fs formed up and dived on the Lufberry circle. As McCampbell expected, as they did so, out of the sun came six Zeros that had been waiting for the Americans. It was a clever trap, but McCampbell had outguessed the enemy. He had left four planes high above his general formation, and as the Americans attacked the four Japanese in the circle and the six Zeros attacked the eight F6Fs, the top cover four F6Fs swooped down on the Zeros. In a minute the air was full of zooming aircraft, splitting into two-plane sections for the most part. For the next half hour, this bit of sky a half mile west of Orote Airfield was an aerial circus.

McCampbell chose to take the dangerous assignment of attacking the Lufberry circle, sure that he in turn would be a target for planes above.

"I made an above, rear, run, at which time I cracked my flaps and was able to stay on the Zeke's tail while he pulled out of the circle in the opposite direction, smoking and heading for Orote Field. I saw him explode in mid-air when only a short distance from the scene. When I pulled off his tail the air seemed full of them and I wondered how four could turn into eight or more so quickly.

"I pulled back into the fight and was able to get on another Zeke's tail as he finished an overhead run on one of our planes. He pulled out to the North and performed a semi-split-S, swinging back around to the south in an effort to scissor me. I had about three bursts at him and stayed on his tail until he burned and went into the water. Ensign Plant pulled onto his tail with me and was firing at him at the same time. I then pulled back into the melee again, singled out and dived on a Zeke 1,000 feet or so below. He headed south at full speed but I was able to overtake him in two minutes using war emergency power. I let out a burst at extreme range which caused him to enter a high wingover to the left. This enabled me to close and get in a good burst before he dove under. I attempted to follow around in a high wingover without the use of my flaps, but due to my excess speed, swung wide, which enabled him to pull back in under me though 500 to 800 feet below. I lost sight of him, so dove out at full gun and headed back in toward the melee. I called all friendly planes that I would pass about a mile off Orote, Angels 4 [4,000 feet] with a Zeke on my tail, and anybody not busy come down and get him off.

"On approaching Orote two or three planes were observed to make a pass in his direction. However, I never saw him again. On arriving back at the melee point, the air was clear of enemy aircraft, so a rendezvous was announced over the point where one friendly parachute was seen. We circled for about ten minutes, got seven planes together and returned to base."

McCampbell added up the results. They had shot down eleven enemy fighters, and probably three others. Two fighter pilots from VF 15 were missing: Lieutenant R.L. Stearns and Lieutenant (jg) J.L. Bruce. The latter had been seen to bail out.

Assessing the fight, McCampbell recognized that the enemy they had faced was well-trained and well-organized. Those fighter pilots knew what they were doing, unlike many who had been encountered on June 19 in the "turkey shoot." The Japanese had also picked off "tail-end Charley" once again, as they had done with Ensign Powers on June 20. McCampbell, in his report, made note of that repetition, and he also gave a cautionary note about Zeros in general: some American fighter pilots could stay with the Zeros in turns by the use of a series of split-Ss, but only some. McCampbell had not been able to see the entire action, but it was apparent that the Japanese had planned this action well; before it was ended, there were at least eighteen Japanese planes in the air against the twelve *Essex* fighter planes.

Bruce had been the one to parachute, and Lieutenant (jg) W.A. Lundin had circled him and seen him alive and kicking, as he went down toward the water. But his life raft fell off the parachute braces almost at the beginning of the descent, which was very bad luck. After he landed the parachute sank quickly, and although several pilots took good looks, there was no sign of anyone in the water.

Lieutenant Stearns's end was certain: others saw his plane hit hard in the cockpit during the fight, and he was last seen slumped over the stick, the plane in a steep glide, heading towards Orote Airfield. Ensign W.J. Clark flew wing on the fighter until he had to break off near the ground, and then Stearn's plane went into a crash.

Stearns had simply been the victim of power: he and Clark were in the high cover division to begin with, and Stearns came down to make a high pass at a Zero while Clark followed through on his wing. That Zero flamed and fell. Stearns and Clark then started a weave, Clark saw a Zero coming onto Stearns's tail, and Clark got in a deflection shot on the Zero, which broke off, smoking, and moved away. But as this happened another Zero came diving across the top of Clark's plane, getting a full deflection shot on Stearns and hitting him in the cockpit. It was hardly a question of skill or lack of it; there were just too many planes going too many directions at one time.

Lieutenant Symmes and his wingman, Ensign Plant, had separated to bracket one Zero they were chasing. Several other F6Fs were on Ensign Plant's side. The Zero turned the wrong way, directly into the other F6Fs (the report called the plane "the dumb Zeke"), and Ensign plant and Commander McCampbell got that one.

Lieutenant Symmes then joined up on three other F6Fs that were chasing one Zero, but he did not have their speed and fell back, whereupon he was tailed by two Zeros who came in hot and heavy. He was able to turn into them enough to ease them off, but one came over in a combination overhead-and-highside pass on his starboard side. He chopped throttle and turned up into the Zero, and the pilot was unable to follow through; Symmes then turned left, cartwheeling onto his tail, and hit the Zero in the cockpit. It went down, did not burn but crash-landed just short of Orote Airfield and smashed into pieces.

The other Zero had tailed Lieutenant Symmes as he went through these gyrations, but Symmes knew he was there and figured he was giving the Zero bad shooting position. But as he pulled out above the crashing Zero, he was attacked from above. He turned left into the Zero, which made only one half-hearted pass and then kept going astern. That gave Symmes a full deflection shot all the way from stem to stern from a little distance above. The Zero burned and went into the beach water at Orote Point.

Ensign Stime caught a Zero on the tail of another F6F (McCampbell's, as it turned out) at 4,000 feet off Orote Point, and made a highside run. The Zero started smoking and headed for the water. Ensign Stime then had a shot at another Zero and hit it hard. It crashed into the side of a cliff.

Lieutenant (jg) Rushing was deep in the melee from the beginning, and he shot down one Zero and probably another. Lieutenant Lundin followed Bruce down in his parachute, and then he found a Zero at low altitude; he fired and the Zero went smoking away. He did not know whether or not the plane was destroyed. Ensign Pigman, who was flying with Ensign Stime, got one Zero with a long burst on the tail, and the Japanese plane went into the ground and blew up.

So that was the fighter squadron's story about Guam for the day. Anyone who said the Japanese were finished was overstating the case a little.

Not all the airmen of the *Essex* who flew that day were assigned to Guam. Eleven fighters, a dozen dive bombers, and eight torpedo bombers were sent on a mission to strike installations at Tinian. They did not run into any enemy aircraft in the air, and the anti-aircraft fire seemed very light. Yet one torpedo bomber got hit hard, and Gunner J.V. Coppola was wounded in the foot by shrapnel.

The third mission of the day was a direct result of the first: when Commander McCampbell ran into all those Japanese planes at Guam, he let it be known back at the carrier, and another strike was sent off at 11:55, fourteen fighters, six torpedo bombers, and twelve dive bombers, to plaster the airfields and knock down any planes in the air. The bombers concentrated on a wooded area next to the runways, where McCampbell had seen sun flashing on propellers that morning. The bombs were dropped but no results were seen. One bomber did spot a pair of planes at one end of the runway and bombed them, destroying both. This strike met no air opposition at all.

A fourth mission went off at 2:45 that afternoon, led by Lieutenant Commander Rigg, who had taken over as acting commander of the fighter squadron on the death of Commander Brewer. The Japanese were in the air again, although the Zeros kept high and out of sight until the dive bombers started their runs. Then four Zeros came out of the clouds and tried to get at the bombers, but Rigg had instructed his fighter pilots to cover those bombers, so they were weaving over them. The fighters stayed between the bombers and the enemy aircraft.

Lieutenant Morris took the first Zero that dived down, and he made three runs on the plane; it began smoking and headed for the deck, but the pilot never managed to pull out, and the Zero smashed into the water and disintegrated. Lieutenant Carr was the next to score on a Zero. He was weaving at 6,000 feet with his wingman, Ensign Berree, when the four Zeros attacked. Carr and Berree jumped on the Zeros, and Carr got on the tail of one and followed it down from 6,000 to 1,000 feet, firing repeatedly. The Zero never pulled out of its initial dive and crashed into the sea.

Berree missed on his first pass at that same Zero but another came up within 200 yards of him and he fired two bursts into its wing roots and started the plane smoking. The Zero started into a split-S turn, but never finished it and fell off into the sea.

The other Zeros in the area, if there were any, disappeared. But on the way home, after all the bombing was finished, the four fighters of Morris's division encountered a single Zero down low. It looked like easy pickings and they dived on him, but this Zero pilot was one of the old school, a real flier, and he flew rings around the Americans. Down on the deck, at 50 to 150 feet, he did turns and banks and flew on his back and completely outmaneuvered all four pilots. "He went through every stunt in the books (and some not in) and as far as is known, escaped unharmed," wrote Lieutenant Commander Rigg in the action report that day.

The attitudes of the fighter pilots of the *Essex* had undergone some revision in the last few days. After the Marianas turkey shoot, most of the pilots thought they could go with any Zero in the world, but in these last days they had learned something. For a good quick bounce from high altitude, what they said was totally accurate. But when it got down on the deck, with the heavier air and heavier F6Fs, the American fighter simply could not maneuver with the Zero, and this old hand on June 23 had proved it beyond doubt. With altitude and resulting high speed, the F6F could stay with a Zero in a dive; the real advantage for the F6F came when a Zero tried zooming and high speed recovery at medium and high altitude.

On June 24, the airmen of the *Essex* were back at Guam on a combination raid, to hit at shipping, bomb military installations, and work over Orote Airfield once more. Commander McCampbell had nineteen fighters, twelve dive bombers, and eight torpedo bombers on the raid. There were no visible aircraft on the field, and none came up to challenge them. There were obviously planes left at Guam, for the fighter pilots had seen them on the 23rd, but they were keeping down.

The Japanese, however, were preparing the defense of Guam, and reinforcements had obviously come in because the American pilots saw one large cargo ship-transport in the harbor and a landing barge filled with Japanese troops coming away from it as they approached. Those Japanese soldiers were unfortunate: the fighters swooped down on the barge, strafing.

Lieutenant (jg) Bentz and Ensign Harry A. Goodwin fired rockets as well as machine gun bullets from their TBFs, as they attacked the merchant ship. All nineteen fighters strafed the landing barge and left it sinking, with many of those Japanese soldiers dead in the water.

Another strike that day was led by Lieutenant Commander James Mini against Agana Airfield. Those planes ran into heavy anti-aircraft fire over Guam, and Lieutenant (jg) James W. Bernitz' dive bomber was forced to land in the sea, but he and Radioman Carl Shetler were rescued.

Since the pilots of McCampbell's first strike had been diverted from Orote Airfield by the sight of that transport and the Japanese soldiers, later in the day, Lieutenant Commander Duncan led another strike against Orote. They bombed the dispersal areas and the runways, and the fighters strafed buildings and in the woods. They may have hit some planes, but the Japanese were so expert at concealment that no one could be sure. Still another strike was made that day against Orote. Two fighters were also sent on that mission to take pictures of activity (if any) on Rota Island.

Ensign Singer was taking oblique photos of Rota village beach when four Zeros came down on him in two sections. Singer pulled up immediately and fired on the first attacker, scoring hits in the wing roots. The Zero exploded. The section behind split off to the right, and Singer turned to meet them so quickly, and put his nose up so suddenly, that he nearly stalled out. He fired head-on at the first Zero, hit it in the engine and it flamed up and fell off into the water.

Singer ducked his nose, put on full power, and headed for the deck, then scudded along toward the *Essex*. He was wounded in the face from enemy fire, but he made it back satisfactorily and later that day was reported recovering nicely. The pictures, said the air intelligence officer, were "just great."

What they showed was that, despite the belief of higher authority that all enemy air activity in the Marianas had been knocked out, there were enemy airplanes around. The American attacks were resumed with a new tenacity.

Lieutenant Commander Rigg then led another strike on the Guam airfields on June 25. Once again the planes found a number of aircraft on the runway and adjacent to it in parking areas. One bomb was seen to destroy three single-engined planes and another destroyed five planes. The aircraft also attacked fuel tanks at Apra Harbor and a ship in the harbor.

On June 27, Commander McCampbell led a strike on Rota, with bombers and fighters. Ensign Frederick Lightner put a 2,000-pound bomb into the west side of the airstrip. The fighters strafed a number of aircraft. But by this time, the Japanese were using dummies very successfully, and the claims of the Americans about plane damage were not always verified later. Still, during the last three raids, no enemy planes had been seen in the air, and that was certainly an indication of a failing Japanese defense effort in the Marianas.

On June 28, planes from the *Essex* and the *Cowpens* combined in a raid to hit Pagan once more. It seemed half-deserted; certainly the airfield was not in operation, and the pilots saw only a few small craft in the harbor as they bombed and strafed. The radio station had been destroyed earlier. It had not been repaired.

The tactic now was to crater the runways with big bombs and thus make sure that the enemy could not use the airfields without major repair work. The dive bombers were good at this. On June 29, they were back at Rota and dropped seven 1,000-pound bombs on the runway. Rota would not operate for a day or two, anyhow. The night fighters went out, too, but at Rota they saw absolutely no air activity. The raids were now almost "milk runs," with only an occasional plane damaged by anti-aircraft fire.

On July 3, the *Essex* was relieved, along with the rest of Admiral Harrill's task group, and steamed to Eniwetok for rearmament and provisioning. The ships arrived on July 6 and remained until July 14. While they were at Eniwetok, the *Langley* was detached from the group and the *Princeton* was substituted. Two old shipmates came back to the *Essex:* Ensign Thomas A. Woods and his radioman, Archie McPherson, who had been shot down in their dive bomber on the Marcus raid. It took that long for a rescued airman to be decanted back to his ship.

On July 15, the carrier was back in operation off Guam, hitting the Guam installations in preparation for the delayed invasion of that island. Since there were no more enemy aircraft to fight, the F6Fs mission changed, they strafed, they bombed, and they were responsible for taking the photographs that helped the senior officers decide what to do next. The greatest danger these days seemed to be in accidents rather than enemy activity.

On July 18, the airmen of the *Essex* sent thirty-four fighters and bombers to hit Japanese installations around Agat on Guam. They dropped bombs from 250 pounds to 1,000 pounds, they used rockets, and they strafed. They left the town of Agat in flames. A lucky Japanese shell (there were few of them) tore a hole in Ensign Otto Bleech's TBF at the wing tank. He jettisoned his bombs immediately and closed the bomb bay doors. His oil pressure dropped to zero and the radio and hydraulic systems went out. The engine went into full low pitch, and in a moment the engine froze up. Bleech called his crewmen, and the radioman came up into the second cockpit and braced his back against the forward armor plating so that he faced aft.

Bleech took the TBF in for a dead stick water landing. The plane hit the water with an airspeed of seventy-five miles per hour, underpinning first, wings and tail, in perfect water-landing technique. The jolt did not seem to be any more than that of a bad carrier landing. All three men got out into the main life raft in about ten seconds.

The plane sank about fifteen seconds later. They were rescued and returned to the carrier that day.

That was enemy action, certainly. But the same day, a dive bomber narrowly escaped destruction when one of its own ammunition boxes fell out during flight and knocked a big hole in the vertical fin. The pilot brought the plane back safely.

The missions were becoming more specific and more closely related to the coming invasion. Commander McCampbell led a mission against Agat town on July 18. The fighters had been told to hit four specific coastal defense guns, but McCampbell could not find any gun installations in the assigned area, and so his planes went after what seemed to be a fuel dump. Targets were growing scarce.

The dive bombers were led on this mission by Lieutenant Roger F. Noyes. They were assigned to strike Bangi Point on the west coast of Guam and Aluton and Yona Islands just off the coast. The object was to destroy positions from which enfilading fire could be directed against the landing troops on invasion day. The photo interpreters had found several machine gun installations, but when the bombers got to the area they could not see them. They plastered the whole area with 100-, 250-, and 500-pound bombs, and they did not believe there were any machine gun nests left down there after they were finished.

The TBFs were loaded with rockets and 100-pound anti-personnel bombs. They struck the islands and Bangi point, and used their rockets against any buildings they could find still standing in Agat town. There were not many.

This was really area bombing, by this time. The fighters on the next mission destroyed a bridge, and burned a building, and strafed trenches that ran from Agat town to Faepi Point. The bomber pilots observed that they seemed to be engaged in clearing trees and brush. They saw only one light anti-aircraft gun, near Bangi Point, and when it was strafed it stopped firing. The pilots came home to report that the island was practically devastated.

But on July 19, they were sent back again, to do even more damage. For days there had been almost no opposition of any sort; they could see nothing moving on the ground below. It was a question of finding and trying to hit pillboxes and mobile artillery, and trucks here and there. It was saturation bombing of possible gun positions and the network of trenches the Japanese had constructed (and were still constructing) around Bangi Point. By the 19th, some of the fighters were bringing their bombs back, since they could not find adequate targets. That meant jettisoning them before coming aboard the *Essex;* almost any place they might have dropped on Guam would have been more useful than that.

In the last few days, the airmen of the *Essex* had been warned to be careful of American underwater and beach demolition experts who were working in the area where the landings would come. On July 19, four battleships started the pre-invasion bombardment. The *Essex* planes were still hard at work.

The fact is that these many air strikes in the middle days of July did not do much damage to the Japanese defense effort on Guam, except in one way. Physically, the Japanese had protected their power plants, and ammunition dumps, underground as well as their communications. The physical damage was limited to installations in the open and about half of these were knocked out. The important factor was the damage to the morale of the Japanese on Guam. Constant harassment, day and night, by bombers and fighters kept the defenders from sleep and gave a constant reminder of the enormous power of the American invading forces.

The *Essex* airmen added to that harassment all day long on July 20, flying one mission after another, trying to hit very small targets, such as narrow road bridges, culverts, and road junctions. All this activity was aimed to make the task of the landing forces easier. In spite of the fact that Japanese anti-aircraft fire was very slight, there were casualties. On July 20, Lieutenant Miles R. Siebert of the bombing squadron winged over for a dive bombing run on a bridge. At 4,000 feet, for some reason not known to the others, the port wing of his Helldiver came off, almost totally intact, and the plane spun crazily down to crash. Siebert and his radioman, Leon Murray, were killed.

The landings were made on July 21 on beaches at Asan, Agat, and Orote. Commander McCampbell led the accompanying air strike. The fighters strafed the beaches between Agat town and Bangi Point, and they also dropped anti-personnel bombs in the area. The Helldivers bombed and strafed the beaches, and so did the TBFs, which concentrated on the wooded land above the beaches, firing rockets into the trees that might conceal Japanese troops.

There was no anti-aircraft fire at all on this early mission nor any on the next, which set out at 8:00 in the morning. This time, the pilots used delayed action bombs, which let them go in very low, without danger of concussion from their own weapons.

After the invasion began, the *Essex* moved up to Tinian Island, where Admiral Harrill's group operated with the escort carriers assigned to protect the invasion forces. On July 23, Commander McCampbell led a strike of planes from the *Essex* and the *Langley,* a maximum effort involving ninety-two aircraft. If any of the *Essex* airmen had begun to believe that the Japanese in the Marianas were finished, this early morning raid of July 23 disabused them. The usual naval bombardment by battleships, cruisers, and other craft had begun at dawn, but was lifted for about an hour, beginning at 8:00, so the bombers and fighters could come in to strike the beaches and Japanese installations. The *Essex* strike was assigned to hit artillery positions, pillboxes, and several villages where Japanese troops were thought to be stationed. They also were to hit the railroad that coursed from the sugar fields to the mill.

The anti-aircraft fire was bothersome; it caused one bomber (Ensign Frederic C. Talbot's) to land at Isely Field on Saipan for repairs. (Isely Field was captured in the first few days of fighting.) The planes also had trouble with their bombs; they were making low runs, and not using fused (delayed action) bombs, so several planes were struck by fragments. Lieutenant Clifford R. Jordan made a water landing off the island. He and gunner Stanley Whitey were picked up by a rescue plane. (Jordan had been seriously wounded by fragments of his own bomb.) Then, when the mission returned, Ensign A.G. Slack's fighter lost power on its final approach to the carrier, and Slack put the plane down in the water near the carrier. He was rescued by a destroyer. Three of the TBFs were hit by some sort of fire, probably anti-aircraft or mortar, and had to be repaired after landing on the *Essex*.

The second mission of July 23 began at 2:00 in the afternoon. Again, the *Essex* and *Langley* planes cooperated. The mission was of a sort now familiar to the airmen of the *Essex*, to hit specific targets that often did not seem to be there. The pilots saw virtually no results of their attacks. Another mission, begun at 3:44, destroyed a sugar mill (there was no evidence of Japanese military use) and concentrated on Tinian town. At the end of that day, through the efforts of the pilots of the *Essex* and other carriers, there was scarcely a building left standing in the town.

On July 24, the airmen of the *Essex* combined with fliers from the *Princeton* to strike the beaches and Japanese installations in support of the landings. A second mission concentrated on gun positions on the cliffs and in the woods above the beaches. There was little enemy activity against the air strikes (none in the air itself), but Ensign David H. Johnson, Jr., was lost when, in the cross-leg of his approach to the *Essex*, he was given a wave-off because his wheels were up. He began his turn, but the plane stalled, rolled on its back and crashed in the sea, nose down. Johnson did not come up.

The dive bombers were assigned to try to knock out a hidden gun position on Guam. Six of them bombed, but did not see any results of the bombing. Then Lieutenant Frank West, the leader of the *Essex* Helldivers on this strike, found a gun and made a direct hit on it. Then he dropped bombs on a railway junction, destroying the tracks and switch.

The *Essex* planes flew some close support that day, hitting mortar positions, trucks, and pillboxes in support of the troops down below on Tinian. There was a good deal of difficulty in locating the targets laid out by the intelligence officers because the Japanese camouflage was masterful. One torpedo plane pilot flew down the island at low altitude after using up his bombs and rockets and from 300 feet saw distinctly two coastal defense guns whose camouflage blended perfectly with the cliff where they were located.

On July 25, the *Essex* was assigned to Guam once more, and early in the morning a strike of Helldivers, along with fighters and torpedo bombers from the *Langley* and the *Princeton,* worked over troop barracks and the main highway south and east of Agana. Later that day, another strike of planes from the three carriers hit a group of buildings on the Orote Peninsula, not far from the airfield.

This was a long mission, and when the pilots came back, after nearly five hours, they were short on gasoline—several planes having less than thirty gallons left in their tanks. Lieutenant Henry H. Kramer had particular difficulty. First his hook did not come down, and he took a wave-off. He came around again, and this time the landing signal officer did not like his approach—too ragged, he said—so Kramer took another wave-off. He never made the third approach: the plane ran out of gas, and he landed in the sea. He and his gunner were rescued by a destroyer.

Someone in intelligence had a hunch that Japanese planes were staging again at Rota for attacks on the American forces, so the planes of the *Essex*, the *Princeton,* and the *Langley* were assigned to make a strike on that island's airstrip. Half the planes

The big battleships like the *Pennsylvania* softened up the beaches for the invading troops at Guam, just as the planes of the *Essex* and other carriers struck at the airfields and troop concentrations.

On the morning of June 19, 1944, Admiral Ozawa's planes found the American carrier fleet and moved in to attack. McCampbell's heroes were busy that day, fighting off the bombers and fighters that threatened their carrier and the fleet. The circled plane is one that got through the fighter screen to be shot down by the fleet's anti-aircraft gunners.

When the fighting was over for Air Group Fifteen, the flying sailors went home on leave. Some then went back to form the nucleus of the "new" Air Group Fifteen. Some went to other units or to schools as instructors. McCampbell stopped to do a little propagandization for the navy. Here he is (left) with Lieutenant Cecil Harris, another of the Navy's "aces." The trophy board they hold is typical of that made by various carrier air groups to show their victories.

Commander McCampbell (left) and three of his heroes—Commander James H. Mini, Lieutenant Commander V. G. Lambert, and Lieutenant Commander James F. Rigg (left to right).

Vice Admiral Marc A. Mitscher (left) commander of the American carrier force, wanted to shake hands with anybody who could shoot down as many Japanese planes as McCampbell had.

June 19. The Japanese gave the attack everything they had. But their fragile planes were no match for the American fighters. Here, a Suisei (Judy) dive bomber goes down in flames after failing in its attack and running into the fighters of VF 15.

Captain Arleigh Burke (left) was virtually commander of the American carrier task force. He was chief of staff to Admiral Marc Mitscher, but Mitscher's health was so poor that most decisions were left to the captain. Here he is with Commander McCampbell aboard the USS *Lexington*.

The men of Air Group Fifteen on the hangar deck of the *Essex* with their scoreboard of Japanese planes shot down, and ships sunk, one of the most impressive of the Pacific War. When this picture was taken, the men of Air Group Fifteen were just about to leave the ship on their way home.

On October 14, the Japanese went after the *Essex* with a vengeance. The photo above shows one of four Tenzan torpedo bombers (Jill) in attack. This plane attacked low on the starboard bow of the carrier, and its torpedo passed close along the starboard side of the ship. It was shot down moments later by anti-aircraft fire.

When the Fighting Fifteen returned to Pearl Harbor after the Leyte invasion, the stories of the pilots became grist for the war correspondents and thrilling tales for the folks back home. Here Commander McCampbell, center, is shown with war correspondent Quentin Reynolds of *Collier's* magazine (right).

The Japanese air installations on Tinian were elaborate, as can be seen in this photo of Ushi Point airfield, the largest on the island. This picture was taken during the carrier raids at the time of invasion.

One of the great honors for any fighting American was presentation to the President of the United States. Here Commander and his mother are shown with President Franklin D. Roosevelt in the oval room of the White House. The occasion was the presentation to McCampbell of the Congressional Medal of Honor on January 10, 1945.

carried delayed-action bombs (with twelve hour fuses) and half carried instant explosives. They bombed in pairs, dive bomber with fighter. The idea was to confuse the Japanese.

Air support for ground troops at Guam was the next order of business, on July 27. It could be dangerous work, and on that day it was. Fighters, dive bombers, and torpedo bombers from the three carriers hit a ridge south of Agana and a quarry where the Japanese were supposed to have some guns. Someone fired back, and Ensign J.C. Crowley's bomber was hit very hard. The shell (apparently from an anti-aircraft gun at Agana Airfield) blew off six inches of the left elevator and broke the windshield above the .30 calibre machine gun. The gunner was wounded by flying glass.

The planes of the three carriers were working together every day now. Another strike on Rota on July 27 was most productive. The targets were rail lines, warehouses, and buildings. But again there were problems. As the mission's planes took off, Ensign L.R. Timberlake's TBF seemed to be in fine shape. It responded to the warm-up and deck check normally, and the manifold pressure was proper as Timberlake took the plane off the deck. Yet when he reached 150 feet of altitude, the engine began cutting out and the rpm needle jumped back and forth. The plane stalled, and Timberlake saw that a water landing was imminent. The TBF was going so slowly that it pancaked down at about seventy knots. The moment the plane hit, the turret gunner, Goren, jumped out onto the wing and then moved to the hatch into the radio compartment. By the time he got there, the water was two-thirds of the way up to the top of the hatch. (The TBF was carrying a 2,000-pound bomb.) The hatch was sprung open, so Goren pulled it off. Inside, radio operator J.D. McAllister was half-unconscious and hurt. He was locked into his safety belt. Goren had to work underwater to get him out, and he did. When he got the injured man out of the plane, he inflated both "Mae Wests" and hung onto McAllister, while Ensign Timberlake was inflating the main life raft. The two got McAllister into the raft, and then they waited, until a Dumbo picked them up. When the aircrew got back to the carrier, McAllister's left leg was found to have a compound fracture.

The other eleven bombers of the *Essex* got off safely that day and hit the assigned target, which was a barrack area on Guam. While one of the planes was passing over the airfield, its turret gunner, William G. Peppel, saw an enemy aircraft hidden in the trees near the airfield. The pilot of his plane went down with two rockets, but both missed. One, however, seemed to move the plane. They went down again, and this time Peppel set fire to the aircraft with shots from the turret gun. So the Japanese, even late in July, were still getting some aircraft into the Marianas.

But the fight was not to last much longer. On July 29, the *Essex* planes again hit supply areas behind the Japanese lines. That day the Marines took possession of Orote Airfield, and the Orote Peninsula was virtually all in American hands. On the afternoon of July 29, Admiral Spruance, General Holland Smith, Lt. General Roy Geiger and Army Brigadier General L.C. Shepherd held a little ceremony at the old American parade grounds to celebrate (prematurely) the recapture of Guam. But the anticipation was not too great; it was just a matter of time before the essential elements of the island would be in American hands.

On August 1, the airmen of the *Essex* were still giving troop support, with bombs, rockets, and strafing. The Japanese had been driven back west of Mount Santa Rosa. Other missions were flown on August 2, one early, one at midday, and one late. On August 3, the *Essex* planes were still delivering bombs and strafing wooded areas where troops were supposed to concentrated. The pilots and crewmen seldom saw any troops. That day, Lieutenant Strane landed at Orote Airfield to deliver some supplies. The Japanese were still fighting.

On August 4, one of the fighters, going in low, was shot up by shrapnel. Sometimes, however, the shrapnel was again from their own bombs as they went in too low. Occasionally Commander McCampbell led his fighters on a quick run over Rota, and usually they saw some activity there (Rota had not been invaded). But for the most part it was slow, tiresome work with very little evidence of any success. Commander McCampbell noted in his final report on these operations that it was hard to maintain pilot morale on such assignments.

By August 8, the Guam campaign was over for the men of the *Essex*. (The island was declared to be secure two days later.) The task group refueled and was reorganized to include the *Essex*, the *Belleau Wood*, the *Langley*, the cruiser *San Diego*, and six destroyers. Captain Ofstie was relieved as commander of the *Essex* by Captain C.W. Weiber. Captain Ofstie left the Guam area for Eniwetok, to become a rear admiral and commander of a group of escort carriers.

While at Eniwetok some more changes were made. Commander McCampbell had noted in his report on the Tinian-Guam operations that replacement pilots sent to a carrier in mid-combat were almost useless. These pilots had as much skill as any pilot could have after about 400 hours of air time, but that was nothing in combat. When the carrier got to Eniwetok, McCampbell managed to get permission to train nine Helldiver pilots as fighter-bomber pilots in Hellcats. The fact was that the Grumman plane had proved itself as a fighter bomber, and that sort of activity was seen as extremely valuable. The complement of fighters on the *Essex* was increased, and that of dive bombers decreased. Also, the dive bomber pilots got a new plane, the SB2C3.

And all concerned, it seemed, were glad to get a new task group commander. Admiral Harrill, known informally (and not very respectfully) on the main deck as "Whiskey," was famous among the pilots for his vacillation. He seemed unable to make up his mind about risks, and consequently the airmen of the *Essex*, in the early Marianas campaign, had wasted a good deal of time on wild goose chases. One day during the campaign, the admiral complained about stomach pains, and the senior surgeon aboard the *Essex* took the problem to Captain Ofstie because it was as much a military as a medical problem. What would they do if the Admiral had to have an operation?

"Do you think there is anything wrong with him?" asked Captain Ofstie.

"He *might* have appendicitis," said the surgeon.

"Good; then put him in the sick bay and take out his appendix," said Captain Ofstie. "He's better off out of the way." The implication was clear that, even if the admiral did not have appendicitis, now was a good time to take out his appendix.

And so, for either military or medical reasons, Admiral Harrill's appendix was removed during the battle of the Marianas, and he was out of action, leaving the running of the ship to Ofstie and the running of the task group to his chief of staff, a more malleable man.

After a few days, the admiral grew a little fretful. He thought he was well, but he was not quite sure. Should he get up and back to duty, or should he stay down in bed?

Once again, the chief surgeon came to Captain Ofstie with the problem.

"Hell," said Captain Ofstie, "let him stay in bed." Then he thought for a moment, recalling the set-up of the *Essex* sick bay, where the senior officer's private room had a head at either end. If the ward on one side was jammed up, the head on that side was opened to the lesser types and closed to the senior's private room. At this particular time the rooms on both sides were vacant.

"I'll tell you what," continued the captain. "Open both heads up. Then Whiskey will get so confused about which one he ought to use that he'll put in for a transfer."

The story may be apocryphal—Commander McCampbell, who told it (long after the war), had a twinkle in his eye as he spoke. In any event, when the *Essex* was getting ready to go back into battle in the Philippines, Admiral Harrill was transferred out to a shore command, and that is how the *Essex* and the other ships of the task group got their new commander, Rear Admiral Frederick Sherman.

CHAPTER NINE

Softening-Up
the Philippines

In September, 1943, the Japanese had begun their withdrawal within the framework of an empire that had once extended to the fringes of Australia. The first realignment created an "absolute national defense" on a line that ran from the middle of the Caroline Islands to the western part of New Guinea on one side, and to the Marianas on the other. In May, 1944, Imperial General Headquarters decreed that the Mobile Fleet would bring about the "decisive battle" in collaboration with the First Air Fleet. In other words, the Americans were to be defeated by the navy and the naval air force.

This was the A-Go Operation, which turned out to be the Battle of the Philippine Sea. It was supposed to so stun the Americans ("utterly crush" was the hyperbole of the Imperial General Staff) that they would come to the peace table humbly, and Japan could retain most of what she had won in 1941 and 1942. Years later, the official Japanese war historians would write: "this plan sadly collapsed, and thereafter the Japanese army also would have to be responsible on the Mainland (Hondo), the Southwest Islands, Taiwan, and the Philippines."

All this was apparent in Tokyo by August, 1944. Army, navy, and air forces all together would have to deal with the next Allied attack "absolutely"; unless these forces—including the army—did so they would be cornered and driven to earth in all these places. "Where ever the Americans and their allies struck, so crushing a blow would have to be dealt them that they would completely alter their strategy for pursuit of the war."

The American attack could come anytime after the first of August. To meet it, no matter where it came, the Imperial General Staff devised four plans, each in anticipation of a different "decisive battle" front. Sho 1 anticipated an attack in the Philippines. Sho 2 foresaw an attack on Kyushu, the Southwest Islands group (near Japan), as well as on Tsiwan. Sho 3 anticipated an attack on Japan proper—all islands, especially Kyushu and (perhaps) the Bonin Islands. Sho 4 suggested an attack on the Northern Sea areas, perhaps on Hokkaido and Sakhalin.

In each case a three-pronged operational plan was developed, involving naval units, the air forces, and the army. Central to each plan was one maneuver: the remaining four aircraft carriers of the Japanese navy would have to be offered as sacrifice.

Admiral Toyoda and the Imperial General Staff were well aware of the U.S. Navy's new preoccupation with carrier warfare. The closer the fighting came to Japan, the less need there was for the Japanese to employ carriers, so they could now be sacrificed, if necessary, in this "decisive battle." They were to be used as lures. Admiral Ozawa was to bring them out and show them, far away from the central scene of operations—which was to be the area of the Allied landings. The watchword was *zemmetsu kokugo* (readiness for complete annihilation, in self-sacrifice for the nation).

In May, as the Japanese prepared, so did the Americans, for the operation to follow the capture of the Marianas. The next allied move, established by the Joint Chiefs of Staff, was to solidify a line running from the Palau Islands to Yap, Ulithi, Morotai, and Halmahera. General MacArthur undertook the last two projects, and the Pacific Fleet undertook the first three. The reason for taking Palau and Ulithi in particular was to establish a new forward base of naval operations for the invasion of the Philippines. This last, the Joint Chiefs had decided, was to be the next and greatest-yet operation of the Pacific War.

It was also to mark the transition of command. Until the summer of 1944, the Central Pacific campaign (the navy) had been paramount in the Joint Chiefs' planning. Then, President Roosevelt made one of his rare but absolute command decisions: the next major action would be to retake the Philippines; not (as General MacArthur seemed to believe) to honor MacArthur's personal promise to return, but because Roosevelt, the consummate politician, could see that the rescue of the Philippines and the return of the pre-war government, with its promise of total independence, would—must—have a positive effect on the war beyond any military victory.

And so the invasion of the Palau Islands was set for September 15, 1944. In the interim, Admiral Halsey took command of the active fleet; its name was changed from Fifth Fleet to Third Fleet, and Task Force 58 became Task Force 38. The ships were the same. The *Essex,* however, was advanced in "rank" to become the flagship of Task Group 38.3, which was commanded by Rear Admiral Frederick C. Sherman and included the *Lexington,* the *Princeton,* and the *Langley.* The larger number of carriers was an indication of the growing power of the American navy in the Pacific.

The *Essex* and the other ships of Sherman's task group left Eniwetok on August 29. There was time for a little horseplay on September 1, when the carrier crossed the equator and Captain Weiber gave permission for a ceremony of King Neptune's court to initiate all the tyros among the sailors into the mysteries of the sea. But on September 3, the deadly business of war began again.

On September 6, Commander McCampbell led a fighter sweep over the Palaus, concentrating on the airfields of Babelthuap and Ngesebus Islands. No aircraft were encountered in the air, and the sky was fairly clear, with broken clouds at 1,500 feet, so it seemed certain there were no Japanese planes aloft that day. This sweep followed the new pattern of using planes together from all the carriers. Actually there were more carriers involved than ever: the *Intrepid,* the *Bunker Hill,* the *Wasp,* and the *Hornet* all participated in this raid. In all, McCampbell had a fighter force of ninety-six planes, a really powerful armada in the air.

The *Essex* fighters bombed and strafed the runways and the buildings, while the fighters of the *Lexington* dropped napalm, a fiery liquid that had come into use after the Marshalls campaign, and which had the horribly effective property of sticking to anything it touched and burning fiercely. The fighters left a number of barges in the harbors burning behind them.

The next day, September 7, the *Essex* fighters were over the Palau Islands again, strafing. This time the mission was led by Lieutenant Commander J.F. Rigg, the new commander of the fighter squadron.

It was surprising to Admiral Halsey and others that the Japanese were making so slight an effort to stop the attacks on the Palaus. They did not know that Imperial General Headquarters had ordained the Sho operations, and that all commanders were waiting for the big American push, conserving their resources. D-Day for the attack by the Marines on Peleliu Island was set for September 15. On the seventh, the *Lexington's* air group leader also took out a group of planes from his carrier and from the *Essex;* mostly torpedo and dive bombers, since there was no air opposition. They hit the airfields and other installations hard on Peleliu, and although the anti-aircraft fire was fairly heavy, the *Essex* lost no planes. There were few targets—mostly anti-aircraft positions.

Commander McCampbell led another strike on the same island the same day with the same results, and the pilots came to the same conclusions: for a major point of attack, Peleliu seemed to be defended only half-heartedly. Since the Palaus not so long before had been the base for the Japanese fleet, it all seemed extremely odd.

There were aircraft on the airfields. The American bombers and fighters damaged a number of them and destroyed others. But they did not come up to fight. A raid that day led by the *Lexington* was almost a carbon copy of the others.

On another raid it was the same, save that one *Essex* TBF pilot misjudged distances in forming up to go home and very nearly cut the tail off another. The damage to the propeller of one and tail of the second was repaired back on board.

A final raid that day smashed the radio station near the airfield at Peleliu, left the runways full of chuck holes, and blew up several buildings. Altogether, on September 7, the *Essex* and the *Lexington* sent 419 planes to Peleliu. Other planes operated in the same manner against other islands.

On the 8th, Gunner Claude Joseph Laborde of the divebomber squadron was wounded by 40mm shrapnel on the day's first bombing raid on Peleliu and Babelthuap islands. The planes were hitting all sorts of military targets, fuel dumps, warehouses, barracks, and other buildings.

The second raid brought real trouble. This raid was led by Commander Mini of the Helldiver squadron. On the way to the target Mini saw that the beaches of Peleliu were going to be hard to get at, a thirty-mile weather front south of Peleliu persuaded him to divert the bombers to Angaur Island.

The anti-aircraft fire over Angaur was heavy. Lieutenant Henry Kramer was flying a fighter-bomber and dived to make his release. As he pulled out of his dive, another pilot saw a fire under his port wing and called on the radio to warn him. Kramer jettisoned his belly tank but the fire spread quickly, soon covering the wing and moving toward the cockpit. The F6F dropped to 1,000 feet. Kramer was seen opening the cover of his cockpit canopy as if to bail out, but then the plane did a wingover and went into a spin. Flames spread to the F6F's tail, and the plane hit in deep water off the shore.

Not all planes hit Angaur. On the western beach at Peleliu, Lt. G.B. Webb and Lieutenant (jg) W.H. Harper went in to bomb and fire rockets from their TBFs. They were hit by anti-aircraft fire from the beaches. Lieutenant Harper's plane caught fire, but he was able to make a water landing, and he and his crewmen were picked up. Lieutenant Webb's plane turned south. Another pilot joining up saw a trail of smoke and then fire under the cowling of Webb's plane. Then he saw Lieutenant Webb jump, but the two crewmen did not. The plane went into the water on a fifteen-degree glide, struck with the right wing, and then broke up. No survivors were seen. Lieutenant (jg) Axman, a torpedo plane pilot, dropped a raft to Lieutenant Webb, who crawled aboard it and remained in it until rescued later by a lifeguard submarine.

That submarine had its own difficulties. The Japanese fired at it when it came near the coast. A call for help was sent to the *Essex,* and Ensign C.W. Plant and Ensign L.S. Hamelin took off to fly air cover above the submarine and protect it from attacks. The planes circled the downed airmen in the area, while the submarine rescued them. When the two fighters were relieved from station, they went north to investigate oil slicks off Babelthuap. The slicks were there, but they did not reveal much. The two pilots then strafed anti-aircraft guns on Babelthuap, Koror, and Malakal Islands. Over one of these, Ensign Hamelin was hit, and his plane crashed into the sea. Ensign Plant circled the area, but saw no sign of Hamelin. He circled again and again, until finally he got dangerously low on fuel and had to return to the carrier.

By the end of the day, it was apparent that there were troops in the Palaus who were ready to fight, but that air opposition was not going to develop. The "softening up" process had been completed to the satisfaction of Admiral Halsey, so, on the afternoon of September 8, the *Essex* and the rest of Task Force 38 moved toward the southern Philippines to make strikes at air bases that might be used to stage planes for the defense of the Palau Islands.

On the morning of September 9, the *Essex* and other carriers were assigned to strike the Mindanao airfields. The first strike took off at 5:35 a.m. against Lumbia and Cagayan Airfields and against shipping in Macajalar and Bislig Bays. The fighters were led by Lieutenant Commander Rigg. Over northeastern Mindanao, the fighters spotted a Japanese patrol plane, which Lieutenant Commander Rigg, Lieutenant B.D. Morris, and Lieutenant R.W. Davis, Jr., attacked and shot down.

Then the fighters came back into escort position and led the bombers against the airfields and the shipping. The Japanese were caught flat-footed on the ground. The dive bombers arrived over Lumbia Airfield at about 7:15; planes from the *Lexington* were also attacking this same area. The bombers went in and when Commander Mini counted a few minutes later, he saw ten planes burning on Lumbia Airfield and five on Cagayan Airfield. The bombers and torpedo bombers also set fire to fuel dumps and barracks. One pilot hit a large tent, which he was sure was cover for mechanics working on planes. Leaving the airfields, the bombers also found a convoy off Mindanao of about thirty-five coastal freighters, luggers and trawlers, loaded with fuel, ammunition, and other cargo. The fighters and bombers sank a number of these ships and left others burning or badly holed.

A few minutes after the first strike took off, Commander McCampbell led a second fighter sweep over the airfields at Del Monte, Lumbia, and three other fields. The only planes they encountered were one large flying boat and two Japanese dive bombers (also used for scouting), probably out on an early morning patrol. Lieutenant Milton shot down the patrol bomber and Ensign Plant shot down the two dive bombers. After the fighter sweep (which did not find many planes on the ground either, except those earlier destroyed), the fighters turned to the convoy near Bislig Bay and attacked it again. They left more ships and smaller vessels burning, but there was a price: Lieutenant J.H. Barry, Jr., went in low to strafe one coastal vessel and hit it squarely. It was carrying either ammunition or depth charges because it promptly blew sky high and in the process blew Lieutenant Barry's plane apart.

Lieutenant Commander Lambert of the TBF squadron led another strike against Del Monte Airfield and shipping in the area. The bombers and strafing fighters sank one escort vessel off Cagayan Light, one cargo ship off Sipaca Point, and a big landing barge loaded with about 150 troops off Salay. The dive bombers found a big cargo ship and set it afire. It beached.

The fighter pilots wasted no sympathy on the men they attacked. They strafed survivors until they ran out of ammunition, and Lieutenant Commander G.C. Duncan, leader of the fighter squadron, emptied his .38 calibre revolver on his last low swoop.

At noon, Commander McCampbell had returned to the carrier, and refueled and taken on ammunition; and he led another strike of twenty fighters, fifteen dive bombers, and six torpedo bombers against Mindanao. The strike was supposed to be made at Cagayan Bay, but on the way Commander McCampbell was informed that all shipping there had been sunk or was burning, so he diverted to Surigao Strait. They attacked dock facilities at Surigao. The only enemy aircraft sighted was again a patrol plane, and Lieutenant G.R. Crittenden and his wingman, Ensign W.R. Johnson, climbed up above it and attacked. Crittenden was given credit for shooting down the plane.

The Helldivers struck the docks with their bombs and set fire to the whole warehouse area, including a gasoline storage tank and an oil storage tank.

The TBFs went in first with their rockets and sank several ships in the harbor, with rockets and bombs. The anti-aircraft fire this time was nothing to sneeze at; five planes were damaged, and one of them landed at sea but both the pilot, Lieutenant Frederick Matthews, and his gunner, Robert A. Erenger, were rescued.

The damage was truly serious; the Japanese on Mindanao that night assessed it: 300 American planes had attacked, they said (the *Essex* alone ran 143 sorties that day, but of course, many planes flew more than once), and they reported that at Mindanao and Davao more than seventy of their aircraft were destroyed and the Mindanao airfields were "crushed." At San Augustin Cape on Davao, the Japanese had a modern radar installation—until the American planes came over. The naval air base there was wiped out, so were a number of planes, and the San Augustin radar station was completely destroyed by fire caused by the bombing.

Here is the way the bombing was see on the ground by one captain of the Japanese air force:

"This morning at Cagayan South airfield, the Korea base squadron's main force and the 66th Squadron's leading units were deployed around the field. At about 8:00, at an altitude of about 3,000 meters [9,000 feet], a group of ten American bombers approached; as we watched, when they were directly above, about half of them suddenly rolled over and dived, coming down in single file to attack the planes and the seaplanes moored at the base. This was the beginning of a systematic enemy attack, and as we watched, our aircraft were destroyed one by one. As if in a daze we saw them catch fire and burn."

The damage was enormous; the Japanese had a false report that day to the effect that the American troops were coming to land at Davao. It was not corrected until very late in the day.

On September 10, a dozen of the *Essex's* F6Fs took off at 6:00 a.m. to join a strike led by the *Lexington's* air group commander. Again the targets were north Mindanao, Macajalar Bay, and Del Monte, Cagayan, and Lumbia Airfields. The *Essex* contingent was led by Lieutenant Commander Rigg. At Macajalar Bay, they encountered one Japanese patrol plane after they had strafed the airfields. At that time, Rigg was preoccupied with the fate of Ensign H.M. Foshee, whose plane was hit by antiaircraft fire over the target. Foshee's engine began acting up, and it was soon apparent that he would have to ditch. He managed to get far enough out to sea to evade capture, then ditched, while Lieutenant Overton, his combat group leader, covered him and reported his position to the lifeguard submarine.

Foshee had been flying on Lieutenant Commander Rigg's wing, so now Rigg had no wingman. He saw a Japanese Nakajima night fighter (Gekko) west of Del Monte Airfield. The Japanese plane first mistook the formation for Japanese and wobbled wings in greeting, but soon enough the pilot saw what he was up against and went into a shallow dive to escape. But with full power the F6F was able to overtake him, which Lieutenant (jg) G.R. Carr proved as he caught up and began firing at the enemy plane, making hits in the engine with his first bursts. The night fighter then jettisoned a pair of 500-pound bombs and tried harder to get away.

Lieutenant R.W. Davis, Jr., and Ensign H.C. Green were trying to get into action against the Japanese plane when they came too close to each other and collided. Ensign's Green's plane burst into flames immediately and burned all the way down. Lieutenant Davis's plane did not burn, but the cockpit was demolished, the whole engine fell out of the plane and crashed separately. Both pilots died.

At about this time, after many bursts, Lieutenant Carr shot down the Japanese night fighter. The American pilots were so used to seeing Zeros explode when hit in the tanks that it was a surprise that it took many bursts to flame the Nakajima fighter.

No long afterward, Lieutenant Commander Rigg "tallyhoed" another Japanese plane over Macajalar Bay. Since he had lost his wingman for the day, Rigg called on Lieutenant Strane's section for help, but he really did not need it. The Japanese pilot, faced with nine American fighters, was a brave man. He turned directly into Rigg, but Rigg still managed to make a few hits on the starboard engine of the twin-engined bomber. Other American fighters herded the Japanese pilot back in front of Rigg, and he began firing again. Once more the Japanese flier turned directly into the F6F, which made shooting most difficult. But then Rigg managed to get on the plane's tail and hit the left engine. Pieces began flying off, and the engine flamed. He also made hits in the cockpit and must have shot the pilot because the plane rolled over into an almost vertical turn to the right at only 200 feet of altitude, the starboard wingtip struck the water, and the Japanese plane cartwheeled across the surface of the sea before stopping suddenly and sinking.

Almost immediately after the first fighter sweep left the *Essex,* the main strike followed: eleven fighters, nine Helldivers, and five TBFs.

Over Macajalar Bay again Lieutenant A. Singer caught a Japanese patrol plane aloft and after a brief fight, shot it down. Two survivors clambered out of the Japanese plane after it made a good water landing, but the Americans strafed them unmercifully. (There was not much camaraderie of the air between American and Japanese pilots; strafing of survivors in the water was a common practice on both sides.)

Lieutenant John Brodhead was leading the Helldivers on this mission. The target for the dive bombers was shipping. He covered Cagayan and several other areas without finding any shipping that day. One pilot, Lieutenant (jg) Calvin Platt, suddenly discovered a fire in his bomb bay. He opened the bomb bay doors and jettisoned his bombs, then headed back toward the carrier. The fire went out and he landed safely.

Del Monte Airfield and its installations became the prime target of the TBFs with their bombs and rockets. They strafed and shot rockets into the barracks there.

Just before 9:00, Commander McCampbell took another mission aloft—another twenty planes to hit the enemy. Lieutenant Morris led eight fighters on a sweep of Cagayan and Lumbia Airfields and found some camouflaged fuel dumps, which blazed furiously after they were hit. The Japanese had put them off in an apparently wooded area—but much of the woods turned out to be clever camouflage. Commander McCampbell led several other planes on a reconnaissance flight over the Surigao area. He found the air bases there deserted, and the runways cratered from previous attacks by other American planes. It seemed as though the Japanese were moving out of the southern area of the Philippines.

On September 9, the weather was spotty and the Japanese search planes that usually went out 650 miles went out only 350 and thus did not sight an American fleet. When attacks came in, the Japanese were literally caught napping.

At First Air Fleet headquarters that morning, a report arrived from the Davao area to the effect that the Americans were about to make a landing. It was greeted with skepticism by the air fleet staff, but Squadron Fifteen was ordered to send fighter planes out to make a reconnaissance. The planes were just taking off when the first wave of American attackers arrived and shot them down. Thus no reconnaissance was made that day, and by the next day it was too late. Most of the air facilities on Mindanao had been destroyed.

It was not quite the same in the Visayan Islands. At 8:00 on the morning of September 12 the first strike involving *Essex* planes took off—eight *Essex* fighters along with eight *Lexington* fighters—to sweep Cebu and Mactan Islands. Once again the Japanese were surprised, but not nearly so greatly as they had been at Mindanao. The fighter sweep arrived over Cebu Airfield at 9:15 and dived down from 10,000 feet through a thin overcast. There on the runways, propellers turning, and on the aprons, nearly ready to take off, were many enemy fighters. The eight *Essex* fighters swooped down and strafed, and on this first pass they accounted for most of the planes on the runway. Two more passes flamed up planes on the taxi-ways and aprons. The *Lexington* fighters, which had been flying cover, came down to join the attack. But while they were attacking Cebu, at Mactan Island's Open Airfield, about five miles away, the Japanese were getting planes into the air. Soon, the sky was filled with Japanese planes, coming to counterattack.

Lieutenant Commander Rigg was leading the *Essex* fighters. He saw two Zeros taking off from Open Airfield, and swooped down. He shot the first as it was 100 feet off the ground; it looped over and crashed at the south end of the runway.

Ahead, he saw a whole group of fighters, which was unusual for this day; the Japanese had apparently scrambled without regard for squadron or flight units, and most of their planes were operating individually, which made life considerably easier for the disciplined American fighters, now used to working in four-plane divisions, splitting off into two plane sections which covered one another. Rigg selected two planes flying in a section, and attacked one. He shot it down turned around; the other plane was gone.

Rigg's wingman had also disappeared in the general melee and he looked around for another F6F to join up on. But things were moving too rapidly; he turned back to Cebu Airfield and saw a Zero taking off low over the harbor. He pounced on the Zero, and shot it into the water. A turn, and Rigg was over Cebu Airfield approach again, where he saw another Zero taking off, very low, between the woods and Cebu town. He dove the F6F on the Zero, which then pulled up directly in front of him and gave him a point blank shot. He fired, and the whole after end of the Zero fell away, just abaft the cockpit. "A beautiful sight," said Lieutenant Commander Rigg.

As the remains of the plane plummeted to the trees, Rigg was already turning back toward Cebu Airfield. Here came another Zero, flying very low, just off the ground, jinking between buildings. He dived on the Zero, which began to flame and then made a crash landing in the water at the end of the airfield.

Lieutenant Commander Rigg then joined up with two F6Fs from the *Lexington*. They found a Zero, and tried to attack. But this pilot was an expert, one of the old hands, and he used a dozen aerobatic tricks, particularly his superior turning ability, to keep the American pilots just off base. They fired, and occasionally they thought they scored hits, but the Zero kept flying. Eventually, after several minutes of this, the Zero escaped into a cloud, and the three American planes went looking for other game. But by that time the excitement was coming to an end. The air strike, which had followed the fighter sweep into the air almost immediately, arrived on the scene with fifteen fighters led by Commander McCampbell.

In all, the fighters of the *Essex* that day downed twenty-seven Japanese planes on the two airfields, and damaged several others. Lieutenant Commander Rigg had the high score of the day with five planes; Commander McCampbell had four. Ensign L.R. Self, Lieutenant Carr, and Ensign W.R. Johnson each shot down three enemy planes, Lieutenant Commander Duncan got two, and eight other *Essex* fighter pilots each claimed one enemy destroyed. Seven of the eight F6F pilots who went off from the *Essex* in the fighter sweep accounted for at least one plane each, but two *Essex* fighters of the sweep were lost: Ensign Plant and Lieutenant (jg) W.V. Henning were listed as "missing in action."

Plant had gone in on Cebu Airfield and Rigg saw him shoot down one Zero. But then Rigg heard a call over the radio: "get him off my tail" and looking down saw Plant's F6F being pursued by a Zero. He and several other pilots swooped down, Rigg took a shot at long distance, fired a burst that alerted the Zero pilot, who then broke away. But it was too late for Plant. Rigg saw a ball of red at the base of the port wing of Plant's plane, and then the F6F burst into flame and crashed on Mactan Island, just south of Open Airfield.

Lieutenant Henning was leading one section in the attack on Cebu Airfield, when he sighted a Zero climbing from the field toward the west. He and Ensign Self, his wingman, headed to attack, first climbing and then making a tail run on the Zero. The Zero pilot turned into them, heading directly toward Self. When the Zero was closing, Self began to fire on it, and the Japanese plane burst into flames. Self pulled up, and Lieutenant Henning slid underneath to avoid collision. Just then an enormous explosion threw Ensign Self's plane a hundred feet in the air; he turned and saw debris floating down and the whole area covered with smoke. He never saw Henning again; the conclusion then was that Henning's plane had been on top of the Zero when it exploded and blew Henning's plane apart as well.

By the time McCampbell led the seventy-plane strike against these fields, the action was half over.

There were plenty of targets for the bombers: cargo ships, tankers, storage tanks that before the war had belonged to Texas Oil Company, Shell Oil, and Asiatic Petroleum, and all the buildings and aircraft facilities of two airfields. Most of the fighters were carrying 500-pound general purpose bombs. There was one exception: Commander McCampbell was trying out rockets on his fighter instead of bombs. The Helldivers were armed with 100-pound anti-personnel bombs and 1,000-pounders, while the TBFs carried 500-pound bombs and rockets. They sank two of the cargo ships in Cebu Harbor, and a sub chaser was left burning and listing. They also sank a barge and many small aircraft. They smashed up the piers, set fire to several of the oil storage tanks, and shot up the barracks and hangars on the airfields. The TBFs attacked the Mactan airfield at low level, bombing and then returning to fire their rockets. When the planes formed up after the attack, Ensign Thomas Carr Maxwell's bomber was missing. No one knew what had happened to it, but Maxwell and crewmen Bernard Schwartz and William Shankle were listed that night as missing in action.

The air strike planes were back aboard the *Essex* well before noon, and the intelligence officers had a chance to look at the pictures and see what damage had been inflicted. They also talked to the pilots and crewmen and got an idea of what had happened over the two islands. The decision was made to give the area another shot to wipe up the remaining ships in the water and port facilities and work over the airfields again. Seventy-two planes, half of them from the *Essex* and the other half from the *Lexington*, went back to Cebu and Mactan Islands. Smoke and fires from the previous strike were still showing when they got over the targets at about 1:45 in the afternoon, and columns of smoke rose to 10,000 feet, making the whole area a little hazy. The fighters strafed. Lieutenant Overton tried out the rockets. He apparently liked them and their effect better than Commander McCampbell did, for he claimed direct hits on one vessel in the water of Cebu Harbor. The dive bombers were supposed to hit Shell Island's storage facilities, but several were diverted by the sight of a tanker, which they attacked and set afire.

The torpedo bombers went after the remaining shipping in the harbor, a 5,000-ton cargo ship, a slightly smaller vessel, and several coastal craft. In a few minutes, bombs and rockets were falling all around the ships. Most of the bombs missed; there were several hits, however, and Lieutenant R.D. Cosgrove made one hit (out of three 500-pound bombs dropped). Later photographs showed the ship partially submerged. Lieutenant (jg) H.D. Jolly fired two rockets into a coastal vessel and left it burning. Lieutenant (jg) Jerome C. Crumley sank a vessel with a crane aboard, and fired rockets into a group of sampans. North of Cebu Rock, Lieutenant (jg) Artman found a group of coastal luggers and claimed a hit and a near miss on two of six ships.

So the attack force returned, to report that there were no enemy aircraft seen in the air and none moving on the ground at the airfields. By that time, Commander McCampbell was already back in the air leading another strike, broadening the area to include the southwest coast of Negros Island. Eighty planes from the *Essex,* the *Lexington,* and the *Langley* made the flight. They found many ships and small vessels at sea and attacked them. They also attacked more airfields, and the Helldivers struck Bohol Island. The fighters and torpedo bombers worked over Dumagusto Airfield on Negros Island, and Lieutenant C.H. Sorensen of the TBF squadron sighted a number of single-engined planes beneath the trees near the runway. He and the pilots following dropped sixty-five 100-pound bombs on these planes and estimated that they destroyed at least twenty-five of them. Photographs showed eleven burning.

For the Japanese, these four days of air strikes against the southern islands had proved truly disastrous. For all practical purposes, Mindanao and Cebu were knocked out as air and naval air bases. In all the confusion about the "invasion" report in the Davao area, the Japanese planes had milled about and most of them had been destroyed. After the attacks of September there were not enough scout planes left in Mindanao to conduct air searches; nor was the damaged radar repaired.

In the attack on Cebu on September 11, the brunt was borne by the 13th Air Group's fighter squadron number thirty, called the Manapua Squadron, and fighter squadron number thirty-one, called the Furaburika squadron. That morning, the two squadrons had been ready for action: the planes were gassed up and were equipped with long-range fuel tanks so that as soon as the enemy carrier task force was discovered they could move to attack. Then, at about 9:30 (9:15 by U.S. estimate), the Cebu army field was struck without warning by the Americans; so was the Cebu naval facility.

As 31st Squadron leader Major Seishin recalled later, it was the perfect ambush. Planes on the runway scarcely had time to jettison their long-range (and very volatile) gas tanks and try to get aloft before the Americans were on them. The Furaburika (31st) Squadron, had four scout planes already in the air, but by the time they were able to sound the alarm it was already too late, and planes trying to take off were shot down scarcely before they reached the end of the runway. Navy planes on their runways were destroyed in a similar fashion. Some of the Furaburika planes had reached high enough altitudes before the strike to be able to come in and help their comrades, but there were too many American planes, and more coming—bombers and fighters.

The first wave of American fighters did enormous damage on the field, but several four-plane divisions of the Furaburika Squadron were able to engage them; still, one by one the Japanese fighters met destruction. Survivors reported that one plane did manage to ram an enemy in a suicide explosion. (This must have been the Japanese explanation for the destruction of Lieutenant Henning's F6F in midair.) As for the Manapua (30th) Squadron, it took the brunt of the first enemy attack, because its planes were just on the point of taking off as the F6Fs roared down by them.

By late afternoon, the ragged remnants of the two squadrons had moved up to Sarabiya Airfield in the Bacolod area, where the Japanese maintained a major army air installation. This was the headquarters of the 13th Air Group and of the 45th Fighter-Bomber Squadron—whose twenty-seven planes were what the Japanese called type 2 twin-seater fighters, and what the Americans called the Kate. By nightfall thirteen of the thirty-one planes of the 31st Squadron and sixteen planes of the 30th Squadron had arrived; about fifty percent of the aircraft had survived the Cebu attack. The shipping loss was assessed at 70,000 tons.

That night, men of all the squadrons in the Bacolod area clamored to be allowed to go off in the darkness to attack the enemy, although all knew that to attack the American carriers alone meant almost certain death and that one or two pilots could scarcely exert much influence on the outcome of the battle. The air group commander let a few of them go. That evening of September 12, two planes of the 30th Squadron were sent off. Later that night, one plane of the 17th Squadron went off alone. Before dawn three planes from the 19th Squadron and two planes from the 31st Squadron took off. These were not kamikaze missions (those were to be invented by the Japanese navy and to come a few weeks later), but the idea was the same—there was virtually no hope of survival. The pilots knew it, and yet they demanded the chance to go. The operation was sufficiently well-defined to have a name (Kanshi Go), but its results are entirely clouded.

From the night attack, only one plane returned safely, and one crashed on landing. The planes of the night raid did not manage to find the enemy. The planes that went out on the dawn attack did not return, and so no results could be assessed. But there was a report very early that morning from Admiral Harrill's task group. A lone bomber had appeared just after 6:00 in the morning and dropped a bomb that near-missed the *Langley*. The gunners of the *Essex* tried to open up on the plane, but the angle was all wrong. The gunners of the battleship *Massachusetts* fired on the plane and claimed to have shot it down. Perhaps they did. In any event, the pilot did not get back to Bacolod.

At 6:00 on the morning of September 13, the airmen of the *Essex* were off again: twelve F6Fs from Air Group Fifteen took off and twelve from the *Lexington's* VF-19 fighter squadron. Commander McCampbell again led the sweep, and he took the planes once more over Cebu to see what might develop. But there were no planes in the air above Cebu; the Japanese had moved all surviving aircraft northward. The *Lexington* air group had a strike coming up so those twelve fighters broke off to cover their bombers, and Commander McCampbell led the *Essex* fighters to Negros Island to see what he could discover there.

They were flying high, but as they approached Negros Island they had to drop down to 6,000 feet to see the Bacolod air complex below because the weather was closing in. It was the beginning of typhoon season in the Philippines, and the weather could change with remarkable speed.

Commander McCampbell looked down. There on the field he saw about twenty planes parked in revetments or camouflaged positions, and one twin-engined Betty bomber just taking off from the field, with a second behind it on the edge of the main runway, ready to take off. McCampbell's division was too far away, but Lieutenant (jg) W.A. Lundin and Lieutenant Commander Duncan were much closer, so their sections nosed down to attack. Lundin shot at the first Betty just after it was airborne; by the time he had made on pass, most of the other *Essex* planes were diving on the bomber. Commander McCampbell's team made three runs on the Betty before it burst into flames and crashed in the water. Lieutenant Commander Duncan turned his attention to the second Betty, and his combat team attacked, scored hits, and the plane crashed and burned about a mile south of the field. The third combat team of four planes remained on top at 6,000 feet, flying cover.

Once again, the Americans of the *Essex* were showing a tight combat discipline.

After this excitement, the fighters settled down to attacking the field below in strafing runs. Altogether they later claimed to have destroyed a dozen twin-engined planes and seven single-engined planes on the ground. These were only planes that burned. Many others, which apparently had no gasoline in the tanks, did not burn and were not claimed.

The sweep fighters strafed the field for about twenty minutes, until 7:30, when the strike group came in sight. Then McCampbell took his dozen fighters up to 7,000 feet and looked around. They were north of the Bacolod air complex when the old cry, "tallyho," came from one of the bombers, whose crew had spotted enemy aircraft as they came in, ten miles west of the field. Part of Commander McCampbell's report:

"We were at 8,000 feet when an Oscar was sighted at one o'clock, slightly below. He must have seen us at about the same time and turned into us and made a half-hearted head-on before pulling out to the right. When in position I pulled over on him and got a rather long burst, starting with 3/4 deflection [allowance for movement of the two aircraft]. He burst into flames in right wing root and spiralled into the water.

"With my combat team behind me we started to gain a little altitude and by the time we reached 8-9 thousand feet two Kates were sighted ahead at 10 o'clock, up. We turned toward them and continued to climb until they rolled over on us. My position was such that by turning sharply to the left neither Kate was able to bear on me. As the first one dove down I followed and got in a short burst as he started his pullout, then another as he turned to the left. It started burning in its right wing root and soon was enveloped in flames as it dove into the bay. Someone on my combat team destroyed the second plane and I saw it hit the water in flames. During this action my wingman, Lieutenant Rushing, became separated from me. He had seen a friendly F6F damaged and smoking badly. He called and said he was accompanying the 'sick chicken' back to base. However, the pilot, Ensign Brex, was forced to land on the island of Negros where he was seen by Lieutenant Rushing to get out of his plane and wave as if uninjured."

Ensign McGraw then came up on Commander McCampbell's wing. Very shortly afterward, they ran into a Nate [Japanese biplane trainer] at their own altitude. This was the first encounter of McCampbell with this particular Japanese army training fighter. (The Bacolod center was a training base.) He found it even more maneuverable than the Zero, and thus even more dangerous. In addition, the Nate could outclimb the F6F at 120 knots. McCampbell learned these facts the hard way:

"After a couple of head-on runs at each other, I managed to beat him to the turn by turning sooner than he and worked onto his tail as he dove away. He was easily overtaken and set afire and crashed into the sea, out of control. During this engagement I became separated from my wingman and so called for an R/Z [rendezvous] at 10 miles south of Bacolod A/D [aerodrome]. While waiting for my flight to R/Z I was attacked from above by a lone Nate, which I did not see until it was too late to counter. After his pass he pulled up in front of me and I got in behind him but was unable to fire because his excess speed had carried him out of my range. I dropped my belly tank, shifted to low blower and WEP [war emergency power (water injection)] and tried to climb up to him. It seemed that he was gaining slightly in altitude and distance when he started a roll over to make an overhead run on me. I split-essed and dived away into a cloud and succeeded in losing him. Although this action seemed to have lasted a long time, other details are too vague to assemble. However the following points stand out:

1. The Nate is even more maneuverable than the Zeke.
2. Nate can outclimb F6F at 110-120 knots airspeed.
3. This 'operational student,' if he was such, will have no trouble completing the course."

Commander McCampbell then returned to the area where he had called the F6Fs to rendezvous, but instead of finding his own planes there, he found five Nates waiting for him at 12,000 feet.

"Although I was alone and below, I felt confident (knowing that I could dive away and into the clouds if necessary) as I tailed in behind and below and had almost climbed to their level when the leader spied me and turned my way. Since he did not dive on me immediately, I simply held my course and violently rocked my wings, hoping that his recognition was as poor as mine and that he would mistake me for a 'friendly.' Apparently he did, because he continued on in a lazy climbing circle. Presently he turned again towards me and again I wobbled my wings, but he wasn't fooled this time and the whole outfit tailed in behind me as I pushed over. While in my dive I saw five friendly F6Fs below me and so I immediately turned to drag the procession across in front of them. The melee was on and it seemed that flaming planes were falling all around, during the course of which I got a long burst from astern at one of the Nates as he dived, smoking, into the clouds. Sometime later, after we got smart, got R/Zd and climbed to 12,000 feet, we chased another Nate into a towering cumulus cloud, but no one got a shot at him. As time and gas were running short we headed for base and arrived without further incident."

Altogether they had encountered in the air about forty Japanese planes, mostly army fighters; very few were the Zeros favored by the navy. The action was continuous for about forty-five minutes, and, at the end, the airmen of the *Essex* claimed twenty-one planes destroyed in the air; they only had lost Ensign Brex. The sweep also covered several airfields to the north, Talisay, which was under construction, Silay, and Tanza.

Lieutenant Commander Duncan shot down the second Betty, and then an Oscar and a Nate, and chased another Oscar for several miles until he realized he was being drawn away from the fighter sweep and that his gas was getting low. Lieutenant Morris attacked a Zero and shot it down. Lieutenant Lundin got credit for half that first Betty and then shot down an Oscar.

Lieutenant Rushing shot down two Oscars and then gave up fighting to try to help Ensign Brex land safely. Ensign Bare did not get any planes on the first round, but on the way home to the *Essex*, when a lone Nate was spotted just above the cloud layer at 6,000 feet, he attacked along with Ensign Flinn and Lieutenant Morris, and the Nate maneuvered right into his guns, Bare fired, and the Nate blew up. There were just too many American planes in the sky to give a Japanese pilot much chance.

Ensign Twelves was the first to notice enemy fighters in the air, just as the strike arrived at around 7:30. He saw a bunch of Nates not far away. As he and his group climbed to attack, he saw even more of them. One rolled over from above to attack, but Twelves moved aside, did a wingover, and got on the enemy's tail. The Japanese plane was hit, started a spiral, and then tried to pull out. Twelves was right behind it, firing every time the Nate came spiraling around into position. The Japanese pilot never managed to pull out of the spin and crashed in the water.

Twelves headed back "upstairs" as doctrine ordered, then saw another Nate, and followed him into a cloud, firing when he could see. They came out of the cloud, the Nate caught fire, went out of control, and crashed into a hill. Twelves was then flying on his back at 3,000 feet. He saw another Nate, which almost ran into him. He recovered, got in two bursts, and the Nate began to smoke, then made a wingover, and headed into a cloud. Twelves could not follow because another Nate was on the tail of his wingman. He hurried over and got a shot into the enemy plane before it could open up on his wingman; it exploded from this one brief, lucky burst. Twelves then heard knocking on his armor plate behind the seat, and his hydraulic system went out. A Nate was on his tail. He ducked into a cloud and his wingman went after the Nate.

Ensign Flinn and Lieutenant Morris pulled up after their first Nate, which they saw 1,500 feet above them at the beginning of the fracas. Morris got in the first burst, which made the Japanese plane begin to smoke, then Flinn fired a long burst into the engine, which broke into flame. Flinn followed and pulled up over the Japanese plane. He saw the pilot slumped over his controls, and the plane then went into a "graveyard spiral" and crashed into the sea.

Morris and Flinn then saw a lone Zero chasing first an F6F and then three other F6Fs, then break off as the American fighters attacked. The F6Fs could not catch up, but Morris and Flinn had altitude so they dived down and Morris exploded the Zero. They saw a Nate just as Ensign Bare and Ensign Davis did, but the Nate turned into Bare and Davis and went by so they could not get in a shot. Morris got one head-on burst in, Flinn turned left to get behind, did so, and knocked pieces off the Nate's cowling, and the Nate burst into flames. Flinn overran the plane and below could see the Japanese pilot trying to bail out of the plane as it dropped into the clouds.

Ensign Davis, Ensign McGraw, and Ensign Self all scored victories or probables, and Self sent one Nate down onto Bacolod Airfield to crash.

The air strike planes were equally busy over this target this day. Sixty-eight planes from the *Essex*, the *Lexington*, and the *Princeton* attacked together at about 7:45 in the morning. Lieutenant Strane, Lieutenant R.L. Hall, and Ensigns Fowler, Duffy, and Bern all either knocked down enemy aircraft or damaged them; the bombers struck the airfield and its buildings, and no one was hurt. On the way back to the carrier, the Helldivers were attacked by ten Japanese fighters near Manapla Airfield and chased about ten miles, but the Japanese did not really try to close with the planes; they were intent only on keeping the Americans away from their field, where one pilot saw about forty Betties and single-engined planes parked.

When the planes returned to base, photos showed only eleven aircraft remaining on Bacolod Airfield. The torpedo bombers had flown down the airstrip, dropping 500-pound bombs on the runway and strafing anything that moved. But pictures also showed that aircraft had been staged in to Fabrica and Saravia Airdromes. So another strike was in order, and it was led by the *Lexington*, with twenty-eight planes from the *Essex* participating.

Only one enemy aircraft was seen in the air; an observation plane took off from Fabrica field at about the time the air strike arrived at 10:30 that morning, but the plane disappeared in the clouds, and no one got a shot at it. First the fighters went in and strafed the airfields at Fabrica and Saravia. They destroyed a number of aircraft, which burned, and they hit a number which did not.

Some fighters strafed Japanese army trucks at San Pablo on Leyte. The dive bombers took the worst beating. At Saravia Airdrome, some thirty twin-engined Japanese bombers were attacked. The anti-aircraft fire was much more severe than usual. Lieutenant (jg) Clyde Gardner dropped a bomb ten feet from one twin-engined bomber, which blew this particular plane up spectacularly. Lieutenant (jg) Alfred DeCesaro's bomber dropped in the middle of a four-plane revetment, and destroyed at least two of the planes.

Lieutenant (jg) Richard Glass dropped his bombs and then made a strafing run. He got one plane afire with his guns, and his gunner, George Duncan, got another. Then a piece of anti-aircraft shrapnel struck Duncan, even as his guns were still firing. Glass pulled up when he discovered that his gunner was hit and headed back at full speed but Duncan was dead by the time they landed. Lieutenant Philip E. Golden went in to bomb and strafe. Anti-aircraft fire caught his port aileron and tore it off, the plane slewed to the right, and down; the altitude was too low for recovery and the Helldiver struck on its right wing, cartwheeled and burned. Lieutenant Golden and Gunner John D. Downey were both killed.

Just before noon another strike of planes from the *Essex,* the *Lexington* and the *Princeton* was led out by Lieutenant Commander Duncan. Once again they worked over the airfields at Fabrica and Saravia, and this time they hit Manapla as well. The Japanese had been moving planes around, and more were destroyed on the ground; none were seen in the air. The damage was by this time so severe on the ground that one Helldiver pilot reported flying through something that looked like gray confetti. It was ashes from the fires below.

At 2:00 in the afternoon, another strike left the *Essex,* to join *Lexington* planes in a search and strike on Cebu and Mactan Islands. They ran into a heavy squall over Cebu and had to turn north to try to find a target. They did find a few small vessels in the Visayan area, and attacked, but the strike was not very effective.

After Ensign Brex's F6F was disabled by a Japanese fighter, and he headed back toward the carrier with Lieutenant Rushing as escort, Brex's plane began to cough as they were over Negros Island. The prop began to run away and finally it seized up. Brex had to make a dead stick landing in a field; one of his shoulder straps broke off from the impact, but he was not hurt.

Brex was still shaking his head and clearing the fog away when the plane was surrounded by Filipinos, most of them aiming rifles at him, and the others carrying knives and bows. They looked particularly fierce and threatening. Two weeks earlier, Brex had gotten a haircut, a short-short crewcut, and in a few minutes it was quite clear that the Filipinos took him for a Japanese. He got out of the plane, hands up, and down onto the ground. The leaders began to search him. When they came to his dogtags and found that he was an American they began shouting, "Americano, Americano!" and almost immediately his situation improved. He had been banged up in the crash, and the rescuers bandaged his cuts and scratches. They took him a little way from the plane and he sat down to rest, while they went through the crashed F6F, taking off everything they could use: the machine guns, ammunition, and whatever came loose. Then they burned the plane, and the whole group escorted Brex to a village nearby.

Next day planes from the carrier came over, circled, saw the crashed and burned plane, and natives waved up at them, trying to tell them that their fellow airman was safe. That day and those following, packages of cigarettes and candy, medicines, and other "goodies" were dropped in the area by planes from the *Essex* and delivered to Brex, who gave them out to his new friends.

Brex stayed in the area for forty days, recovering from the effects of the crash, and then he started on a trip to a contact point set up by the guerillas. On November 6, Ensign Brex reached a communications center where the guerillas had a radio. By this time the Leyte invasion was well established. By radio, Brex's friends got in touch with the U.S. Army Air Force 5th Fighter Command, which sent an army Dumbo (amphibious plane) on November 17 to pick up Ensign Brex. He was taken to Morotai and then to Manus, where he received orders to report to ComAirPac (Commander, Air Force, Pacific Fleet) at Pearl Harbor. He went to Pearl Harbor, and on November 29, 1944, Ensign Brex rejoined Fighting Fifteen.

CHAPTER TEN

Paper Tigers

On September 12 and 13, Admiral Halsey's planes had flown a total of 2,400 sorties, or individual flights. They had hit all the airfields in the south and central Philippines, and they had been surprised by the general lack of opposition. On the evening of September 13, Admiral Halsey and his staff assessed the strength of the enemy and decided it was really minimal. Why not, then, abandon the whole idea of the preliminary assault on the Palau Islands, and advance the attack on Leyte by several weeks? Halsey made that suggestion that very night to Admiral Nimitz at Peral Harbor, by radio.

By September 13, however, two days before the planned landings, everything was in place for the assault by sea, air, and land on the Palau Islands. At 5:30 on the morning of September 12, the battleships and cruisers of the naval bombardment force had begun their work. Underwater demolition teams were swimming around the beaches, clearing out boulders and mines and underwater obstacles placed by the Japanese. Minesweepers were working in Kossol Passage and around Peleliu and Angaur, and the minesweeper *Perry* was sunk that day.

Vice Admiral T.S. Wilkinson was busting to get into the Palaus, and Rear Admiral J.B. Oldendorf, commander of the bombardment squadron, was bragging about the great job his ships were doing in setting up the invasion. So the forces in motion prevented Admiral Nimitz from stopping to listen to what was undoubtedly very sound advice. The invasion of the Palaus would continue—and it would be extremely costly in terms of lives and would turn out to be just as unnecessary as Admiral Halsey believed.

On the night of September 13, the Japanese, who were far more aware of the weakness of their Philippine defenses than the Americans were, expected an invasion in the Philippines at almost any moment.

One of the reasons that the defense in the southern Philippines was so slight was a report received at Clark Field near Manila (the center of Japanese air operations in the Philippines) on the night of September 12 that American carrier forces had been seen moving north—which would mean an assault on Luzon Island in all probability. Thus, late on the night of September 12, the 30th Air Group was transferred north to Clark Field, and so was the 22nd Air Group. The 2nd Air Division also received similar orders.

Early on the morning of September 13, the 13th Air Group (which had been taking a heavy beating for two days) was told that it would have to be responsible for the southern air defenses, and the Furaburika Squadron was told that its mission was primary. The squadron was nearly decimated; this news did not make much difference in its conduct of operations that day; bravery was the common factor, but gallantry and willingness—even eagerness—to die for emperor and homeland did not tip the balance.

At 6:00 in the morning, the usual Japanese morning patrol set out from the Bacolod complex—a mixed patrol of eight planes, some Zeros, some two-seater fighter-bombers. They went to high altitude, 15,000 feet. Suddenly at 8:00 without the slightest radio warning, the first wave of American planes appeared over the field, coming in over the mountains to the east of the field. "They appeared to rub against the peaks," said one Japanese officer who saw the American attackers appear. (That was Commander McCampbell's fighter sweep, dropping down to 6,000 feet to get a good view of the air complex, since the weather was closing in.)

And then, as this officer (the commander of the 31st Squadron) watched, like ships, the planes began sailing at one another and in moments the sky was filled with planes cartwheeling and turning, and the field was rutted with machine gun fire as the American fighters swooped in to strafe the parked planes near the runway.

That first wave lasted an hour. (The Japanese did not differentiate between the fighter sweep and the air strike that came in on its heels.) "Three times more that day we were attacked," the commander recalled, and all day long the men, from the officers down to the lowest enlisted man, cried out for a chance to wreak vengeance on the enemy.

The Furaburika (31st) Squadron's commander finally could stand the strain no longer. He agreed to draw names of men who would be allowed to man the handful of remaining planes and fight back. Two commissioned officers were chosen and three non-commissioned officers. (Unlike the American services at that time, the Japanese still used many non-commissioned officers as pilots. In fact, Saburo Sakai, who survived the war as Japan's leading fighter ace, served for most of the war as a petty officer, and only late in the war was rewarded with a commission in recognition of his valuable service.) So hard had the 31st Squadron been hit, that this contingent of five represented half of the squadron's remaining pilot strength.

The runway was badly pitted by the 500-pound bombs dropped by the *Essex* bombers. The 45th Squadron, which had come up the previous day from Puerto Princesa, had lost all its planes. The 27th Squadron, at Sarabiya, had lost most of its planes. The 31st Squadron still had two of its radar-equipped planes, and these might make it possible to make an attack on a carrier. The planes took off. They did not manage to sink any carriers.

As September 13 came to a close, the staff of the 13th Air Group began to assess the damages incurred and those inflicted. The Bacolod headquarters complex was in shambles. Only sixteen planes remained, and they could only claim for all this damage (eighty-seven of their aircraft in the area destroyed) that they had shot down six American aircraft. That the odds were about three to one against them was taken into account, but the real problem, as assessed by the Japanese airmen, was their intelligence system, which failed to warn them of the approach of the enemy so that planes could be airborne to fight and at least escape the ignominy of destruction on the ground—as though they were honeycarts. The one outstanding act of the day was that of the pilot who had crashed his plane into one of the Americans.

On the night of the 13th, more changes came to the Japanese air forces in the Philippines. The 10th Air Group that day was moved from Puerto Princesa on Palawan, to the west of the Philippines, up to Clark Field on Luzon to strengthen the air defenses there. The 45th Squadron (what remained of it) and the 27th Squadron were also moved up to Luzon. The Visayas and the whole southern Philippine area suddenly became very lonely.

On the morning of September 14, Commander McCampbell led a fighter sweep over the Visayas again, hitting airfields in the Iloilo, Negros, and Panay areas. Not a single enemy airplane was encountered in the air. The Americans found about twenty-five planes on the ground at Santa Barbara Airfield and strafed them. Five runs were made, but disappointingly only nine planes flamed up. Apparently the others had no gas in the tanks. The planes were camouflaged but not very well and they were of a different color than the airmen of the *Essex* were used to seeing—that was probably because these were new planes just staged in. Before leaving the Iloilo area, the fighters strafed the harbor and burned a few small craft. The sweep then moved to northern Negros, to hit Saravia and Fabrica Airfields. There were new planes there too, twenty-two at Saravia and sixteen seen at Fabrica. All were strafed and some burned.

Lieutenant Commander Rigg led off a second strike that morning against Santa Barbara air installation on Panay. The fighters went down first and found the fires still burning from McCampbell's raid. They could not get any of the other planes to burn. The bombers joined those of the *Lexington* and the *Langley* to attack Iloilo, then broke off and hit Santa Barbara. But there was not much to hit, just a few small wooden shacks.

The TBFs were assigned to bomb the barracks on the western side of Santa Barbara Airfield and the shops on the north side. They blew up most of them. Another strike went out at about 9:00 in the morning, but by this time the targets were extremely skimpy. A noon strike on northern Negros was the same; the greatest excitement was making a drop to Ensign Brex's rescuers. Lieutenant Commander Duncan of VF-15 and Lieutenant Carr escorted Lieutenant Brodhead of the Helldiver squadron to the spot, where Brodhead dropped cartons of cigarettes and medical supplies and money in a parachute devised from a pilot's chute. When they first came over Brex's clearing it was empty, but they circled, and waggled their wings, and in a few minutes about 100 Filipinos came out of the trees and began to wave, and then spread an American flag on the ground.

On the night of September 13, the Japanese air high command began to reassess the situation in the Philippines. The whole ambience was oriented toward an air attack in the Halmahera area against the new landings to be made by General MacArthur. It was quite apparent that MacArthur was planning to land there. The Japanese were aware of MacArthur's long-range plan to move from northern New Guinea (the Vogelkop) to Halmahera, and then to Mindanao. But as the American planners looked at the intelligence reports, they saw that Halmahera was stoutly defended and that the Japanese were building more airfields. (A total of nine either existed or were under construction.) The Halmahera adventure would be very expensive for the Americans, and so Morotai, ten miles off the northern tip of Halmahera, was chosen as the new target and then advance base.

On September 13, once again undetected by the Japanese, the American fleet units moved from various points to the north of new Guinea to begin the operation, and then the Japanese knew the fat was in the fire. They still expected the landing at Halmahera, however.

On the evening of September 13, the Japanese were aware of the coming landings. The chief of staff of the 2nd Air Division and officers of the 4th Air Army met with the chief officers of the Southern Area Army at Manila to chart a course of action. They were ready to put their Halmahera air defense plan into action. But on that same day came the enormous destruction of the southern Philippines air facilities by the American carrier planes.

That night, the conferees in Manila had the latest of a series of reports about a group of carriers that had been seen traveling northward, east of the Philippines. To these officers, it seemed quite likely that an invasion of Luzon was being planned. At least that issue was raised, and it was agreed that it had to be taken seriously.

The Halmahera air operations plan was approved and all but put into effect on the 13th, but that night it collapsed in the concern for the northern Philippines. By this time, news of the gunfire at the Palaus had also been transmitted to Manila, so it was known that the Americans were making two landings in the south; but it was also sensed that these were mere preliminaries, and that the major battle had to be fought in the Philippines. The Halmahera air defense plan was abandoned and it was agreed that no further efforts would be wasted at the Palau Islands. The defenders would have to shift for themselves and fight to the end.

The attempts to strike back at the American carriers had failed uniformly; air losses were enormous, and it was perceived at the meeting that rather than continue to expend aircraft in the south, the 4th Air Army had to regroup its resources and strengthen them.

On the morning of September 14, the 4th Air Army put out a general air raid warning in the Manila area. Three different carrier groups were now identified, one traveling north and two others close to the southern and central Philippines. That day the air forces in southern areas tried to stage a counterattack on the American planes.

From Legaspi, and from Mindanao, Leyte, and the Bacolod complex on Negros, a ragged group of planes tried to make an assault on the carriers. They failed. The 13th Air Group sent out ten planes, but they straggled back late in the day to land at fields around Manila, unsuccessful. That day, from headquarters went out orders to bring the air strength north, and so Puerto Princesa and other bases were virtually abandoned. One by one, the planes made—or tried to make—their way to the Clark Field complex.

On the night of September 14, the *Essex* got a respite from action. She steamed out to the fueling rendezvous that night and the next day, and on September 16 took on oil, supplies, and replacements for lost crews. On the 17th, standing off Palau to support the landings there, the *Essex* was "snooped" by a lone Japanese plane just at dusk, but the plane turned back while still thirty-five miles away from the carrier. Undoubtedly this was one of the Japanese patrol planes that belatedly were keeping better track of the American carrier forces.

The wheels, however, were now in motion for Japan's answer to the growingly powerful drive of the American forces. On September 15, Imperial General Headquarters issued an assessment of the situation in the region and stated that the Palau and Morotai (they called it Makassar) invasions made it quite clear that what the headquarters called "Nimitz" and "MacArthur's" armies were converging toward the Philippines and that is where the major decisive battle was going to be fought. No special action was taken—to move naval forces—for it was too early for that, and Imperial General Headquarters was cautious in such matters. But the area commanders were alerted, and the pipeline of planes and supplies was replenished as rapidly as it could be from the Tokyo end. The "decisive battle" was not far away.

The battle for Peleliu began with the marine landings on September 15, and it was a much harder job than any Americans had anticipated. The Japanese had developed a defense technique here that was quite new to the Americans. Neither naval bombardment nor aerial action could do much good against troops who were dug deep into the ground, sometimes with three or four layers of caves and tunnels. The landings at Morotai were unopposed and the going there was easy compared to the Palaus.

The admirals and the generals were really out on a limb, having predicted that Peleliu would be a "pushover." Instead, it was late November, 1944, before organized resistance was declared ended, and it was well into 1945 before the last of the Japanese on the island surrendered. Angaur was another bitter Palau to swallow; and in the end Admiral Halsey's recommendation that they all be bypassed proved the wiser course.

The really valuable piece of real estate taken at about this time was the atoll of Ulithi, about 900 miles from the Philippines. It had an enormous protected harbor surrounded by coral reef and islets, and would provide the Americans with a useful forward naval and air base. Here the Japanese had completely miscalculated; they had abandoned Ulithi at the beginning of September as of no possible use to the enemy or themselves. Halsey's forces took the island on September 23 without resistance.

By this time the *Essex* and other carriers were back in action. On September 19, they set course for the Philippines, having stood by the Palau invasion until it was apparent there would be no Japanese air opposition. On the night of September 20, the *Essex* was nearly in position to make an air strike.

By 10:00 on the morning of September 15, the news of the Morotai and Peleliu landings had reached the headquarters of the Japanese 4th Area Army at Manila, and major decisions were being made. The Japanese 4th Air Army (air force) had to decide what, if any, action would be taken by the army air forces to stop the Americans. Actually, until the battle for the Marianas the air defenses in the Philippines and all the other islands outside the perimeter of inner empire had been in the hands of the navy. Now the army air forces had agreed to take a hand, and, as it happened up to this point in the Philippines, most of the planes faced by the airmen of the *Essex* had been army planes.

It was decided on that morning of the Allied landings that the 13th Army Air Group would take the responsibility for repelling the assaults in the Halmahera and Palau areas, along with the 15th Squadron and the 7th Air Group heavy bombers. But this attack force was rapidly diminished by the American carrier planes, so nothing came of the plans.

On the night of September 15, the Japanese army air forces in the Philippines consisted of 250 operational aircraft and another 100 that had been damaged but could be repaired. On the 15th and 16th the weather turned bad again. By the 17th, the authorities in Manila were convinced that a landing on Luzon was imminent, and so all aircraft were consolidated to repel the American forces in the north. Most planes were ordered up to the Clark airbase complex outside Manila.

By the night of September 20, the Japanese air command planned a "surprise attack" on the American invasion forces. The available aircraft numbered about 300. The disposition was as follows (damaged planes in parentheses):

35th Squadron: 6 planes (6), Zeros
31st Squadron: 14 planes (7), Zeros
22nd Air Group: 44 planes (17), dive bombers
17th Squadron: 21 planes (8), Zeros
19th Squadron: 23 planes (9), Zeros
10th Air Group: 38 planes, mixed types, mostly bombers
27th Squadron: 25 planes, Zeros
45th Squadron: 13 planes, biplane trainers
6th Air Group: 44 planes (24), dive bombers and torpedo bombers
65th Squadron: 29 planes (18), fighters
66th Squadron: 15 planes (6), fighters
7th Air Group: 29 planes (17), bombers
2nd Squadron: 13 planes (2), scout bombers
36th Mixed Squadron: 5 planes (2), radar-equipped bombers

So this was the army air force available to Lieutenant General Tominaga, the commander of the 4th Air Army. The navy's air force was even smaller because the Philippines defense had been considered largely an army problem, and the navy was just now beginning to move its air units into the region. The principal naval air unit was the 5th Base Air Force, under Vice Admiral Teraoka.

On September 20, General Tominaga made an inspection tour of the Clark base airfields. The main purpose of the tour was to inspire the officers and men of the squadrons to do their duty in the days to come. He went about, giving a few inspirational words to each unit. The aviators responded patriotically and promised to do their best for the emperor and their country.

The next morning, shortly after dawn, the navy air forces sent out search planes to find the enemy carriers, which were reported steaming north toward Luzon.

At 8:05 in the morning, Commander McCampbell led the first strike of the day against the Clark base complex. He was flying a new F6F-5 with rocket-launchers under the wings, and so were eleven of the other fighter pilots. The Helldivers were carrying 1,000-pound bombs for the runways and 250-pound bombs for aircraft and personnel. The torpedo bombers carried 500-pound bombs and rockets. Thirty-six planes from the *Essex* flew in this raid, with thirty-six planes from the *Lexington.*

At 9:05, another search set out on a course of sixty degrees from Manila, just as Commander McCampbell's raiders were zeroing in on Nichols Field in the Clark complex, and Las Pinas Field not far away. The latter received the most of the Americans' attention in the beginning, but it was apparently inoperative and the fighters soon moved off.

On the way to the target, the *Essex* airmen encountered three Tojos (Nakajima type 2 fighter) and one Tony (Kawasaki type 3 fighter). The three Tojos were too far off for any action, but the Tony was not. More than a dozen of the F6Fs swooped down on Las Pinas Field, and on the way back to the rendezvous Ensign H.R. Berree and Ensign G.W. Pigman, Jr., saw this Tony chasing a lone F6F. They closed as rapidly as possible, and to get the Tony off their friend's tail they fired long bursts while still out of range. The Tony pulled up in a steep wingover and then began evasive action. The Japanese plane could out-turn the F6Fs, and as long as the pilot maneuvered thus he kept the two fighter pilots off his back. But he made the error of diving with the F6Fs, and this was one area of aerobatics in which the American plane was superb. Berree and Pigman both began firing and their bullets hit the enemy plane hard, in the cockpit and at one wing root. Apparently the pilot was injured or killed because the plane immediately went out of control and crashed in Laguna de Bay.

Meanwhile Commander Mini led a dozen Helldivers in the first air attack on Manila. They came in at 13,000 feet, and expecting trouble here they were equipped for the first time with "window"—aluminum strings that deflected anti-aircraft gunners' radar and helped protect the attacking planes from the enemy gunners' fire. The "window" seemed to work: much of the anti-aircraft fire burst behind the planes, although the fire was intense. But no one could be sure of the results, happy as they seemed to be, because the *Essex* pilots were used to Japanese inaccuracy in anti-aircraft fire at long range (the enemy gunners gave too little lead).

The Japanese tried a trick of their own. They lit smudgepots in the city and on the hillsides. But the result was a general haze and not a blackout of the targets.

Lieutenant Commander Lambert led the torpedo bombers, which also attacked Nichols Field, starting from 12,000 feet and gliding down to 7,000 feet. The TBFs' primary targets were the aircraft on the ground at Nichols Field and the shops and hangars. Several planes bombed the hangars on the northern end of the field. They could not see the results. One plane bombed in the revetment area at the southern end of the field, and the pilot noted two Topsies [Mitsubishi transports] parked in a revetment, but he apparently did not hit them.

The aircrews had been leery of Manila. It was a big city and they expected the anti-aircraft fire to be intense. It was, but either the "window" or the bad gunnery of the Japanese on the ground (who had not before fired at many planes in anger) prevented any damage. One Helldiver returned to the *Essex* with a nick in the bomb bay doors, and that was all.

The *Essex* planes left buildings burning at both airfields. Around one hangar, which blew up and smoked furiously, several parked planes were at least damaged.

The second strike that morning was led by the air group commander of the *Lexington,* but the *Essex* furnished sixteen fighters, twelve dive bombers, and seven TBFs. Lieutenant Commander Rigg led the Air Group Fifteen component. The mission was the same: knock out the airfields around Manila. By the time the second strike arrived at Manila, a pall of smoke hung over the city and the airfields, the result of the bombing and strafing of the previous strike. Again the "window" saved the airmen many casualties. The Japanese range was excellent, but the anti-aircraft fire again burst on the "window" and not on the American planes. The general smoky atmosphere made it hard for the attackers to pinpoint targets, and the Japanese had their smudgepots in the hills going full tilt by this time, which added to the confused condition of the air.

Lieutenant Roger Noyes was leader of the *Essex* Helldivers on this strike, but his radio failed before they reached the target and he turned the lead over to Lieutenant Richard Mills. All went well, until pull-out from the area, when a Zero got on the tail of Ensign M.G. Livesay's Helldiver. But above the Helldivers sat the F6Fs of the *Lexington* squadron, flying high cover, and one F6F came down in a hurry and shot down the Zero with a single pass. Ensign Livesay flew home unscathed. On this strike someone hit a fuel dump, and the greasy black smoke burst up through the general pall to prove it. The TBFs also claimed further damage to one of the Nichols Field hangars and a half-dozen planes parked nearby.

In the afternoon, Commander McCampbell led another strike out, but this time the target was a Japanese ship convoy near Salvador Island, off the west coast of Luzon. It was a fast convoy, moving north at a speed of fifteen knots, seven ships in column. The lead ship was a destroyer, then came a large cargo ship, followed by two smaller ones, then a large ship that seemed to be a tanker, and finally two more escorts roughly equivalent to American destroyer-escorts.

Commander McCampbell's twenty-four fighters (twelve from the *Essex*, twelve from the *Lexington*) led the way. They carried rockets (at least the F6F-5s did) and 350-pound depth bombs. Lieutenant (jg) M.M. Gunter, Jr., got a direct hit on the lead ship—the destroyer—and four other pilots made near misses. The result was that the destroyer lost way, and went dead in the water, and began to list, and probably sank after they left the scene.

Commander McCampbell got hits with his four rockets on one of the smaller cargo ships. Lieutenant Richard Glass got a direct bomb hit on the stern of another, which was also left dead in the water. Lieutenant (jg) John Storrs Foote of the Helldiver squadron got a direct hit on that second big ship, and several of Commander Mini's other dive bomber pilots scored hits. The destroyer and the escorts put up a heavy volume of anti-aircraft fire, but none of the planes was seriously damaged.

For the first time since the torpedo squadron of the *Essex* had gone into combat, the TBF pilots carried torpedoes. They went after the ships on the southern end of the convoy. First they came in circling, and then attacked from west to east, dropping at 400 feet and then down at 250 feet in some cases. One plane managed to reach 250 knots coming in, and the drops were made at distances from 1,000 to 1,200 yards out. The results were not spectacular: Lieutenant (jg) S.M. Holladay scored a hit on the port bow of one of the ships, but three other pilots who launched torpedoes at that same ship missed; one of the torpedoes was seen to pass under the ship, and the two others simply disappeared. But Holladay's torpedo and the bombers from above had done the job; Commander McCampbell saw the crew abandon ship, and later only the superstructure showed above water.

Five other torpedo bombers attacked a second ship, but only one of those torpedos had a normal run, and this torpedo missed astern. The other four torpedoes all porpoised; the Americans were still having trouble with aerial torpedoes. No one could figure out the reason for the porpoising and sudden turns of the torpedoes; the pilots had followed doctrine and maintained level flight on the approach, and the drop was not too high. The trouble was the machine; they were still using the mark 13 torpedo, a World War I design, though equipped now with a newer ring and stabilizer, which were supposed to give the torpedo stability in the run but which did not work well.

The *Lexington* led the next strike, which came in on the heels of the first hit on the convoy. Lieutenant Commander Rigg was in charge of the *Essex* contingent again. The fighters hit the fighting ships and managed to score with ten rockets. But the destroyer and escorts fought back with their anti-aircraft guns. The Helldivers and the TBFs both carried bombs this time. They sank several of the ships that had been badly damaged before and left the others smoking. They sank two small luggers in the vicinity as well.

On this strike, they saw no Japanese aircraft at all. During the previous one—Commander McCampbell's first strike on the convoy—pilots had spotted a formation of eight Japanese fighters over Luzon, but the Japanese made no attempt to close on the sixty American planes from the *Essex* and the *Lexington*.

From the ground, the attacks on the Clark Field area seemed devastating. The ground crews watched that first *Essex-Lexington* raid on Nichols Field with dismay, and thereafter the complex was attacked until 6:00 in the afternoon; the Japanese counted more than 400 aircraft above Manila, the harbor, and the airfields.

The 17th Squadron was stationed at the south end of the Clark complex, as was the 19th Squadron. Starting on September 12, every day the fighters and bombers made patrols, but they were singularly ineffectual. One reason for this was the quality of the Japanese army pilots. They had very little experience. Since they were not very well trained, their organization was unable to keep up with this spate of unusual activity. "The succession of air attacks," wrote the official Japanese historian, "and the constant strain of upkeep of the air-craft began to take its toll." The airmen of the *Essex* helped keep this pressure on, and the Japanese 4th Air Army was unable to respond.

Early on the morning of September 21, the 17th Squadron was alerted by 6:00 to the presence of the enemy carriers coming north, and the sirens on the airfield began to blare. The weather was not kind; a heavy mist hung low over Anheresa Field, where the 17th was stationed, and the overcast was thick and low. But at 8:30, a division of four planes from the 17th Squadron got off the ground for the morning patrol. Over Clark Field this morning the rain was falling gently and the overcast continued. The patrol moved around the area until 9:00, and then suddenly out of the cloudy sky from on high, ten carrier planes (the Japanese called them "Grummans") attacked.

The 17th Squadron suffered badly that day. The four-plane patrol met enemy fighters and was lost. From the ground, it appeared that comets were falling around the whole Clark area, and the Japanese planes were the comets. Most of these pilots were getting their "baptism of fire" that day, and they had very little luck. The airmen of the *Essex* and of the other carriers had been in combat since May, and in the dogfights and melees that developed about the city, one Japanese plane after another fell. As noted, the *Essex* fliers encountered virtually no Japanese planes in the air, but other pilots did, and in the fighting most of the 17th Squadron's pilots were lost.

The 19th Squadron did no better. Its morning patrol was attacked by 110 planes (the survivors reported), which swooped down from high altitude. At the end of the first attack on the area, four of the squadron's planes had been shot down, and three more were apparently shot down. The Japanese claimed one victory only. By the end of the morning they had lost eighteen planes from that field.

Commander McCampbell led the morning strike of Admiral Sherman's task group against the Manila Harbor area and Nichols Field. It consisted of thirty-five *Essex* planes and thirty-six *Lexington* aircraft, a mixture of fighters, dive bombers, and torpedo bombers. Although they were going to hit the ships in the harbor, the group's experience with torpedoes had been so dismal on the day before that the TBFs carried bombs, not torpedoes; the dive bombers had 1,000-pound bombs, and the TBFs had 500-pounders.

After takeoff at 6:25, one Helldiver pilot discovered that he could not retract the wheels of his plane, and he had to abort, landing again on the carrier. The other planes went on, climbed to 13,000 feet, and in just a little over an hour were over Manila.

The Japanese had run up barrage balloons from the ships in the harbor, which were supposed to create difficulty for the attackers, but they did not; the planes simply jinked around them in their attacks.

Lieutenant William S. Burns led the torpedo bombers in their attack on the aircraft shops west of the north-south run way on Nichols field. They got one solid hit on the hangar and two on the shops, and the rest of the bombs dug holes in the runway. They used the "window" again, although some of the pilots were still not sure it did any good. But the proof of its effectiveness was that virtually no one got shot up by the heavy anti-aircraft fire.

Lieutenant Roger F. Noyes led the Helldivers in their dive bombing attack. They bombed fuel tanks located between Earnshaw's Docks, owned by the Honolulu Iron works, and the inner harbor. The tanks caught fire and black smoke rose thousands of feet in the sky. The tanks began to explode and started other fires in the dock area.

Most of the fighters were equipped with rocket-launchers and rockets. Lieutenants Morris and Singer found an I-boat, one of the big Japanese fleet submarines, at a dock in the inner harbor, and unleashed their rockets. They scored hits, and later the submarine was seen moved out into the outer harbor, at anchor, with a large oil slick all around it.

Commander McCampbell shepherded his planes out of the area, on their way home, and tagged along behind, looking over the damage. He saw a twin-engined bomber over Manila Bay, up at 20,000 feet, heading south. He took his combat division of four planes to make the attack. It took them ten minutes to climb up to 18,000 feet, but they were still three miles behind the enemy plane. Perhaps the Japanese pilot did not see them, for he suddenly reversed course and came right back toward the four pursuing F6Fs. By that time McCampbell had renewed hope of catching the plane. The fighters used emergency power and caught up with the Japanese aircraft. By this time the Japanese pilot had seen them and was pouring on the gas, trying to get away.

McCampbell had not fired his rockets at ground targets; these rockets were air to ground missiles, not designed for attack on aircraft, but he decided to give it a whirl, so he fired two 5-inch rockets at the enemy plane. One rocket struck the starboard stabilizer and knocked off the top third of it, although the rocket did not explode. The Japanese pilot must have wondered what sort of new weapon the Americans had; he began fishtailing to keep the fighters from getting a clear shot and increased his efforts to get away. McCampbell got on his tail, gave him a burst in the right engine and wing root (where the gas tanks were located) and the plane burst into flames. The right wing broke away from the fuselage and the right engine tore loose, and the various parts of the big plane plummeted down to crash in Manila Bay.

Following the pattern, the second strike, which came on the heels of the first, was led by the *Lexington's* air group commander, Commander T.H. Winters; the *Essex* contingent was supervised by Lieutenant Commander Rigg. This attack was concentrated against the port facilities in Manila Harbor and three Japanese cargo ships at the docks. The piers were bombed and strafed, and so were the ships, which were damaged but not sunk.

On the way back to the carrier, the fighters flying cover saw ten Japanese fighter planes at 10,000 to 12,000 feet. At first it appeared that they were engaged in a melee with American fighters, but on closer look it turned out that they were practicing— another indication of the sad state of training of these Japanese army pilots. When they saw the size of the American force, they did not attack, except for one lone Tony, which decided to make a pass at the formation possibly with the hope of knocking off a "tail-end Charlie." But as the Japanese fighter approached, Lieutenant Crittenden and his wingman, Ensign Slack, turned directly into it, and met it head-on at 4,000 feet. Crittenden got in one burst as the enemy plane rolled over to make a run, and the Tony began smoking heavily and turned away. Crittenden did not follow it down or see it crash, but claimed only a "probable" for the records.

The planes flew on, back across Luzon, toward the carriers. Another five Tonys were seen over central Luzon, but they seemed hesitant about attacking so many planes, and when the fighter pilots of the strike turned out to intercept, the Japanese flight sped away.

These were planes of the 22nd Air Group's 17th and 19th Squadrons, or perhaps both were planes from the 17th Squadron, for that morning the leader of the 17th Squadron took off with eight fighters to attack the enemy, and found them, and started an attack along the eastern shore of Luzon. According to his report, he pursued the Americans, but no definite results came from the action. Nothing was said about the one plane damaged and perhaps shot down by Lieutenant Crittenden. But by the end of the day (September 22) the 17th Squadron had been virtually decimated. The commanding general himself came to sympathize, and personally commended ten non-commissioned officers for the bravery they had shown in the unequal battle with the Americans.

The 2nd Scout Squadron had moved up to Clark Field on September 21, and late on that afternoon the Squadron's Captain Yuko Nitsuko discovered the American carriers off Cape Encanto. It was too late that day to launch an attack, and the squadron had been hard hit in the afternoon by an American bombing raid. On the morning of September 22, the 15th Scout Squadron was sent off from Nichols Field to find the enemy again. Every plane of the 2nd Squadron that could fly was put in the air. That morning, one Zero was spotted by the lookouts aboard the *Essex,* but the guns could not be brought to bear because the *Essex* and *Lexington* were launching their air strikes, and the plane turned and left the area. Perhaps it was one of Captain Nitsuko's planes.

For squadron after squadron, September 21 and 22 were days of frustration and dreadful losses for the Japanese. Every squadron of the 4th Air Division had received great damage, and the 107th Education Group (training) was almost totally destroyed. This unit had lost all its fighting planes, but several of the pilots went up in training planes (Nates) to try to ram the enemy. American reports indicate that they seldom succeeded.

On the night of the 22nd, the Japanese assessed the damage. At the time of the *Essex* attack on Manila Bay, some thirty ships had been anchored or moored in the bay. Seventeen of them and one destroyer were sunk or burned. One 10,000-ton cargo ship was lost, and one 8,000-ton ship. Three other big ships were damaged so badly as to be immobilized for months. At the end of that day, the destruction by fire had been so great that the whole harbor rang with explosions and the ships blazed, and throughout the capital city of Manila the air was polluted. The Japanese described the atmosphere in the city that night as "ghostly."

Regarding that convoy discovered by the *Essex* heading north along the Philippines shore (Convoy Tama 27), the Japanese ruefully reported at the end of the day that it had been totally destroyed—six ships, two of them more than 5,000 tons.

So the Manila attack came to an end, and on the night of September 22, the *Essex* moved away from the coast to fuel once more.

On the night of September 23, the carriers moved again toward the Visayas for another round of attacks on these islands so near to Leyte, which would be the next target of American invasion. This was the largest coordinated attack yet put forth by these carriers. It included twenty fighters and dive bombers from the *Essex,* twelve dive bombers from the *Lexington,* twenty-four fighters from the *Princeton* and the *Langley,* and thirty-two fighters from the four carriers of Admiral McCain's group, Task Group 38.1.

The Japanese had beefed up their anti-aircraft defenses in the Visayas by this time. The fighters encountered intense fire from the ground at Coron Bay and particularly from the ships they were hitting. The *Essex* contingent attacked two cargo ships in the north cove of Basuanga Island. So many American planes were now available that the strike planners and the air group coordinator in the air could pick and choose: the airmen of the *Essex* were assigned to two ships only, while those of the *Lexington* were given four other ships in the same anchorage. The results were not very conclusive, the *Essex* Helldivers claimed near misses on their ships, but no sinkings. They under-estimated: the official Japanese history speaks mournfully of six ships badly damaged in Coron Bay that day.

As soon as the Visayan shipping strike had left the decks of the *Essex* that morning, the carriers launched another strike, led by Commander McCampbell, against Cebu and Mactan, familiar island targets. A dozen *Essex* fighters and a dozen torpedo bombers joined twelve *Lexington* fighters and eight *Lexington* dive bombers.

If they expected to find a rush of enemy aircraft to the area, the pilots of the *Essex* were sadly disappointed. Nothing arose to oppose them as they neared Mactan and Cebu. They led the torpedo bombers down in attacks on shipping and strafed as they went.

Over Cebu Harbor, Commander McCampbell flushed a pair of seaplanes (Petes) and dived down from 12,000 feet with his combat team to attack. They dived through clouds, lost the Petes, and then found them again, down low, heading south in close formation at 500 feet. These were Japanese search planes, carrying depth charges for use against the spate of American submarines that had been working Philippines waters in recent weeks. As McCampbell and wingmate Rushing attacked, the two seaplanes turned off in opposite directions, to wheel around and head back for their base. They never made it. McCampbell and Lieutenant (jg) Roy L. Nall got on the tail of one of them, and Lieutenant Rushing got on the tail of the other. Both seaplanes flamed up and crashed in the water.

Each of the six *Essex* torpedo bombers carried a 2,000-pound blockbuster that day, as well as the usual quota of rockets. Two of the pilots attacked a cargo ship in the open water between Mactan Island and Cebu, but both missed. But Lieutenant (jg) J.C. Huggins and Lieutenant (jg) E.F. Lightner put their two bombs into a 3,000-ton freighter south of Cebu. Four thousand tons of explosive on a 3,000-ton ship has a remarkable effect, and this cargo ship sank *immediately*.

Then, Lieutenant (jg) J. Smyth secured a direct hit on the northern pier at Cebu. The results again were spectacular. An enormous hole appeared in the pier, and the cranes and dock facilities all around it were shattered. So, in spite of the misses by half the planes of the torpedo squadron strike, the enemy was again seriously hurt.

Three hours later, another strike of *Essex* planes arrived in the Cebu area, along with *Lexington* planes. Cebu Harbor was the major target, and the fighters and dive bombers hit the piers and warehouses with everything from machine gun fire to 2,000-pound bombs. One lugger (100 feet long) was sunk and five were damaged. One tanker tied up at the Philippine Refining Company dock was damaged, and the pier next to it was seriously damaged. Fires were started in a coconut oil refinery and in several other buildings around the pier area. When the bombers and fighters left the scene, smoke billowed up behind them and the view aft was punctuated by the yellow and red of burning buildings.

But there was a price this day. Ensign H.C. Gaver, one of the pilots who had converted aboard the *Essex* from the Helldiver to the F6F, was hit by anti-aircraft fire over the target. He notified his division leader that his engine was missing and that he could not make the carrier, but would have to land just a few miles off Cebu in the water. The lifeguard submarine was in the area, and he had a good chance of making it back alive to the *Essex*. But as he brought the plane down toward the water and was just about to settle it, one wing dropped, and struck, the plane cartwheeled and burst into flames, hit the water, and sank. Gaver's fellow-pilots circled, but no head came up.

The dive bombers made their standard attack, and did damage to the Cebu city port. But again those 2,000-pound bombs carried by some of the torpedo bombers were spectacular: one landed on the port's central pier, and smashed not only the pier but a building across the way. Another blockbuster landed among several small buildings by the marine railroad on Mactan Island and flattened all of them.

A third strike left the decks of the *Essex* at 1:00 in the afternoon to join more planes of the *Lexington*. Once again, Cebu Harbor, Mactan Island, and all between points were targets. And Lieutenant Morris led a fighter sweep over Panay Island. They found no fighters or any aircraft, but did manage to expend their ammunition against several small coastal vessels near Iloilo Island and Antayan Island.

That was the end of a long day. The task force retired toward Kossol Passage in the Palaus, and then to Ulithi, the new big American harbor and forward base, where the carriers would receive new planes to replace those lost, new pilots, and ammunition and supplies for the next assignment to Task Force 38. Ensign Gaver's body washed up from the deep and was recovered by Filipinos and buried in the Maniawe Municipal Cemetery.

As far as Admiral Halsey was concerned, the Philippines had been sufficiently softened up to the point of no return. After the first few days of this running battle, the Japanese opposition had been minuscule. Whatever the Japanese air power in the area had once been, at this point it looked very much like a "paper tiger."

CHAPTER ELEVEN

Action Off Formosa

On October 6, 1944, Task Force 38 again moved out, this time from Ulithi. The next step was to make air strikes at the Japanese "air pipeline"—that series of islands between the Japanese homeland and the Philippines which could be used to bring down aircraft to oppose the coming American landings on Leyte.

On October 9, Admiral Sherman's task group began a high speed run toward Okinawa in the Ryukyus, the islands the Japanese call the Nansei Shoto (Southwest Archipelago). At that same time, the first elements of the American invasion force—the minesweepers—were moving out from Manus toward the entrance to Leyte Gulf. The American battle plan was in motion.

This time, the whole Third Fleet carrier contingent was together, four task groups, including seventeen carriers, with Vice Admiral Marc Mitscher in command, riding in the *Lexington,* which was the flagship of the task group in which the *Essex* served.

Early on the morning of October 10, Commander McCampbell and his wingman, Lieutenant Rushing, took off from the *Essex* to lead the attack waves over central Okinawa and Kume Shima (island). McCampbell's job was to coordinate the early morning fighter sweep and two strikes by bombers and fighters that would follow almost immediately. They did not encounter any enemy aircraft in the sky as they flew to the target area.

Immediately after they took off, so did fourteen fighters from the *Essex* and sixteen from the *Lexington.* The *Essex* contingent was led by Lieutenant Commander Rigg, leader of the fighter squadron. The fighter pilots looked for enemy planes in the air but did not see any. Their main target was Yontan Air Base, which they attacked straightway, catching at least a dozen aircraft on the ground. Apparently these planes were getting ready to take off, because they were on or near the runways, and fully

116

gassed. Several of them burned and exploded. The sweep then moved on to Yontan South Air Base, where the fighters again strafed, but this time they had more difficulty in getting at the planes, which were parked in stout revetments. They also destroyed one fuel truck and on the shore found a small coastal steamer, which they left trailing oil.

Meanwhile Commander McCampbell and Lieutenant Rushing were having a field day strafing shipping at Okinawa. They found four cargo ships, the largest about 6,000 tons, and they attacked with machine guns and rockets: two rockets hit the first ship. They exploded depth charges on the stern of a second, which began to burn aft. Half an hour later, this ship was found dead in the water, south of Kume Shima. The third ship began trailing oil after being strafed, and the fourth went dead in the water off Nago Wan (bay).

The first air strike included another thirty-two fighters from the *Essex*, the *Lexington,* and the *Princeton,* and twenty-seven dive bombers and twenty-seven torpedo bombers from the three carriers. The bombers plastered the Yontan airfields, destroyed barracks, hangars, and shops, and put holes in runways.

Obviously the first strike and the fighter sweep had caught the Japanese by surprise, but by the time the second air strike left the decks of the three carriers, the Japanese were getting into the air, and when the American planes arrived over Okinawa again, it was a different story. Lieutenant Morris was leading the dozen fighters from the *Essex.* They found the target and looked around, but saw no enemy aircraft. The fighters attacked shipping in Nago Wan with 500-pound bombs and sank one 8,000-ton freighter, three small freighters, and damaged two more small freighters. Two of these ships went up in a spectacular explosion; they were moored together and a direct hit on one of them sent them both sky-high, perhaps blown up by ammunition they were carrying.

At about this point, the enemy planes showed up—a combination of fighters and fighter bombers, ranging from Zero fighters to biplane trainers. Lieutenant Morris attacked the first plane to get within range, a Tony. He swooped down, taking advantage of altitude, got on the enemy plane's tail and shot the plane down into the water.

Over the airfield, Lieutenant (jg) Milton found another Tony just taking off, and after several bursts shot it down. It crashed into trees not far from the runway.

Lieutenant Berree and his wingman found an Oscar (Nakajima army fighter) down low on the water, heading for interception of the American bombers, which were working over the port facilities and the harbor shipping. The plane did not burn as Berree poured shells into it, but he apparently wounded or killed the pilot because the fighter nosed over and went straight into the water.

On the way to the airfield to find more enemy planes, Berree and his wingman spotted another army plane, and Berree shot it down. This was really very easy picking; the plane was a Nate, an army trainer never designed to face F6F-5s in combat.

The Japanese by this time were beginning to get organized, but it did not do them much good. Ensign Flinn's division spotted four planes in formation down low, apparently just after takeoff. Flinn shot down one Tony, whose pilot put his wheels down and tried to make a forced landing, but never made the land and splashed into the water. Ensign Pigman shot down another Tony. Oddly, when Pigman's shells burst into the wing roots they did not start fires, or least not the sort of fires that usually exploded a Japanese plane. Instead, on this plane a long column of white smoke began to exude from the wing root, and the plane did not burn but cartwheeled back onto the airfield and then broke up into small pieces.

Ensign Borley's division spotted five enemy aircraft below, and he attacked one Zero. The Zero pilot banked sharply to the right and Borley lost him. But the Zero pilot outfoxed himself; instead of breaking off, he came all the way around, and Borley met him again and this time got in several good bursts. The Zero, true to type, burned nicely before it crashed in the water.

Ensign Frazelle and his section leader saw an Oscar level with them at nine o'clock and turned into it. They started shooting, but the Oscar went right through their fire, apparently unharmed. Frazelle then got behind the Japanese plane and gave it a long burst from astern. The Oscar smoked and then burned, and crashed on its back in the water.

Lieutenant Nall was leading a division, and his real task that day was to take photographs, but the Japanese planes were coming thick and fast and he and his division made several passes at planes to keep them away from the bombers, before several other fighters joined and then Nall went "upstairs" for high cover and protection of the bombers.

Commander Mini led the dive bombers, which hit one beached ship and made near misses on several others. Lieutenant C.H. Sorensen led the torpedo bombers, which were carrying 4- to 6-second delayed-fuse 500-pound bombs. Commander McCampbell sent them into the channel between Okinawa and the little island of Yahagi Shima, where he had seen a number of barges and small vessels. The torpedo bombers went in from south to north in glide attacks. Sorensen bombed the first oil barge, which came up suddenly—it had been camouflaged with branches and nets. He made direct hits and the barge began to burn. Lieutenant Goodwin made a hit on the bow of the second barge, and then made another run and hit the third barge. Lieutenant William S. Burns bombed a lugger and set it afire.

As these pilots returned, another strike was setting out from the carriers. These planes destroyed more planes on the ground, but met none in the air, and then concentrated on hangars, barracks, and buildings around the airfield, and on the small craft around the island. Many of them passed over burning, beached, and sunk vessels; the targets were getting harder to find.

On the fourth strike, Lieutenant E.W. Overton, Jr. led the *Essex* fighters out. They were supposed to hit Yontan Airbase again, but the target coordinator decided there was nothing left there to attack, so he sent them south to the next complex, Yontan South Air Base. It was hard to see over the whole area because of the haze from fires burning on the ground.

Two of the fighter pilots were sent out to take pictures. Lieutenant Singer was one of them, and as he was returning from Kume Shima, he looked down at little Ie Shima off the Okinawa coast and saw an airfield clustered with aircraft, mostly navy two-engined Nakajima bombers (Frans). One had just landed and the others were in a landing circle, one following another. Singer made a diving turn onto the first plane in the line, and with one burst sent that Fran flaming to the ground. The pilot never knew what hit him. Singer had chopped his throttle, but he quickly overtook the second landing plane, passed it by and concentrated on another that turned out to the left to evade him. He shot that one down. It exploded with such a bang that it shook the whole F6F.

Singer had dropped down to about 1,500 feet, and now he climbed up again and looked around for the rest of the planes from that landing circle. He saw one, a Sally (flying boat), heading low across the water north. Singer chased, began to fire, his port guns jammed, and the impact and recoil of his starboard guns threw off his aim. He missed. The Sally turned back toward the Ie Shima field. Singer was having trouble with his guns still—one port gun was not firing, and it disturbed his aim—but he managed to get enough hits into the Sally so that as it tried to land, pieces began to fall off, the landing gear folded up, and the plane skidded in, plowed up the runway and nosed up. It seemed doubtful that particular plane would fly again.

Singer then pulled up and saw another Fran heading for the clouds near Okinawa. He chased, trying to recharge his guns. The Fran came out of the cloud directly in front of him, and the pilot probably did not even know that Singer was there. Singer began firing again—only three guns fired but they were enough, the Fran burst into flames just aft of the engine and went into a diving spiral that ended with a crash into the water. Singer looked around. There were no more enemy aircraft in the air, so he went back to the carrier. In just a few minutes he had shot down four planes, single-handedly.

The Japanese at Okinawa should not have been so badly surprised, it would seem. They had warning that something was coming, part by American intent, part by accident. Admiral Halsey had sent a bombardment force to Marcus Island to confuse the Japanese. It arrived off Marcus at 4:15 on the morning of the 9th. A bombardment force without carriers was certainly an indication that something was going on. Quite by accident that same day a Japanese search plane out of Kyushu was shot down by a patrol bomber working out of the Marianas. The knowledge that the plane had not returned was coupled with the news of the American carriers, and the Sasebo naval district issued an alert.

But the alert did not get to the defenders of Okinawa in time, and consequently they were surprised that morning by the appearance of hundreds of American carrier planes. (The Japanese counted 900 planes; the Americans claimed nearly 1,400 flights or sorties.)

At the end of the day, the American pilots claimed to have destroyed more than 100 Japanese aircraft. The claim of the airmen of the *Essex* was twenty-three, including Singer's four planes shot out of the air. The Japanese figures showed thirty navy planes shot down or destroyed on the ground and fifteen army planes. But the truly shocking damage to the Japanese was the virtual destruction of the big new air base at Yontan, and the annihilation of virtually everything that moved on or under the water that was in the area. The Japanese counted four major ships sunk (including a 10,000-ton freighter), the submarine tender *Jinggyo,* thirteen torpedo boats, two special attack (midget) submarines, and twenty-two miscellaneous small naval vessels.

The airmen of the *Essex* had suffered two casualties, both wounded. ARM2C S.C. Peterson, Jr., of the torpedo squadron, was hit by 7.7mm bullets when his pilot zoomed down low and drew anti-aircraft fire on the second air strike. ARM2c Charles Rowland of the Helldiver squadron, flying that day with the torpedo bombers, was not so lucky. He was hit by bullets in the left arm, and, when the plane got back safely to the carrier, he was rushed into sick bay, where the doctors had to amputate his arm above the elbow. There were no other *Essex* casualties. One TBF went into the sea on takeoff, but all three crew members were picked up. The reason for the crash, said the pilot, was too much slipstream from planes ahead of him. If the reason was greeted with some incredulity, there was too much to be done for anyone to pay much attention to the accident.

The success of the Okinawa strike (twenty-one American planes lost, but only five pilots and four aircrewmen) was encouraging to Admiral Halsey; but even had the losses been much greater, he was still already committed to the next effort, which was to be the sweep of Formosa with its twenty-four major air bases. On October 11, the *Essex* and some other carriers fueled, while about half the carrier task force doubled back to make a strike at Aparri Airfield on Luzon. All this did was confuse the Japanese a little: they were not quite sure whether the American invasion was coming to Formosa or whether it was coming to the Philippines, but they were already planning for both.

On September 19, the Imperial General Staff's army section had issued orders to the army air forces to prepare for Sho 1, which was the Philippines attack. The navy was also getting into position to move air and sea units to the Philippines area, but all planes headed from Japan could easily enough be diverted at Kyushu and sent down to Formosa if that was how the battle went.

In Formosa on October 11, the wheels were already in motion to counter the American attack. Admiral Toyoda, the Japanese navy's chief of staff, happened to be in Formosa at that time on an inspection trip. Tokyo informed him of all the American activities of recent days. As of the 11th, the Americans' next move was not quite certain, but, at 6:45 on the morning of October 12, the planes of Task Force 38 struck Formosa.

The area assigned to the planes of the *Essex* was the west coast of Formosa and the Pescadores Islands offshore. It was a grim day, clouds hanging low and the sea choppy with the wind.

Commander McCampbell led the first air sweep out that morning. He took off with three other F6Fs to be first at the target. His mission was to coordinate attacks and observe shipping and other potential targets in the Pescadores area, and that is what he did. When he and his division arrived over the enemy territory nothing was stirring. But by the time the thirty-two fighters of the air sweep arrived, the Japanese were putting hundreds of planes in the air.

Lieutenant Commander Rigg led the *Essex* fighters. They met the *Lexington* fighters and were flying above them for cover at 19,000 feet when over Formosa they saw the first defenders ready to intercept. The Japanese planes had the altitude advantage this time; they were at 23,000 feet, and the fighters from both American carriers had to climb to reach them. But in spite of that advantage, the Japanese threw their luck to the winds: these were not the tightly disciplined Japanese pilots of the Pearl Harbor and Guadalcanal days, but mostly tyros, and almost uniformly they violated the first law of the fighter pilot, which was to maintain formation discipline. The Americans swooped in divisions of four planes and split off into two plane sections. "At no time was there noticed a single friendly VF alone, unless he was joining up on other F6Fs; the Enemy Aircraft did not follow this procedure, consequently it was easy to pick them out and off," wrote Lieutenant Commander Rigg in his action report that day.

The melee was staged at altitudes from 25,000 down to 15,000 feet, and here the F6Fs could keep up with the Zeros and the other Japanese fighters that might be more maneuverable at lower altitudes.

The Japanese began well enough. It looked as though they were going to fight in units of four and six planes, but almost immediately they began breaking off. "No trouble was experienced in outmaneuvering the Enemy Aircraft. After two scissors with a Zeke or a Tojo [Army Zero] it was possible to get on the tail." Down low, at 8,000 feet and below, it was a different story, and the Japanese had the maneuvering advantage in the heavier air, which negatively affected the flight characteristics of the heavy F6F fighters.

The Japanese had some tricks up their sleeves, too. Several planes carried phosphorus bombs, which they dropped toward American planes. Had they hit, they would undoubtedly have started fires that could not have been put out, but they did not score any hits. Bombing a moving target in the air is not a very easy task. One pilot was sure the Japanese had some sort of rocket weapon in the tails of their aircraft, for he saw a red flash and smoke come from one of them. But if there was such a weapon, it was no more effective on American planes than the phosphorus bombs that day.

The action in the melee was so fast and furious that the actual count of planes shot down was lost. Lieutenant Commander Rigg was the first to get in a shot. Climbing up from 19,000 feet, he attacked a Zero that was coming down at him, and got in one burst. His wingman finished the job with another, and the Zero flamed. Rigg then made passes at several other enemy aircraft, and three of them started smoking, but he was so busy he could not stop to follow them down and so did not know if they actually crashed. He did see one other Zero flame and crash after several bursts from his guns.

Lieutenant Commander Duncan had a rare experience that day. A Japanese army fighter came at him head-on, firing. Duncan stayed right with him, and they moved on a collision course until it was apparent to Duncan that the Japanese pilot was prepared to ram, and he pulled up. As the Tojo went beneath the F6F, Duncan saw it burst into flames.

Lieutenant Carr went after a Tojo, which pulled a new maneuver: the pilot dropped his wheels to increase drag and slow down during the flight. It did not help the Japanese pilot much, though. Carr started the plane to smoking and it fell off on one wing. Then a fighter from the *Lexington* group put more bullets into it and it crashed. Carr got credit for half of that plane.

Lieutenant (jg) R.P. Fush saw a Zero make a run on a group of F6Fs and then break off and swoop down. He went after the Zero, and shot it down, then found a Tojo, which made the mistake of trying to dive away from the F6F. Fush caught the Tojo and shot out the engine. The plane went into a tight spiral and crashed.

Lieutenant Twelves had a narrow escape in an encounter with another Zero. This plane was evading several F6Fs above, which had been chasing it. The pilot came head-on at Twelves, and scored hits in the cockpit, engine, and wings. One bullet went through the plotting board on Twelves's knee. Another smashed the cylinder head temperature gauge right out of the instrument panel. The Zero pilot put many more holes in Twelves's plane—wings, ailerons, a propeller blade, elevators, stabilizer, and rudder—but finally the Japanese made the mistake of turning directly in front of the F6F, and Twelves got in one burst that set the plane afire. The pilot bailed out, and his parachute opened down below.

The F6Fs encountered one extremely fast and maneuverable plane, the Raider, which they called a Jack. They saw four of these planes but engaged only one. Four of them were in tight formation, maneuvering to come after Twelves's division, and this one came at Twelves. The Jack outclimbed the F6F at 18,000 feet which *was* unusual, but the F6Fs stayed in formation, and when the plane dropped below after its run and started to recover altitude, Twelves was able to get in one burst, which knocked the Jack down. It did not flame.

Lieutenant (jg) J.P. Van Altena shot down two Tojos in the fighting, and Lieutenant (jg) M.M. Gunter, Jr., shot down two Zeros.

Lieutenant (jg) W.S. Deming, Jr., got down low and had to climb when he and his section leader saw several Tojos up above them at 18,000 feet. The Tojos were making runs on F6Fs behind them. Deming chose one and shot it down. He noticed then what other pilots were beginning to see—that after a divisional pass or two the Japanese pilots became defensive in their maneuvers and tried to engage the American pilots in individual dogfights.

Ensign Hoey came upon a Tojo that was chasing an F6F that had fallen out of formation. He shot the Tojo off the other fighter's tail; the Japanese pilot made a desperate attempt to ram Hoey, but his engine quit, luckily for the American pilot, and the Tojo crashed.

Ensign Pigman and his division were climbing to meet the enemy when a group of Tojos made a pass at them. Pigman got on the tail of one Tojo and shot it down, the empennage came off, and the pilot bailed out. Pigman rejoined his formation, saw a Zero below, fired, and it exploded. He then fired on another Zero, but was too busy staying in formation to see what happened to it.

Ensign C.A. Borley was flying at 17,000 feet and climbing for altitude when he saw a Tojo about 3,000 feet below and made a high side run on the plane. When he got in range, he opened fire. Even at 1,500 feet he managed to put bullets into the Tojo's cockpit and the wings, and the plane smoked. Small bursts of flame erupted from the cowling. The plane then dove straight into the sea.

Borley recovered at 14,000 feet and as he started to climb again, he saw a Zero nearby on the opposite course. He made an overhead run, and the Zero flew right into his tracers. It went into a lazy spiral, caught fire, crashed, and exploded. Borley then saw a group of F6Fs at about 8,000 feet and joined up. Five hundred feet below, they spotted several Oscars dead ahead, on a parallel course. Borley chose one Oscar and increased his speed. He saw the enemy pilot look over his shoulder at the American plane just as he opened fire. The pilot rolled the plane over—it was hard for Borley to believe he had actually hit the Japanese plane from extreme range—and then the pilot bailed out.

Borley was down to 7,000 feet then. He saw an Oscar flying toward land, apparently leaving the fight. Borley went after him. The Oscar pilot saw him and increased his speed. Borley closed in at 280 knots (to the enemy's 200-225) and opened fire at 800 feet. He sprayed every part of the plane, and it caught fire, then went into a shallow dive, and crashed on land. Ensign Borley, with four planes to his credit in a few minutes, rejoined his division.

Ensign P. Bugg got into a dogfight with a Tojo at 19,000 feet and had no trouble in out-turning it. He shot down the enemy plane, the Japanese pilot bailed out, but his parachute did not open. Down he went toward the sea, the long white trail of the unopened parachute tagging after him.

Ensign J.C. Taylor's section leader shot down one Zero of the many that attacked them at 20,000 feet. Taylor stayed in formation covering, then they saw two Tojos on the tail of an F6F below them and went after them. The section leader made a pass at one, and Taylor took the other. He shot it down, and then reclimbed to 20,000 feet, and saw three more Tojos at 12,000 feet. Taylor went after them and shot one down.

The Japanese broke off the battle, and the fighters continued their sweep and moved in to attack Keishu Airdrome. On the ground they found a number of fighters, engines running, preparing to take off, and they strafed all of them. Some burned. They also strafed the revetments around the field, hitting many twin-engined bombers. In some revetments there were two or three planes. As they moved away from the strafing attacks, Lieutenant Commander Rigg saw a dozen fires on the fields itself from burning aircraft and more fires in the revetments.

The F6Fs came in low, and they found the anti-aircraft fire heavy and accurate. Lieutenant Van Altena's plane was hit, and on the way back to the carrier he had to ditch in the water. His wingman, Ensign Dorn, circled the downed plane and saw Van Altena get out and into his life raft. He continued to circle until assured that Van Altena would be rescued by the lifeguard submarine and then flew back toward the *Essex.* But the circling had taken too much fuel, and Dorn had to land in the water about twenty miles from the carrier group. Van Altena was rescued that day, but Dorn was not; he was listed as missing in action—sacrificing himself for a comrade.

Ensign Borley had kept his belly tank throughout the aerial fighting, although this was regarded as unwise and dangerous procedure, since the tank was vulnerable and if it caught fire could destroy the F6F. During the attack of the airfield, Borley went down with his division to strafe the airfield in formation. As he pulled out, at 2,000 feet, his F6F was suddenly hit by what he thought was a 40mm anti-aircraft shell. The cockpit filled with smoke, and he felt an intense pain in his left leg: shrapnel.

The smell of burning rubber filled his nostrils, and he sensed that the belly tank was burning. He jettisoned it, but it stuck, and before it came off the F6Fs engine had stopped. The propeller was still windmilling, and the plane vibrated badly. Borley turned off the fuel supply, pulled the mixture back to idle cut-off, and switched off the magnetos to prevent a fire.

When the plane was hit he was travelling at about 300 knots and was over land. His only hope was to get out over water and make a landing, without power. He did get about two miles offshore, but then the plane stalled out at thirty feet above the water, travelling at ninety knots, and pancaked onto the surface. The F6F broke in half and sank in five seconds. Borley jumped out with all his gear, and inflated his yellow Mae West life preserver.

Borley realized that so close to shore he might draw the attention of the Japanese, who would try to capture him. He released his parachute and the raft, back pack, gloves, canteen and helmet, and began swimming toward the open sea.

Sure enough, it was not long before he saw a sampan headed his way. He deflated the bright yellow life jacket about halfway and hoped that he could lie low enough so that they would pass him by. But no, they saw him and came toward him. There were several men in the boat and they seemed bent on his capture. He unholstered his .38 calibre revolver, not knowing what would happen since it had been immersed in salt water, and when the boat approached he fired.

His aim was good; he knocked the first man out of the boat with one shot. Three more shots, and he hit the second man in the bow, who also fell overboard. The sampan then drew away from Borley, and he began swimming again, out to sea. His one hope was to get out far enough, and have the luck of rescue by a lifeguard submarine.

By heading directly out to sea, Ensign Borley managed to save himself from capture and possible death (the Japanese "tried" and executed several American fliers who were unlucky enough to crash or parachute onto Formosa during these raids). Several times that day, Borley saw small craft not far away, but the Japanese did not believe he could have swum as far as he did, apparently, because they remained closer to the shore, and he escaped further detection.

Late in the morning (the fighters' mission ended at around 9:00) Ensign Borley saw a lone F6F flying over and waved to attract attention. The pilot saw the yellow Mae West and circled, waggling his wings to show that he had identified the man in the water as American. But nothing happened, until late afternoon when a pair of F6Fs came over low and purposeful, found him, and dropped a life raft.

In that rough sea, warm though the water was, it seems improbable that Borley could have survived the night without the raft. He clambered aboard, and secured himself inside. That night he drifted. He could see lights ashore, and particularly the flashing and ragged light of fires burning, with occasional explosions.

All the next day he drifted slowly away from the land. Several American fighters came over, and all waggled their wings, so he still hoped for a quick rescue. But at nightfall he was still in his raft, and the weather was growing worse. That night he was tossed by the stiffening sea, and the next morning when dawn broke, he saw that he was out of sight of land. His spirits fell.

On that third day he saw nothing but sea and sky and birds and a few fish. The sea grew rougher, and during the third night the raft capsized twice. He lost his extra dye markers and his water canteen, the new one, that had been dropped with the raft, but the lashings held and he did not lose the raft.

At the time the loss of the canteen did not bother him because he had not been thirsty or hungry since the ditching. But on the fourth morning he was both, and thirst particularly bothered him. A flying fish landed in the raft, and he decided to try *sashimi*, the Japanese way of eating raw fish. But one bite was enough: he decided he wasn't yet that hungry and dropped the fish. On the fourth night, again Ensign Borley was tossed badly by the seas, but his raft stayed afloat. He was thirsty, but he had no water.

Next morning, he was still afloat. He thought he saw something on the horizon and pulled out his .38 again. It was rusty, but it fired, and he hoped, without really believing, that the sound might have carried to someone, somewhere. It did not, but in mid-afternoon on this fifth day, the submarine *Sawfish* spotted the yellow raft and came alongside. Ensign Borley was rescued and taken back to Pearl Harbor to await the coming of the men of the *Essex*. His was one remarkable saga of the sea war.

At about the time that Ensign Borley received the yellow life raft, the Imperial General Staff was deep in conference. It was still arguable whether the Americans intended to invade Formosa or the Philippines, but certain orders were issued on October 12 that would be valid in either case. Principally, at the moment they involved the naval air forces. The base air forces in Formosa and the Philippines were alerted to prepare for their various chores under either Sho 1 or Sho 2. The 3rd Naval Air Squadron and the 4th Naval Air Squadron were transferred from Kyushu to Formosa and the 7th Base Air Force was placed under the command of Admiral Fukudome, of the 6th Base Air Force. Also, the 1st Submarine Squadron was ordered into action to destroy the enemy, and Admiral Fukudome brought the most famous of Japan's air attack units, T Force, to Formosa to strike the American carriers.

A few minutes after the fighter sweep went off that morning of October 12 the first air strike of fighters, dive bombers, and torpedo bombers took off from the *Essex*, met a similar force from the *Lexington* and the *Langley*, and together the planes moved toward central Formosa and the Pescadores.

Up above Formosa, Commander McCampbell was sorting out the attack areas. The fighters were to come in over the mountains and hit Kobi Air Base. But where was Kobi Air Base? The American intelligence on Formosa was woefully inadequate, the result largely of submarine observations and reports from long-range bombers in the past. The maps showed three air bases in this general region. Actually there were about fifteen. But with some difficulty the fighters located their assigned target. Matters were not helped any by the Japanese jamming of the fighter control frequency, which Commander McCampbell noted. The fighters swooped down on the field, and strafed and fired rockets at all the aircraft they could find. Many of the planes were twin-engined Betty bombers, and were full of gasoline, so it was hard to assess the damage. Nor could the fighters make repeated passes, since the bombers were coming in, and in view of the Japanese interception of the fighter sweep, McCampbell ordered the fighters "upstairs" to look after the bombers as they did their work.

Commander Mini led his dive bombers on this mission; one Helldiver began to heat up and had to return to the carrier, but nine went on to the target. They were scheduled to bomb Toyohara air base, but the fog over the field was too thick, so they looked around and found a hole above the Kobi base and bombed it instead.

The torpedo squadron was led out by Lieutenant (jg) R.L. Bentz. Seven torpedo planes made the mission; one had to turn back with engine trouble. They, too, were supposed to bomb Toyohara airfield, but frankly they did not know what they bombed—it was a square airfield with anti-aircraft positions in the center. Their briefing had indicated they should aim for the hangars and buildings. They did, and destroyed two hangars, three small buildings, and one revetment. But not until they were coming out of dives did anyone realize that there were about a hundred Japanese aircraft parked on that field, and they were not hit at all!

The next mission to go off was a search, or rather several searches, northeast of Formosa, to see if elements of the Japanese fleet might be out. The searches were carried out by teams: one Helldiver and one F6F fighter in each team. One search found nothing at all. One discovered a new X-shaped airfield on Miyako Shima, in the Okinawa area. No search planes found any warships, or even any cargo ships or convoys.

Two of the searches did encounter enemy aircraft aloft. Ensign M.H. Frazelle shot down one Nakajima 96—or Nell, as the Americans called the plane. Ensign K.L. Lee found a twin-engined Betty bomber at about 4,000 feet, 150 miles from the carrier. He made a pass at it, and the turret gunner began firing back at him. But Lee's shots went into the wing roots and the gas tanks, and the plane began to blaze and crashed into the sea.

At 8:14 that morning, the second strike from Admiral Sherman's carrier group set out sixty-five aircraft from the *Essex,* the *Lexington,* and the *Langley.* Their attack was directed at Boko Harbor and the Pescadores Islands. They found the harbor full of ships, and attacked. At least five of the vessels were destroyer escort types or minesweepers. Lieutenant Commander Lambert dropped delayed-fuse bombs under the bow of one, and it apparently sank immediately after the explosions.

They sank one 750-ton ship and one of about 500 tons, strafed aircraft on an airfield and one flying boat on the water, and destroyed them. They then sank a 10,000-ton freighter and a 3,000-ton ship and damaged most of the warships.

The planes retired south of the harbor, which was an error, for the anti-aircraft fire there was intense, so much so that Ensign H.C. Copeland's torpedo bomber was hit in the engine, and three cylinders were blown off. The plane began shuddering and missing, and it seemed the crew would have to bail out over enemy territory, but somehow Ensign Copeland managed to get the plane down to the end of Formosa and out to sea before making a water landing. He and his crewmen, R.J. Bradley and W.C. Poppel, clambered out of the sinking plane and into their life raft.

Then complications set in. A 1,200-ton freighter nearby changed course, as if to come and pick up the hated American survivors. But up above, this move was seen by

Lieutenant (jg) Symmes who dropped a raft to the survivors, and included with it a note to the pilot about what was happening. Then he attacked the Japanese freighter repeatedly and finally sank the ship. But the survivors of the sunken ship got into a power boat, and again purposefully headed toward the downed airmen of the *Essex*. Symmes had left his wingman circling over the raft; now Symmes strafed the power boat, and sank it. Next, he found the lifeguard submarine and led it to his survivors. Then he and his wingman went back to the carrier, strafing another small freighter they found on the way.

The third strike of October 12 left the *Essex* at 11:25 in the morning to destroy facilities and planes at Rokko Airfield Number 1. The primary target was Toyohara Airfield, but it was still socked in; so Rokko head been chosen as the alternative. Actually they found the field by accident, it was not on their maps, but there it was, an unreported airstrip still under construction, below Taichu. They destroyed most of its buildings and installations.

On the next strike, just before 2:00 in the afternoon, the carrier planes hit Niko-sho Airfield, as directed by the target coordinator, the commander of the *Lexington's* air group. They also bombed and strafed several ships they found offshore. With the return of this group of planes just after 5:15, the *Essex* air operations came to an end for the day, and the ship began to batten down for the night. There was a chance that the Japanese might try a night attack on the carriers.

The Japanese had just that thought in mind. The celebrated T Force was to make the valiant effort to destroy the American carriers. The Thunderbolt Torpedo Squadron, with about 100 planes, would set off to find ways through the American screen of destroyers, cruisers, and combat air patrols, and get at the carriers. Several planes did in fact get close enough to the *Essex* to see the carrier and drop flares.

Afternoon search planes reported back to Japanese headquarters that they had found three groups of carriers on the east side of Formosa (they did not find the fourth one that night). At abut 2:00, the Japanese attack force began to move, taking off from several air bases. The weather that afternoon and evening was threatening, with heavy clouds in the sky. The plan of attack was called the Milky Way Plan and it involved fifty-five planes, many of them type fours as the Japanese called them, or Tenzan torpedo bombers (Jills). But that night the bombers did not get through to the carriers, and twenty-six Japanese attack planes failed to return to their bases.

On the morning of October 13, once again the *Essex* dispatched sixteen fighters, which joined up with another sixteen F6Fs from the *Lexington*, to continue the attack on north and west Formosa and to discover what might be worth attacking later in the day. Lieutenant Commander Rigg led the *Essex* section again. There was a good reason for this. Rigg commanded the fighter squadron, but until the Philippines air strikes Commander McCampbell had been inclined to see himself as commander of both the whole *Essex* air group and of the fighter squadron that he had trained and built up. But Admiral Sherman had straightened McCampbell out on that matter; what was good tactics could be terrible strategy, and although McCampbell was the best fighter pilot in the air group, he was *commander* of the air group, and his task therefore was to command and not to get involved in chasing after Japanese aircraft.

This was the opposite of the instructions issued McCampbell so long ago by Captain Miles Browning, but Admiral Sherman was in charge, and furthermore he was also on the *Essex,* flagship of Task Group 38.3. So since the Philippines strikes, McCampbell had been obeying the letter and spirit of his admiral's instructions.

The fighter sweep was a disappointment to the pilots who wanted air action. Only three enemy aircraft were seen in the air, and the moment the American fighters appeared the Japanese planes ducked into the low cloud cover that hung over Formosa that day. It was not a question of cowardice (against odds of 30-1?) as some pilots might have believed, but of orders. Admiral Fukudome, entrusted with the battle against the American carrier force, was planning a major effort for the following day, and all Japanese air strength was to be conserved for this effort.

Since there was so little action over the Formosa air bases, the first air strike of the day was devoted to the Ansan Naval Base in the Pescadores. Commander McCampbell took off with his division of fighters, but he was not actually leading the strike; again his job was to be target coordinator, or manager, while Commander Winters of the *Lexington* led the air strike. Lieutenant Morris led the fighters from the *Essex.*

The weather had grown noticeably worse since the fighter sweep of early morning, and by the time the planes arrived over the naval base the cloud cover was a distinct hampering factor. The fighters had escorted the bombers carefully to the target; seeing no enemy aircraft in the air, they swooped down to strike with bombs and strafe. The results were not very satisfactory.

A destroyer and a battleship were located inside the base's graving dock (an excavated drydock with a lock which could be opened and closed), and were attacked. The damage was not known, largely because the bad visibility prevented the pictures from coming out. A pair of the fighter-bombers dropped their 500-pound bombs in a skip-bombing attack against a destroyer escort outside the base, and they thought they did some damage.

The dive bombers and torpedo bombers were hampered even more by the bad weather. It was a question of finding a hole in the clouds, trying to get through before it closed up again, and then trying to find a target in a hurry and hit it. It wasn't easy. The dive bombers did not do very well. Worse, in his dive, Lieutenant (jg) Earl Clifford was hit by anti-aircraft fire, he managed to level off at 200 feet above the base and headed for the water. There was no question about getting out to sea, he was too low and would never make it. He did not even manage the water landing, the plane came down, one wing dipped, it struck, and the Helldiver cartwheeled and went in. All that appeared was an oil slick. Lieutenant Clifford and his gunner, Stanley N. Whitby, were marked down that night on the report as killed in action.

Lieutenant (jg) M.P. Deputy, who lived up to his name and took over from torpedo squadron strike leader Lieutenant R.D. Cosgrove when the latter's radio went out, found a hole in the clouds over the target area and led his eight torpedo planes down. Only half the planes got through that hole and found themselves in position to make the glide attack on the naval base. They dropped a dozen incendiary clusters and started a number of fires. The second division, having missed that first hole in the clouds, found another, but then found themselves in no position to hit the naval base, so they went instead to the Chomosui airfield. Actually this is precisely what they were supposed to do; Commander McCampbell had radioed Cosgrove to split his force and attack those two targets, but Cosgrove had not gotten the word. The air base attack set fire to one hangar.

By the time the second strike came along, McCampbell was rushing back toward Formosa from the Pescadores to try to direct its activity. The selected target was Bukai Dam at Lake Jitsugetsutan on Formosa, one of the main sources of power for the island. But the strike arrived so rapidly on the heels of the first that McCampbell did not make it in time.

Unfortunately, the strike leader made a mistake in identification and the *Essex* torpedo planes missed the mark entirely. They dropped their torpedoes, but not against Bukai dam; they were over Lake Kanan instead. There was a dam, a tiny one of very little importance. The damage even to that dam seemed nonexistent. As for the powerhouses and other installations, they could not be found by the dive bombers either, so they attacked a sugar-alcohol refinery in the town of Mato.

Early in the afternoon, the admiral changed his focus and sent a fighter sweep over the southern Nansei Shoto, specifically Miyaki and Ishigaki Islands, to see what could be found there. Fourteen planes were involved, ten from the *Essex* and four from the USS *Cabot* of Admiral Bogan's strike group.

Lieutenant Commander Duncan led this sweep, which covered the area 200 miles south of Formosa. They found several previously unknown (to the Americans) air fields on Miyaki Island and a small seaplane base. They strafed the planes on the ground but not one burned. And tragedy struck the fighter squadron again: Ensign Flinn's F6F was hit by anti-aircraft fire, and he had to land on the water near Miyaki Island, just offshore in fact, in about six feet of water. He made a good landing, and then got out on the wing of his plane and waved to his friends up above. There was very little question about his future; the only real one being whether or not he would survive the initial fury of his captors.

The final strike of the day was against Kagi Airfield on Formosa, where a number of aircraft had been seen on the field that morning. Seventy-two planes from the *Essex*, the *Lexington*, and the *Princeton* attacked the field, and they strafed and bombed a large number of Japanese aircraft on the ground. They also raised hob with the field's facilities, destroying a hangar and several other buildings. On the way home, the Helldivers were jumped by several Zeros, but were saved by fighters from the *Princeton*, which drove them off and shot down one. The torpedo bombers also saw Japanese planes as they started home, but the enemy planes did not attack them.

Admiral Halsey had more or less concluded that the job at Formosa was done. The claims of his pilots added up to an enormous number of Japanese aircraft destroyed, in the air and on the ground. (In that big air battle of the 12th the *Essex* airmen claimed twenty and a half planes—the half being shared with a *Lexington* fighter pilot.) The fact was that the Japanese had been very hard hit, but they still had a powerful punch particularly in southern Kyushu, which could be delivered when Admiral Fukudome was ready.

The Japanese had kept "snooping" the American carriers that day, and on the evening of October 13, they launched another attack which was supposed to arrive on target just at dark—the most vulnerable time. The strike force set out from several bases on Formosa starting at about 1:30 in the afternoon. The weather was just what the attackers wanted; heavy cloud cover over the carrier force, which was bunched up. The idea was to hide among the clouds until the proper time and then strike. That, said the commander of the attack force, offered them the best chance of success.

That evening, the *Essex* and her fellow ships of Admiral Sherman's task force were busy. A number of Japanese snoopers were routed, and two Betty bombers and one Judy (torpedo bomber) were shot down by the fighters of the combat air patrol. But Admiral McCain's task group was not so lucky. The Australian heavy cruiser *Canberra* was torpedoed by one plane. In Admiral Davison's task group, the carrier *Franklin* was attacked by four bombers of the T force, carrying torpedoes. Three of these were shot down before they could do any damage (and one torpedo was skillfully avoided by the captain), but the fourth bomber, badly damaged, was brought in over the *Franklin* by a brave Japanese pilot, who smashed it into the flight deck. Fortunately for the men of the *Franklin*, the Japanese plane had already dropped its torpedo, which missed the ship. But the burning, exploding plane skidded across the flight deck and then slipped over the side.

The Japanese were delighted. All sorts of wild stories were taken back by the surviving pilots about the success of the attack, and claims about the sinking of two carriers were actually believed at the highest levels. Eighteen Japanese planes failed to return from this mission, but it seemed a small price to pay for those carriers.

The damage to the *Canberra* created some problems for the task force. It was apparent that the Japanese still had a lot of air strength in Formosa, and the *Canberra's* task group was only about eighty-five miles offshore. The ship was crippled and dead in the water. What to do? That was the question that assailed Admiral Halsey.

The answer could have been to abandon the ship and take the men aboard other warships for safety. But that was not Halsey's way. He decided they would get the *Canberra* back to Ulithi, come hell or high water, and he set about the preparations. The first of these was to order another air strike for the next day, although it would have to be quite limited in view of the shortage of his supply of aircraft and the damage done to many planes. But he could put about 150 fighters in the air the next day and perhaps 100 bombers, and these should keep the Japanese so busy that they would leave the Americans alone as they started homeward with their crippled cruiser.

On the morning of October 14, three of the four carrier air groups sent fighter sweeps and air strikes over Formosa. Admiral Sherman's sector was the central part of the island, and the *Essex*, the *Lexington*, the *Princeton* and the *Langley* all put up planes for the effort: eighty-three planes in all. The targets were airfields in the Shinchiku area, which might put up aircraft to harry the slow-moving *Canberra*, which was under tow by the cruiser *Wichita* at four knots. Columbus's *Santa Maria* could have moved faster.

Commander McCampbell led the planes from the four carriers. The *Essex* planes struck three airfields and destroyed hangars, a few buildings, and even fewer aircraft.

There just weren't very many Japanese planes in view that day. The reason was, first, that the Japanese planes not destroyed in the two days of furious air strikes were well hidden, but more, that the Japanese effort against the carrier force had now switched over to southern Kyushu.

The 6th Base Air Force was entrusted with the task of destroying the American carriers. That day the headquarters issued an order:

"1. The enemy carrier force has been hard hit by our heavy blows.
   2. The Base Air Force as well as the No. 2 attack squadron will exert their full capacity together to annihilate the remnants of the enemy."

Admiral Toyoda saw in this affair a chance to slow down the Americans by exerting his full air strength. At least a thousand planes were to be used from the base air forces and special squadrons. The T Force, which had already lost about thirty planes in its abortive attack of October 12, was again to try to show its highly advertised skill.

A dozen of the *Essex* contingent of fighters were put up over the task group that day as combat air patrol. All day long the Japanese were snooping around, but not attacking. Admiral Toyoda was saving his strength for the evening. The combat air patrol did locate one enemy patrol bomber near the ships and Ensign J.D. Mooney, Jr., shot it down.

For a time, as the day wore on, except for the problems of the tow, not very much happened. The hope was that the *Canberra* could be out of range of Formosa's land-based aircraft by dusk, the dangerous time.

On Formosa, the various commands reported to Admiral Toyoda in Taihoku the results of the morning attacks by the Americans. The first American planes had appeared over the island at 7:00 (those were *Lexington* and *Essex* planes), and the attack continued until 9:30 that morning. But the damage was not regarded as very great; or, to put it another way, the previous damage had been so great that for all practical purposes the Formosa airfields had been reduced to the status of temporary airstrips. After the last planes buzzed away that morning, it was reported that the American carriers were moving off, and there would be no more raids.

However, to augment the carrier force, Admiral Halsey had asked for support from the army air forces, and the result was a raid by 100 B-29s that flew the long distance from western China to bomb the southern Formosa area that day. They appeared around Takao at 12:30 and attacked for nearly two hours.

During the afternoon of October 14, three more "snoopers" were shot down by carrier planes of Task Group 38.3 on combat air patrol. Then, just after 3:00, a battle began.

For this day, the Japanese 6th Base Air Force had assembled 430 planes to attack the American carrier task force. In southern Kyushu the 6th and 7th Base Air Forces combined some units; the 6th Base Air Force got the 51st Squadron with some 250 planes, and 150 planes were immediately dispatched as reinforcements. On the morning of the 14th, units of the general attack force of 380 planes began moving out from their southern Kyushu bases. They landed at Okinawa for gas.

The American fleet had been discovered at just about the time that Ensign Mooney of the *Essex* combat air patrol was shooting down the search plane—perhaps by that very plane. The fleet was reported to be about 100 kilometers (sixty-five miles) southwest of Ishigaki Island, and the base at Okinawa sent the air strike planes out to begin hitting the enemy.

At 3:09 in the afternoon, the *Essex* had its first taste of the desperate attack. A single "bogy" was discovered on the radar screen, about twelve miles out and closing fast. Probably this plane was one of the dozen scout planes sent out by the 6th Base Air Force. One minute later, the sound of "general quarters" rang through the carrier, and men scurried to their battle stations. The Japanese plane continued to come in, tracked on the radar but invisible in the clouds that hung spottily over the carrier group. As the plane came out of the clouds, high above the *Essex*, the spotters identified it as a Judy—an Aichi navy dive bomber. The *Essex* and the ships around her put up a tremendous barrage of anti-aircraft fire, and the Japanese bomber pilot apparently had some second thoughts, for he pulled out of his dive at 1,500 feet and skirted off, later to make an attack on the *Lexington.*

The Japanese planes were attacking all the carrier groups at this point, and they continued, through the afternoon, evening, and night.

As the Japanese planes that survived came back from the attack on the U.S. carrier force, they reported glowingly that they had secured wonderful results. The first wave, of some 100 planes, attacking at between 2:00 and 3:00, returned to Japanese bases to report direct hits on two enemy cruisers and the destruction of one destroyer, which was said to have burned before the eyes of the Japanese airmen.

That afternoon the second attack unit, which consisted of a dozen scout planes, 110 fighter bombers, and another 100 torpedo bombers and heavy bombers, came back reporting another two cruisers burned. The T Force attacked with about twenty-five planes, and claimed to have sunk one carrier.

The reports continued the rest of the day, and from the Japanese point of view they seemed most favorable. The Okinawa relay station, which was monitoring the radio broadcasts of the pilots as they came away from the American fleet, kept reporting victory after victory.

Just after 5:00, the radarmen of the *Essex* reported a new set of bogies heading in. This time there were more, about a dozen planes. Ten miles out, they stopped and began orbiting, as if preparing for attack. The formation separated into two sets of planes, and two units of five planes came hurtling toward the *Essex.* Just at that time another group of seven Jills (Nakajima torpedo bombers) was sighted in attack approach on the ship. The first set of bombers came in range and the 5-inch anti-aircraft guns opened up. The Japanese planes were five miles away. When they cut that distance in half, the 40mm guns began to fire, and when they got closer the popping of the 20mm guns joined the clamor.

At 5:10, Captain Weiber ordered the call to general quarters and men began running across the decks. A few seconds later, the first torpedo bomber launched its "fish" at the starboard beam of the ship. The captain ordered an emergency turn to starboard, and the torpedo passed beneath the ship's stern. Six more torpedo bombers came in on the *Essex* in the next few minutes, and the lookouts spotted four torpedo tracks. All missed.

In three minutes, it was all over and the sky was quiet. Four of the torpedo planes had been sent smoking or exploding into the sea by the gunners. The rest had veered away and begun the return trip to their land bases.

At Admiral Toyoda's headquarters, the news kept coming in all the rest of the day and all evening. It was wonderful news: a stream of reports of sinking American ships. As nightfall came and the heavy bombers from Okinawa continued the attack, the reports began again. One dive bomber squadron after another reported marvelous results.

When the results came in so well, there seemed no reason to keep them quiet, and soon Tokyo knew that an enormous victory had been won. "The people went mad"— that is the verdict of the official Japanese war historians. All night long, they paraded in the streets and shouted for more good news. Nine carriers, the pilots reported, had been sunk.

The fact, however, was that in all these attacks by perhaps 600 aircraft on October 14, only one U.S. ship was badly hurt, the cruiser *Houston*. She was torpedoed in the midst of the battle, just eighty miles south of the Sakishima Gunto, and well within range of more Japanese attackers.

The problem for the Americans was still to get the crippled ships back to friendly waters. The problem for the Japanese was to try to destroy the rest of the fleet. On the night of October 14, the Japanese went astray, led partly by their own optimism and the careless reporting of the pilots, and partly by a basic misunderstanding of the American force, its composition, and its organization.

On the morning of the 15th, Rear Admiral Ralph Davison's Task Group 38.4 turned off to begin attacks on the Luzon airfields to prevent the Japanese from mounting attacks from there against the stricken ships. The Sherman task group and Bogan's group milled around the Japanese seas, hoping thus to attract the Japanese surface fleet to come out and fight. But Admiral Toyoda was not to be thus tempted. He had already put into effect the Sho plan—whether it was to be directed to Formosa or the Philippines would depend on where the enemy landings came, and the surface fleet was not to be used in a purely naval engagement, but to attack the next landing and "annihilate" the forces.

The reports came in all night long. The Okinawa relay station, reporting on the attack of the T Force, claimed a battleship sunk, and two carriers, one armored cruiser, one carrier, and two light cruisers damaged and "certainly sinking." The air of celebration was enhanced, and the euphoria of the Japanese continued.

On the morning of October 15, the Japanese set out to find the crippled American ships and sink them. At 9:30 that morning, search planes from Formosa found a carrier in an oil slick, two warships of some size, and two destroyers. (Apparently this was the *Canberra* flotilla, which the carrier had just recently joined.) When Admiral Toyoda had this news, he reiterated his inspirational message: various damaged units were now apparently still afloat at various areas in the sea, and the 6th Base Air Force and its attached units must devote all their energy to continuing and repeating the attack.

That morning, the 6th Base Air Force sent off about 100 planes to find and attack the enemy squadron that was moving so slowly. But again bad weather was given as the reason for the failure to discover the ships, and so no attack was made.

By this time, the American Third Fleet was widely scattered. The damaged *Houston* and *Canberra,* called informally "Crip Div One" (Cripples, Division One) were struggling to get into safe waters. Rear Admiral Laurance DuBose had been assigned the task of protecting them, with three cruisers and eight destroyers. The carriers *Cowpens* and *Cabot* were also assigned this task, and they were hurrying to the area, while the *Houston* and the *Canberra* were drawing together. As the forces converged, the Japanese got the impression that these ships represented the major American elements left afloat. Actually, Admiral Davison's task group was preparing to strike Luzon that morning, and Admiral Sherman's group, including the *Lexington,* was fueling.

On the morning of October 15, the planes from Admiral Davison's carriers began hitting the Luzon airfields early. Japanese search planes from the Manila area fields were also out, and at 8:00, 240 kilometers off Luzon, the Japanese scout planes discovered four carriers and their support ships. Then, at 11:22, patrol bombers discovered four carriers and seven other warships at a point 600 kilometers from Manila. Was it one force or two? The Japanese tried to find out.

Admiral Teraoka, the commander of the 5th Base Air Force in the Philippines, ordered an attack, and the day's battle began. Literally hundreds of Japanese planes flew from bases in Kyushu, Formosa, Okinawa, and the Philippines to find and destroy the American carrier force. They did not do so. But that day, from the Inland Sea, Admiral Shima, the commander of the 2nd Striking Force, brought three cruisers and a division of destroyers out to find the crippled ships and sink them.

None of this action directly concerned the *Essex* and its airmen that day. But on October 16, American radio intelligence found the Japanese cruiser force, and the alert was on. Admiral McCain divided the search area into pie-shaped pieces. The *Essex* portion involved a fifty-degree spread, out 300 miles from the carrier; five teams were sent out on patrol. Each team consisted of two fighters and a dive bomber, with the dive bomber pilot in command. One such team (Lieutenants Matthews and Berree, and Ensign Craig) shot down a Japanese dive bomber, and damaged a Nakajima two-engined P1Y navy bomber, but the bomber was faster than the fighters at low altitude and got away.

Another team (Lieutenants McCutcheon and Milton, and Ensign Pigman) shot down another Nakajima bomber. But the searchers did not find the Japanese task force. The rest of the searches that day and the next were carried out by other carrier groups. No one found the Japanese, except for some Japanese search planes, because Admiral Shima had a feeling that there were many more carriers still afloat than his headquarters admitted, and so he turned about and went back to Japanese waters.

On October 17, as the *Essex* and other carriers moved toward the Philippines, an American force moved into the entrance to Leyte Gulf and landed at Suluan Island. That morning, the Japanese garrison on Suluan sighted the American ships and reported to Tokyo. It all became clear to Admiral Toyoda: the target was the Philippines and the Sho 1 plan was put in motion.

The carrier groups separated to carry out different tasks in support of the coming landings on Leyte Island. Admiral Sherman's group fueled again on October 18, and then moved up to the east side of Luzon Island for operations. On October 20, as American troops began the landings at Leyte, Admiral Sherman's carriers met Admiral Bogan's off Cape San Ildefonso, on Luzon, and prepared to intercept any Japanese naval forces that might come down to try to stop the landings.

Officially, the Japanese were still bemused by their "great victory" in the battle of Formosa's air space. The Navy claimed to have sunk eleven carriers, two battleships, three cruisers, and one destroyer, and to have damaged eight carriers, two battleships, four cruisers, and fourteen other ships seriously, and to have set fires in another dozen ships.

The word was out in Tokyo that the Americans' air power had been destroyed; that there could not possibly be an American landing anywhere, and that the Sho plan was not going to be implemented. Then came a fateful word from a Suluan Sea outpost.

CHAPTER TWELVE

The Battle of Leyte Gulf

The U.S. Army's forces began landing on Leyte Island on the morning of October 20, after several hours of bombardment by American naval vessels. The Japanese did not have many units in this area and fewer field guns, so the initial reaction came from mortars and anti-tank guns in the hills behind the Leyte beaches. Up above, planes of Task Force 38 prevented the Japanese air forces from reaching the troops. The Japanese 16th Division troops were to fight a delaying action at Leyte, giving the 4th Army time to prepare for the "decisive land battle" on Luzon.

As far as the air was concerned, on the day of the landings all seemed to go well. A few planes appeared around the landing areas but not close enough to fire upon. They seemed more concerned with watching than with action. During the afternoon, the situation was regarded as safe enough for General MacArthur to make his celebrated "return" by wading ashore on Leyte, thus putting the political stamp on the invasion as symbolic of America's determination to return U.S. sovereignty and then freedom to the Filipinos. On the home front this was heralded as one of the high points of the war.

Several of the other task groups were in action that day, but not Admiral Sherman's. Its power was being saved for the next morning, when the Japanese were expected to begin attempts to destroy the invasion ships. At least one Japanese plane did get through on the 20th, and torpedoed the cruiser *Honolulu*. Thus it was seen as important for Admiral Halsey's planes to begin clearing off those Visayan airfields and try to make sure that no planes were available for the Japanese to use. That was an impossible task, of course, but it was possible to harry the enemy airmen on the ground, and shoot them down if they came near the landing area.

At dawn on October 21, the *Essex* put up its first fighter sweep, and Commander McCampbell, not precisely in accord with the wishes of the admiral, led it.

The first target was San Jose Airfield on Mindoro Island. On the way, Commander McCampbell saw a Japanese freighter at anchor, and warned the strike that was following them. Over Tablas Island, looking for airfields, McCampbell's combat team was attacked by a pair of those old-fashioned biplanes (Nates), which were no match for F6Fs under any conditions. The Japanese pilots must have known, but word had come from Imperial General Headquarters that the invasion of the Philippines was to be met by the Sho 1 Operation, and that every man was to do his utmost for emperor and country. Consequently, the Japanese of all services were fired up to a point very near hysteria, and acts of extreme (even if irrational) valor were common from this point forward.

McCampbell's official report of the incident reflects the tone with which the Americans viewed the attack: "two Nates, both of which were quickly disposed of. . . ."

McCampbell shot down one Nate, and his wingman, Lieutenant Rushing, shot down the other. Then McCampbell spotted a twin-engined scout plane, gave chase and overhauled it and shot it down as well.

Meanwhile, the other fighters were becoming engaged with enemy aircraft. Lieutenant Crittenden and Lieutenant (jg) A.C. Slack shot down a Sally (Mitsubishi heavy bomber), and then Lieutenant Slack found another army trainer (Nate) and shot it down. Ensign Minor A. Craig found a Dinah (Mitsubishi reconnaissance plane) and shot it down.

These were all observation planes or scout bombers or trainers, and most of them were army planes. The Japanese naval air force had not yet begun major operation against the American landings, possibly because the air force was in the midst of a change of command. Admiral Teraoka's performance had not been regarded in Tokyo as adequate to assure victory in the air during the Sho 1 operation. From Tokyo, Imperial General Headquarters sent Vice Admiral Takajiro Ohnishi, a valued member of the staff and a tried operational officer, to survey and take over the naval air forces in the Philippines. He had actually arrived a few days earlier and was making the survey when the first moves came against Suluan Island. He was aghast to learn that instead of the 500 or 600 planes he had expected to find on the fields, the naval air force totaled fewer than 100 aircraft. With these he was supposed to support the desperate naval gambit of the next week and win victory!

Soon the *Essex* fighters and bombers of the air strike followed the fighter sweep to the area. They joined planes of the *Lexington* to knock out shipping and air bases in the western Visayan Islands. Their first target was the freighter McCampbell had reported off Romblon Island. Several fighters swooped down to strafe the freighter and left it burning.

Lieutenant Brodhead led the Helldivers on this mission. They had been instructed to hit shipping in the Coron Bay area, and they were carrying single 1,000-pound bombs. When they arrived in the area, the strike leader (Commander Winters) assigned the *Essex* bombers to two cargo ships. They made glide attacks, since they were using 5-second delayed action fuses, and they sank one cargo ship and damaged the other. On the way out they strafed a smaller cargo ship.

While passing over a section of southern Luzon Island on the route, the fighters came across an airfield at Legaspi and strafed a number of planes they saw on the ground. They spotted some dummies, too—they were growing more sophisticated. But if they saw some planes, there must be other planes in the area, they concluded and radioed their findings back to the carrier. The next strike was sent out to hit the southern Luzon airfields.

Forty-three aircraft left the deck of the *Essex* on this raid. There were the usual abortions; on every mission one or two planes acted up and returned to the carrier before meeting the enemy. This day, one fighter and one dive bomber did not finish the mission, but forty-one planes hit four airfields. They found many covered revetments, whose contents would remain a mystery, and they saw more evidence than usual of Japanese camouflage. But the raid really was not very satisfactory, as Commander Mini's report indicates:

"The assigned target was Naga air field in southern Luzon. When no worthy targets were found there, the strike group was split and assigned other fields in the general area as targets. Eight VB [Helldivers] attacked Legaspi air field, damaging two buildings. Five attacked a hitherto unreported single strip, apparently non-operational, on Iahuy Island, where a metal hangar was destroyed and a small fuel dump fired. One VB unable to select [operate] diving flaps, joined VT [torpedo bombers] in attacking Antayan air field and damaged a barracks building. . . ."

For the next two days, the *Essex* was out of it. The Leyte battle-front was quiet. One disturbing report was made on the 21st about three Japanese planes that came diving in on Admiral Daniel Barbey's Northern Attack Force off Leyte, apparently bent on crashing into the ships. Two of the Japanese planes were shot down, but one did crash into the foremast of the Australian cruiser *Australia.*

The air action around the beachhead was minor, and was handled by the escort carriers. Admiral Sherman's task group fueled, searched for the enemy fleet that was supposed to be coming out of the north, and waited. The airmen of the *Essex* had a little rest.

The Japanese official history shows that, by October 21, the naval air force was almost entirely moribund. Intelligence was a major problem. Everywhere the Japanese search planes went, it seemed, they found the American carriers, and this was most confusing. The 21st was the day when the war in the air also changed character: Admiral Ohnishi sent up his first kamikaze suicide plane (the plane was never seen again), and from that moment the 5th Base Air Force ceased to exist as a conventional air unit.

The army had not yet been reduced to such desperate straits. That day, it put seventeen planes into Leyte Gulf to attack the enemy fleet, and they claimed to have destroyed one transport and two destroyers with direct hits; two carriers were also "near missed," they said. This report of course did not agree at all with American reports. One reason was probably that the Japanese army fliers were even less experienced at reporting their activities accurately than the new Japanese navy pilots.

But the result was calamitous for the high command, engendering an optimism that was totally misplaced.

On October 22, as the airmen of the *Essex* waited, air activity was at a low key on both sides. About fifty American carrier planes attacked Cebu, the Japanese reported, and elsewhere about fifty land-based American heavy bombers and a number of medium bombers also struck at widely separated targets. The Japanese were still confused by the many sightings of American carriers in disparate positions. They had not yet come to grips with the fact that Admiral Halsey's Third Fleet was scattered at the moment, and that there existed an entirely separate force of carriers, eighteen escort carriers, that were in close support of the invasion forces.

At 8:07 on the morning of October 22, for the first time the 5th Base Air Force learned of the existence of eighty transports off the Leyte coast. But even then, neither army nor navy managed to launch a major air attack during the entire day.

On October 23, the Japanese official war history shows, the Japanese high command was once again puzzled by the low level of American carrier action. They did not understand that the radio intelligence reports had let the Americans know that Sho 1 was in operation, and the American fleet was waiting for the arrival of the Japanese Imperial Navy.

The American army already had matters well in hand on Leyte, and the landings were secure, barring some disaster which could only come from Japanese air or naval forces. After the Formosa battle, the naval air forces were in no position to make such attack, because back in Tokyo the belief persisted that the American carriers had been sorely hurt and did not constitute a major threat, and because the heavy losses of the Formosa air battle would take some time to repair. More planes and more pilots had to be brought together and then moved across the island chain that was becoming ever more dangerous. In the meantime, the defenders would have to work with what they had; a handful of navy planes, and several hundred army planes that were far less effective.

Admiral Ohnishi did schedule a kamikaze attack by the 5th Base Air Force on October 23, but because of bad weather he called it back. A Japanese search plane that morning sighted two battleships, four cruisers, and eight transports inside Leyte Gulf, but by then it was too late. Operations had already been suspended.

What everyone was waiting for—both sides—was the appearance of the Japanese fleet. In the early hours of the morning of October 23, Admiral Kurita was leading the main force of the Japanese fleet to attack the Americans by coming south of Luzon Island and then skirting down along the coast of Samar Island. His ships were in the Palawan Passage when American submarines torpedoed the cruisers *Atago, Takao,* and *Maya,* just as if going bang, bang, bang! Since the *Atago* was the flagship of the task force, the whole force was thrown into confusion because the *Atago was* sinking. Of the three, only the *Takao* survived, and she had to go home for repairs.

On the night of October 23, Admiral Halsey had many reports of different Japanese naval units at different places. The reports were confusing, there was no doubt about that. Nothing would be better than to have an actual sighting by a plane from the task force, and, for the early morning operations of October 24, Halsey made sure the search planes were out, ranging far and wide, and out early.

On the afternoon of October 23, fully expecting the arrival of the Imperial fleet, which would proceed to destroy the enemy transports, Japanese army commanders in the southern area, including those of the 2nd Air Division, held a meeting, and then went back to their units with the orders from Imperial General Headquarters. They called their subordinate officers together and made plans for the next day, which, Imperial General Headquarters said, was to see the route of the enemy and turn the war around. On October 24 a general attack would begin, and that meant cooperative effort by army and navy to secure an immediate victory.

Operation Victory (Sho 1) would begin with a general land, air, and sea assault, just after morning light.

The Imperial Japanese Naval Air Force's first attack group, which was to start the assault on the enemy aircraft carriers the next morning, consisted of several coordinated units. First there was the Air Mastery Squadron, which on the night of October 23 comprised fifty-four Zero fighters, and twenty-eight torpedo bombers. The other units of the attack force were the 1st Attack Squadron, consisting of six bomb-carrying Zeros, and the No. 2 Special Attack Squadron, which meant kamikaze—ten Zeros loaded with dynamite. Besides those, the attack would include the No. 3 Protective Squadron of fifty-one Zeros and the No. 3 Bombardment Squadron with thirty-eight bombers.

Admiral Sherman's task group had been pinpointed, and at dawn it was toward this group that the 1st Attack Group headed from the Manila airfields at Mabalacat and Bamu Bamu.

The debacle began at 6:35 in the morning at Mabalacat Airfield, when the fighter sweep took off—and the ten planes from Bamu Bamu Field that were supposed to join up got behind. Then the Tenzan (torpedo plane) and kamikaze units took off at 8:30, with the bombardment squadron. By this time the interval between the units was large and growing constantly greater.

By the time they reached the sea, the units were in complete disarray; and at Polillo Island, for some reason, only the bombers turned to the northeast. At that point, the bombardment group was still behind the protective fighters, but again, for some reason, the bombers went straight in toward their targets. The fighter sweep that was supposed to pave the way for the bombers never appeared at all. The units stuck together, but no unit had any liaison with any other.

Lieutenant Commander Jitsu Kobayashi was the overall air group commander this morning. He was out in front with his division of Zeros, and the Air Mastery Squadron, the No. 3 Protective Squadron, the No. 3 Bombardment Squadron and the No. 2 Special Attack Squadron (kamikazes) were flying in formation, when they encountered about fifty planes from an American carrier group and fighting began.

Lieutenant Commander Kobayashi was shot down, and Captain Fuchi Oshi, commander of the Protective Squadron, took over, rallied the planes to disengage from the fighting, and headed them out toward the carriers, which had been located ninety degrees east of Manila, 150 kilometers out at sea. They moved in. At 8:07, the *Essex* radar screen blacked up with pips.

That was when Commander McCampbell (after some initial confusion) joined his six-man fighter force from the *Essex* as the first fighters from Admiral Sherman's task group to intercept the Japanese strike. They found the enemy off Polillo Island and hit them as described on pp. 1 and 2. The fighting was fierce. McCampbell shot down at least nine enemy planes that day, and his wingman, Lieutenant Rushing, shot down six. Lieutenant Black, who came to help them with the job, shot down five before he ran out of ammunition and had to quit.

Lieutenant Crittenden led the second division of five planes that peeled off to go after the torpedo bombers down on the deck. Lieutenant Crittenden shot down five bombers, and Lieutenant (jg) W.A. Lundin shot down a bomber and a Zero. Lieutenant E.B. West destroyed two Zeros, and Ensign McGraw shot down one bomber.

Another part of the force that assailed Lieutenant Commander Kobayashi's attack group was the *Essex*'s combat air patrol of sixteen F6Fs—not all of them operating at once, but up and down. Lieutenant Morris led eight planes off at 10:50, when the fighting was getting hot. One fighter's engine began to miss, and that pilot went back to the carrier, but the other six continued after Morris.

Just before the combat air patrol took off, one of the planes from the No. 3 Bombardment Squadron scored against the Americans. The sky was overcast and squally that day, and the Japanese attack force had difficulty keeping together. When they came to within sight of the carriers, the bombers separated from the fighters, which remained above, and that is how Commander McCampbell and the others found them.

Most of the bombers rushed in, either to destruction or to dropping and escaping through the overcast. But one lurked in the clouds high above the carrier force, watching the carriers make wide, sweeping turns and moving through squalls. When the air action had moved elsewhere, and the sky above the carrier group seemed clear, suddenly out of a cloud appeared the one bomber which cropped a 250-kilogram (550-pound) bomb on the flight deck of the *Princeton*, which had just recovered its combat air patrol. The bomb penetrated the ship's interior and did an enormous amount of damage because it started fires in the torpedo storage room and the torpedoes began to explode and blow up parts of the ship.

Lieutenant Morris and his six companions circled over the task force, giving special attention to the damaged *Princeton*, which was already pouring out smoke. Three fighters were vectored out to meet a new part of the attack force that was coming in—about thirty planes. When they saw the Americans, the dive bombers and torpedo bombers broke off and ducked away, while the "rats" (fighters) formed a Lufbery circle and went around, nose to tail. This was a standard maneuver for the Japanese fighters in the Philippines; the purpose was to draw enemy fighter attention to the Zeros (they were all Zeros this time, Morris noted). That way, the dive bombers and torpedo bombers were given a better chance to slip through the screen.

In fact, Morris was giving the enemy more credit than they deserved for planning, because as Japan's official war historians would late note, the attack that day was a fiasco from start to finish.

Admiral Fukudome, considering the matter of attacking the enemy fleet on this first day of the Sho 1 operation, decided to undertake a mass daytime attack with 180 aircraft. Because of this decision only the kamikaze units were to attack singly; virtually all of the 6th Base Air Force was committed to the daytime mass raid. This new policy was begun on October 23. On October 24, it ended ignominiously.

Fukudome's theory was that, with a force of 180 planes, the group attack would overwhelm the enemy. The theory was appropriate if all worked as planned; but as it turned out, the air strength as presented was weak, and the plan failed.

These were the conclusions reached by the Japanese Self Defense Agency historians years later, based on wartime diaries, action reports, and interviews with survivors. The problem from the beginning was disorganization; for example, the 99th Bombardment Group's No. 3 Bombardment Squadron was eighty kilometers behind its protectors, and the kamikaze unit's protective fighters somehow fell sixty kilometers behind the suicide planes.

If the bombers could have come in from high altitude on the American carriers and executed their mission, there was a good chance of inflicting serious damage. But the fact was that the fighters did absolutely nothing to protect the bombers. Not a single fighter squadron went in to attack the enemy.

The American fighters caught them in this situation, and the opportunity to affect the outcome of the struggle was lost. The principal factor in all this, according to the participants who survived, was the bad weather; deserted by its goddess of good luck the attack group of the 6th Base Air Force that day turned its back on confrontation with the enemy. The fighter sweep did not live up to its responsibility, and the No. 3 Bombardment Squadron was slack.

To be sure, said the Japanese historian, there was a problem of limited visibility, with towering thunderheads rising to 11,000 meters (30,000 feet), but over Manila that day, there was heavy cloud cover, too, and yet after a while it lifted. So 180 planes, a large battle force, went out to meet the enemy and did not succeed, and the remnants came home claiming that weather conditions were responsible. (The historian's tone indicates that it was hardly the weather at all.)

Lieutenant Morris and his fellow fighter pilots saw this disintegration in action, with the Japanese fighters staying high and going into a defensive circle, and the bombers breaking off to go it alone in the face of American fighters and the deadly anti-aircraft barrage put up by the ships. Morris, like Commander McCampbell, did not concern himself with the logic of the Japanese. He was too busy shooting them down.

As the Japanese fighters moved in their Lufberry circle, Lieutenant Morris led his four plane division to attack. Four bombers broke out and sped for the deck, and as the Americans came up, the Japanese broke off into two plane sections. Morris chose the leader of one Zero section, made a high side run, and saw four bursts strike the Zero. It flamed up, and crashed.

His wingman broke off just then to chase one of the four bombers that slipped out of the Lufberry circle, and shot it down, then rejoined. Morris then made a pass at a pair of Zeros coming toward him. He missed on that first pass and turned, to find the Zeros turning with him and firing shots that were hitting his aircraft. He tried to turn with the Zeros for a few seconds, but then saw that he was not going to win that way, and ducked into a cloud. He was beginning to have a fine respect for those pilots—"part of the first team," he later reported.

Inside his cloud, Lieutenant Morris made a 360-degree turn, and came back out where he had gone in. The two Zeros were circling out toward the other side where he could be expected to come out, and he got on the tail of one, and in a few seconds shot it down. By this time the damage done by the Japanese fighters to Morris's plane in that brief dogfight began to tell. The engine began to cough, and when Morris looked down in the cockpit he saw hydraulic fluid, which meant trouble. He broke off the action and headed back toward the *Essex.*

Lieutenant (jg) J.B. Bare had gone up high above the Japanese Lufberry circle, and he kept coming down, making passes at planes as he did. He saw a Zero on the tail of an F6F and made a pass, which caused the Zero to break away. He got on the tail of another Zero and saw it fall off in a spin after making a split-S, and then go smoking into the sea.

The fight was moving south, but off to one side, Bare saw one F6F moving toward three Zeros. The F6F turned into the Zeros and they split. The F6F got on the tail of one, and Bare got on the tail of another that did a wingover and got on the first America pilot's tail. He shot that plane down, then found himself bracketed by a pair of Zeros; he turned into one and shot his way out of the trap.

Lieutenant Twelves saw a Jill straggling after the original formation and attacked. The Jill exploded with a mightly roar. Either it was a torpedo bomber and he had hit the torpedo (which was likely, since the aircraft was a Nakajima B6N Navy torpedo plane) or it was a kamikaze. Two Zeros then started down on Twelves, so he put on full power to join Lieutenant Morris up above. They got above the Zero group and began pouncing down on them from above. Twelves made a quick run on one Zero and fired a handful of shots, then was past, firing into another Zero. The first Zero went out of control and spun in and so did the second.

The majority of Zeros were still trying to keep the Lufberry circle going, and Twelves hung on the edge, waiting for a plane to get a little behind. But his plane had been shot up during his earlier exertions, and his oil lines were in trouble. One of them gave way and spattered oil all over his windshield so that he could see only dimly around the edges. He broke off and was led back to the *Essex* by another F6F.

Above the *Princeton,* other planes of the *Essex* fighter squadron flew protection, as captain and crew of the stricken carrier tried to save it. The Japanese sent more torpedo bombers to try to get at the *Princeton* again, but these American fighters protected the ship. Lieutenant (jg) N.B. Voorhest found one Aichi dive bomber above the carrier getting ready to make a dive at 19,000 feet. Voorhest climbed and attacked, the Judy went into a shallow dive, and then crashed.

Ensign W.R. Johnson saw a torpedo bomber off to one side, and went after it. He stayed with the plane as it dived for the deck and finally shot it down just above the water.

Lieutenant (jg) W.N. Anderson saw a two-engined heavy Nakajima bomber (of the No. 3 Bombardment Squadron) and chased it at 2,000 feet. He caught the slower bomber and began pouring shots into the wing root and starboard engine, trying to hit the gas tanks. The bomber went into the water at an angle and exploded. One parachute was seen trailing out on the sea, but there were no survivors.

After Commander McCampbell took off from the *Essex* that morning with the seven fighters of the "emergency squad," he climbed high and the others followed. There was a good deal of trouble with radio frequencies, and before anyone knew, Lieutenant Strane and four other fighters moved down to 18,000 feet while Commander McCampbell and Lieutenant Rushing moved on to 25,000 feet and encountered the big Lufberry circle there.

Strane got out of touch with the others and did not see any aircraft to attack until he was close to the ship formation. There at 5,500 feet, he found a lone Zero heading back toward Manila. The clouds were very thick at 5,000 and 6,000 feet, and Strane feared that before he could get down (he was at 9,000 feet) the Zero would duck into cloud cover. But the Zero pilot did not see the F6F, and Strane came down fast, got on the plane's tail, and shot down the Japanese fighter. First the stabilizer and parts of the wing flew off, and then the pilot decided the end had come and bailed out. His parachute opened and he drifted toward the water. Strane saw a destroyer come over to pick up the Japanese pilot, but he never discovered whether or not the man was rescued.

By this time the fight was over, and the American planes were heading back toward the *Essex*. The great group attack of the Japanese first air striking force had nearly completely failed—though not quite, because the *Princeton* kept burning, the fires grew worse, and later in the day she had to be abandoned and finally sunk by an American ship.

Meanwhile, the Japanese remnants of the formidable air armada straggled back to their Manila-area bases.

The story of Lieutenant Commander Yasushi Ema, published several years after the war in Japan, gives an indication of the Japanese difficulties. Commander Ema was commander of the No. 3 Bombardment Squadron. He took off from the Clark Field complex and joined the force orbiting above, which was to head as a unit toward the enemy. But almost immediately, the engine of the leader of the protective fighters began to act up and the fighters began to lag behind the bombers. An hour passed and they did not catch up.

By the time the bombers got to land's end and passed over the sea, the fighters were far behind, and it was not long before enemy fighters jumped the unescorted bombers from the rear and from above. Ema led his division in the attack on the carriers, which they could see, but they were totally exposed to the enemy fighters. Two or three American fighters started the attack, and immediately one plane began to flame ("like a potbellied stove"). It then went into a dive and broke up in the air.

Lieutenant Commander Ema was one of the next to feel the sting of the F6Fs. An enemy attacked and shot up his left wing so badly that the aileron refused to respond. He could still fly and he jettisoned his belly tank. Just then fire broke out in the plane, and it went into a tailspin. He was sure he was going to crash. Perhaps because of the speed, however, the fire went out, and he managed to recover and level off at 2,500 feet. He started home, nursing his damaged aircraft, and was again attacked by American fighters, but got away, with many holes in the bomber, by ducking into the cloud cover that appeared almost miraculously.

He tried to radio his situation back to the base, but by this time gasoline fumes had penetrated the cockpit and nearly choked him so he could not speak. Somehow he made it back to the Clark base complex and landed. In retrospect, he considered the entire attack a complete blunder, which meant the sacrifice of most of the attack unit to the enemy's fighters. From the beginning the attack was disjointed, and the Americans had their own way in the air. The confusion was complete. By the time Ema returned to his base, the others who had come down before were already talking about his crash and giving him posthumous credit for having dived his plane into the enemy in a suicidal gesture.

In Admiral Sherman's task group, major emphasis that day was on protecting and saving the *Princeton* and preventing the enemy from reaching the other carriers. In the latter effort, the force was successful; the combat air patrol and other fighters sent out to help chased away another major air attack later in the day from Admiral Ozawa's carrier force, one of the four fleet units sent out to win the "decisive battle" for Japan on this crucial day.

Most of the carrier planes were busy on other business, however, and for most of the *Essex* pilots that was an attack on Admiral Kurita's main battle force, which had come up south of Luzon in spite of its mishaps of the day before, to try to go through San Bernardino Strait and attack the American landing force from the north, down along Samar, to Leyte. That morning of October 24, Admiral Kurita's ships were discovered in the Sibuyan Sea, just about to turn into Tablas Strait. The attack on these Japanese ships was begun in mid-morning by planes from other task groups.

During all the morning, the *Essex* had been on the alert. At 10:15, a twin-engined bomber broke through the combat air patrol screen and came down on the formation to attack the *Langley*. This Betty bomber was pursued by an F6F which dared the anti-aircraft fire of the ships to come in. But the AA guns got the Betty in the end, and it crashed between the *Essex* and the *Langley*. They nearly got the F6F, too, until it banked and waggled its wings to show its markings.

The next raid came twenty minutes later; five Japanese bombers moved in fast, but two were shot down and the other three chased off before they could drop torpedoes or bombs. Another raid came at 11:00. The *Essex* was preparing a strike. In some ways, it seems a wonder that the beleaguered carrier could mount a strike.

Admiral Sherman's first strike was launched at 10:53 on the morning of the 24th and discovered two groups of Japanese ships, totaling twenty-six vessels in all, about three miles apart. Ten *Essex* Helldivers were involved in that strike and two of them, Lieutenant (jg) Matthews and Lieutenant (jg) Parrish, found the *Musashi,* one of the world's two largest battleships (her sister ship, the *Yamato,* was the other). They each put a bomb into her. Commander Mini, Lieutenant (jg) Nelson, and Lieutenant (jg)

Fontaine scored hits on the *Nagato*, a battleship. Someone hit the *Yamato* twice. Lieutenant (jg) Kelley found a cruiser and bombed it.

Very noticeable on this attack was something the bombing pilots were not used to: heavy and accurate anti-aircraft fire. Commander Mini was hit hard and barely made it back to the carrier group; even so, he could not get aboard the *Essex*, but had to land in the water and was picked up by a destroyer.

The main *Essex* strike got off at 12:59 p.m., consisting of eight fighters and a dozen Helldivers. The *Essex* pilots went after the big ships. There was some confusion because both the *Yamato* and *Musashi* were in action that day, and several pilots reported hitting battleships of this class, but which one was not quite certain at the time. The *Musashi* was the ship that took the beating, and finally the combined efforts of the planes of Task Force 38 sank her that evening. The fighters were bombers that day, dropping from 2,500 feet. The dive bombers were carrying 1,000-pound bombs.

Like the Japanese pilots of the first attack group, the American pilots had trouble with the weather and had to change course many times to get away from heavy cloud cover. But unlike the Japanese, they did not let the weather deter them from their mission. All of the *Essex* dive bombers went after the *Musashi* with their 1,000-pound bombs. While still out of range they were taken under fire by the ships below, and the fire never slackened. All the planes were bounced around, and that of Lieutenant (jg) Conrad W. Crellin took a direct hit just after he had dropped his bomb (it hit the battleship and contributed to her later sinking). The Helldiver burst into flames and crashed near the enemy ships, and Crellin and his gunner, E.E. Shetler, were both killed.

At the time of these air strikes, the Japanese main attack force was steaming along on the Sibuyan Sea, about twenty miles north of Tablas Island. Late in the afternoon, Admiral Kurita turned his fleet around and radioed Admiral Toyoda in Tokyo that he had been under heavy attack by more than 250 planes, and that the *Musashi* was sinking. The implication was that things were very bad and that Admiral Toyoda ought to order them home to safety.

But Toyoda had no such intention, and after some hours of vacillation Admiral Kurita remembered that he had a rendezvous with two other Japanese naval forces in Leyte Gulf in the next morning. Coming from the Dutch East Indies through the Sulu Sea was Admiral Shoji Nishimura, with a heavy cruiser force and two battleships. Coming along from Japan with a force of cruisers and destroyers was Admiral Kiychidei Shima. Like three packs of wolves, they were all supposed to meet at the point where the Americans were standing off the beaches, and massacre the enemy, destroy all the transports and support ships, and then watch as the army pushed the helpless American soldiers into the sea.

So with this vision in his head, Admiral Kurita turned around again and headed for San Bernardino Strait.

That afternoon of October 24, search planes sighted a Japanese carrier force coming down on the outside of Luzon Island. This was Admiral Ozawa's contribution to the Sho 1 plan; his force of carriers were "paper tigers," carriers with virtually no aircraft aboard and incapable of giving more than a token blow to the enemy. In fact, Admiral Ozawa had already very nearly shot his wad with the abortive air strike he launched that day to assist in the destruction of the American carrier fleet. None of his planes got through, apparently, and very few of them made it back to the carriers. But that was never the point: the Japanese had made of Ozawa a sacrificial lamb in reality (unlike Lieutenant Commander Ema, who was a sacrificial lamb because of Admiral Fukudome's blunder in strategy).

In the Sho plan it was quite clear that Admiral Ozawa's force was to decoy the American carriers into an attack, thus keeping them away from the surface units coming south and east to destroy the transports at Leyte. In retrospect, some historians have indicated that the Japanese figured Halsey would be the commander and thus the U.S. force would be easy to dupe. But that could not have been true, because the Sho plan was drawn in its essence (the decoy part) long before the Japanese could have known who would be in charge of the fleet on that particular day. No, the Japanese tactic was simply good sense on their part, and if Admiral Kurita had not spent half a day milling about in confusion under American attack, and if Admiral Fukudome had not committed his major resources to a fiasco, then they might have gotten further with it. But if, if, if—if wishes were victories then the Japanese would have won the war. The fact was that as of October, 1944, the Japanese Imperial Navy had very little use for its carriers. It had planes, but an enormous shortage of pilots. Before the war, and in the beginning, the average Japanese naval pilot had seven years of training behind him. Nearly all these skilled men were gone and the Japanese training program had never responded to the exigencies of the war the way the American program did.

Once an American carrier air group had served its six-month stint in the line, it was returned to the United States, for leave. Then, a third of the group's personnel were retained in that air group, as a cadre to train newcomers; a third were reassigned to other combat units, strengthening them; and a third were assigned to training programs. Thus, for example, Commander McCampbell, having served as landing signal officer of the carrier *Wasp* at the time she was sunk off Guadalcanal in 1942, was sent home as an instructor at a fighter pilot school at Melbourne, Florida. There he was able to give young pilots a first-hand view of the deadly Zero and Japanese air tactics. After a stint there, he went back into combat.

In contrast, take the story of Saburo Sakai, Japan's leading aviator to survive the war. The only reason he survived was that he was so badly shot up during the Guadalcanal air battle that he had to be invalided home. Meanwhile, other pilots who were as good or better remained in the battle zone long after fatigue had set in and fell in combat.

There was another reason for the Japanese willingness to sacrifice the remaining carriers. After Saipan, the battle zone had moved almost to the shores of inner empire, and there were plenty of air bases on the islands. The carriers really were not needed any more.

On the afternoon of October 24, when the American pilots came back to Halsey's carriers to report that Admiral Kurita had turned his ships around and was heading west in the general direction of Manila or Japan, Halsey ceased to worry much about San Bernardino Strait. It seemed clear that the Japanese had taken a disastrous blow that day. Then, when a search plane sighted a Japanese carrier force 200 miles east of the northeast tip of Luzon, all three of Halsey's operating task groups (McCain's was just coming back from the Ulithi area) were ordered to find and destroy the enemy, and the battleships and cruisers of the Third Fleet were formed into a separate task force that was assigned to seek a surface battle with the battleships and cruisers accompanying Admiral Ozawa's carriers.

During the early morning hours of October 25, a night fighter from the *Independence* found the Japanese force, and the alert was on.

Just before 6:00 in the morning the first strike against the carrier force was launched by the *Essex*. Four fighters were detached from the combat air patrol and sent streaking out to find the Japanese fleet for the strike, and at 7:10 that morning they did so. The discoverer was Lieutenant (jg) Homer Voorhest of the Helldiver squadron, who was flying an F6F that day as a fighter-bomber pilot. He saw two battleships, four carriers, five cruisers, and half a dozen destroyers. Lieutenant Collins, the leader of the flight, stayed high and observed the Japanese fleet until he ran low on fuel. By that time the air strike had come in.

Leader of the air strike was Commander McCampbell; the strike force consisted of 101 planes from the carriers *Essex, Lexington,* and *Langley.* When the location of the enemy was confirmed, McCampbell's planes were only fifty miles from the Japanese, orbiting and awaiting instructions. It did not take them long to close and attack. First down came ten fighters, carrying 500-pound bombs. They dropped and scurried away, low on the water, strafing as they went. The anti-aircraft fire was intense and accurate. Commander McCampbell and Lieutenant Rushing stayed high, to cover the attack, and McCampbell served as target coordinator for the attack of his force and also for the second air strike, from other carriers.

During this first strike, one Japanese carrier did launch about twenty Zeros, and the F6Fs went after them. Lieutenant Strane saw them first, half a dozen Zeros at 9,000 feet, above the American dive bombers. The Zeros moved to attack the bombers, and Strane led his planes to attack the Zeros. On Strane's first burst he knocked down a Zero. Then Strane saw his wingman start a diving turn to the left, and as Strane's plane rolled over saw two Zeros firing at his wingman; he got into an excellent position above the two Zeros and shot them both down. Then, looking around for his wingman or some other F6F on which to join up, Strane found himself in a whole flight of Zeros.

He turned into the first one, fired, and saw smoke and flames, but he did not see a crash because by that time another Zero was attacking him, making a high run from dead ahead. He tried to pull away, but the Zero put some 20mm shells into his engine, and the power failed. Then the plane caught fire behind the engine, and Strane bailed out, giving his position over the radio, which still worked, although another Zero was shooting at him and knocked off the whole instrument panel.

Strane's F6F was at 2,500 feet when he parachuted. His parachute caught on the rim of the cockpit for a moment, then came loose, and he was away. Two Zeros circled, and so he refrained from pulling the rip cord so he would not be shot down while dangling from the parachute. He almost waited too long; he pulled, the 'chute opened, made one swing, and he splashed into the water. He went down and swallowed a lot of salt water. Then he came up and got into his raft, and after giving the salt water back to the sea, he settled down to wait, hopefully, for rescue.

At first, he fired some flare cartridges from his Very pistol, but the sun was too bright, and the planes above did not see him. He settled down then to watch, as about 350 planes, by his count, attacked the enemy ships.

Lieutenant (jg) C. White was also turning above the Helldivers when three Zeros appeared, attacking. He pulled up and fired at one head-on, the Zero flamed and crashed. White then dropped the nose of his F6F to regain speed and saw a Zero directly ahead of him. He began shooting, the Zero began to come apart in mid-air, and spun off on a wing and crashed.

Lieutenant (jg) R.E. Foltz was climbing when he saw his first Zero. He turned so sharply he nearly went into a spin, but recovered, shot down one Zero, and then began chasing another.

Lieutenant Singer shot down one Zero, went after another that was making a Chandelle turn, and saw pieces fly off. His wingman then started after four other Zeros; he followed. One got on his tail, and he saw tracers come by beneath his wing. He made a snap right turn to get away, but the Zero was right after him, and then joined by another. Singer managed to get a long deflection shot at the second Zero, and it began to smoke, but he didn't see what happened because he was to busy trying to get away from the first Zero. He dove from 7,000 to 3,000 feet, and pulled out violently to the right. His windshield fogged up, but around the edge he could see a Zero coming straight at him; he fired, and the Zero blew up nearly in his face.

The Helldivers were led in by Lieutenant John David Bridgers and hearing Commander McCampbell's directions, they attacked a carrier of the *Chitose* class. They dropped twelve 1,000-pound bombs on the carrier and made eight hits. By the time they finished the attack the carrier was burning fiercely and listing.

For the first time in the war, the *Essex* torpedo planes had a real chance. The attack of the *Essex* dive bombers on the carrier had been so effective that Commander McCampbell, who had previously instructed the torpedo planes to attack the same ship, canceled the order and directed them to one of the battleships instead, on the starboard side of the Japanese formation. Lieutenant Commander Lambert then split his force so half could attack from each side. However, four of the TBFs had already committed themselves to attacking the carrier and they did. They scored at least two hits. By the time the planes began retiring at the end of the strike, this carrier sank. The other pilots attacked the battleships, and Lieutenant (jg) L.G. Muskin, Lieutenant J.G. Huggins, and Ensign Kenneth B. Horton all claimed hits.

Lieutenant (jg) H.D. Jolly dropped his torpedo against the *Ise*-class battleship. So did Ensign D.J. Ward and Lieutenant (jg) J. Smyth. Two geysers sprang up alongside the ship.

Lieutenant Charles W. Sorensen and Lieutenant (jg) L.R. Timberlake dropped their torpedoes against another carrier and one of them hit amidships. And the last two pilots, Lieutenant Commander Lambert and Lieutenant (jg) S.M. Holladay, dropped against a carrier, which turned just right for them as they were zeroing in on the battleship. Lambert got a hit, and Holladay thought he did too.

The flak was very thick all around the Japanese ships, and as the torpedo bombers came out of the attack, a group of Zeros moved in to attack, but once more the superior formation technique of the Americans saved them. The torpedo planes closed up on each other, which meant the tail gunners could give a good account of themselves, and the Zeros decided not to attack.

As the *Essex* attack ended, Lieutenant Strane was still in the water in his raft, waiting for rescue and trying to attract attention with his mirror and his Very pistol. But nothing happened. The planes went home—to be replaced immediately by a whole new set of aircraft from other carriers, which did the same sort of attacking, with bombs, strafing, and torpedoes, against the hapless Japanese decoys. Again the attack was under the supervision of Commander McCampbell, who circled the action and gave directions, performing masterfully what Sherman insisted was his task.

The pressure on the Japanese fleet was never-ending. By the time the second strike had completed its destructive work, the third strike was coming in, again from the *Essex,* the *Lexington* and the *Langley.* Ninety-eight planes arrived this time, Commander Winters of the *Lexington* was the air coordinator this time, Commander McCampbell having flown back to the *Essex* for gas. The *Essex* contingent was led out by Lieutenant Commander Duncan.

They found Admiral Ozawa's fleet retiring to the north, leaving the cripples behind. But the cripples could be taken care of by the surface fleet and submarines, so the carrier planes went after the undamaged ships. Since Commander Mini was somewhere at sea, pacing up and down the deck of a destroyer, Lieutenant Roger Noyes was in charge of the Helldivers.

They were given a *Chitose*-class carrier on the west side of the Japanese disposition. Six planes attacked the carrier, which swung around to the southeast to avoid the bombs. The four TBFs carrying torpedoes were also assigned to that ship. They attacked, and several bombs and torpedoes from the *Essex* group and from others hit the ship. As they left the scene, the target coordinator reported the vessel sinking.

Nine Helldivers from the *Essex* attacked the *Zuikaku,* the pride of the Pearl Harbor attack fleet that had come on evil days. She had already been hit hard by previous strikes and seemed to be laboring in the water as she maneuvered to escape—quite fruitlessly. It did not help when Lieutenant H.A. Goodwin and Ensign A.R. Hodges dropped 2,000-pound blockbusters that struck squarely on the carrier's flight deck. As they pulled up, their gunners could see the holes in the deck with flames pouring through.

Lieutenant Noyes ran into trouble as he began pulling out from his bombing dive. The anti-aircraft fire followed the pattern of the Japanese navy: intense and accurate, and Noyes was hit. His bomb bay was still open. Flame shot out from both wings, and it appeared that the Helldiver was a casualty. The shock sent the plane into a vertical right bank, and Noyes let it go and dropped almost down to the water to gain speed. He went so fast and so far that several of his pilots swore he had crashed.

But, as with Lieutenant Commander Ema, the gods of war were sitting on Noyes's shoulder; the speed put out the fire, and he pulled out of the dive and headed back for the *Essex,* limping along at 125 knots. The impact of the shell had severed the control cables to the port aileron and it was stuck in full left position; to compensate he had to use full aileron tab, rudder, and right stick to keep the plane on an even keel. The hydraulic system was in shambles, and he could not close the bomb bay doors or use flaps. But with all that drag the flaps weren't precisely a necessity. Somehow he got back all the way, got a wave-on, came in, and put the plane down on deck. After a good look, the air officer had it pushed overboard, "surveyed by the deep six method."

Late afternoon brought still another *Essex* strike on the remnants of the Japanese carrier fleet. Again with planes of the *Langley* and the *Lexington,* forty-one *Essex* fighters and bombers hurried to attack. This time the strike leader was Commander M.T. Wordell of the *Langley* air group. Also by this time, three of the four Japanese carriers had sunk, and the pickings were much slimmer. The fourth carrier was so badly damaged that Wordell assigned the bombers of the air strike to hit the two *Ise*-class battleships. The fighters strafed the battleships and other ships, and eight of the fifteen dive bombers scored hits.

One battleship was a conversion: in their earlier need for carriers, the Japanese had removed one turret and put in a short flight deck. The ship was as tough as any battleship, however, and although the *Essex* crowd said they put about fifteen bombs into her, and she almost stopped once, soon she was going again. The Japanese reported a somewhat different story: that all of the planes that attacked her on this raid, she had taken no hits and had thirty-four near misses. In fact, Admiral Ozawa's chief of staff had some unkind comment for the American bomber pilots: "I saw all this bombing and thought the American pilot is not so good."

Whatever their accuracy, the planes of Task Force 38 did sink four carriers and a destroyer that day, and the *Essex* team played its part. And late in the day, Lieutenant Strane was rescued by a destroyer of the surface force that had come up to the scene looking for crippled Japanese ships.

After the battle, and continuing long after the war ended, a dispute arose as to whether or not Admiral Halsey should have left San Bernardino Strait unguarded to go after the Japanese carrier force. The dispute was engendered by the actions of Admiral Kurita, who turned about from his retreat, on orders from Admiral Toyoda, went back into San Bernardino Strait, through the strait, and the next morning (October 25) descended on the American forces off Leyte. In the battle that followed, the escort carrier *Gambier Bay* was sunk by naval gunfire (the only aircraft carrier ever thus destroyed), and the destroyers *Johnston* and *Hoel* and the destroyer escort *Samuel B. Roberts* were also sunk.

But the Kurita fleet was routed and sent limping back through San Bernardino Strait once more, to be harried all the way back to Manila by American aircraft and submarines, and the whole point of the action was negated. Admiral Halsey never had much to say in the argument against his detractors, but his loyal staff and officers did, and they (with some notable exceptions) were strong in their belief that "given the information Halsey had about the situation of the Kurita fleet, his action was justified," as Commander McCampbell put it.

History may go farther in Halsey's defense in later years: at Admiral Kinkaid's disposal that day were eighteen escort carriers, which carried a total of 493 aircraft, and whose sole purpose for existence was support and protection of the landing. True, the *Chenango* and *Saginaw Bay* had left the area for Morotai on the evening of the 24th, which deprived the force of fifty-eight planes, and the successful attack on the *Gambier Bay* prevented her from getting off more than a few of her fighters. Even so, in the argument among historians and navy men, sight seemed to have been lost of the old Nelsonian theory that the object of a naval battle is to destroy the other fellow's ships.

In the end, the proof was in the pudding. At the small cost of one "jeep" carrier and three destroyer-type vessels, the battle was won, and both the airmen of the escort carriers and the men of the destroyers made it a glorious day for the U.S. Navy. In fact, the destroyer action of December 25, 1944, was the high point of the destroyer war and did much to erase the many blots on the copybook made in the days of Guadalcanal.

If the soft-hearted cringe at the thought of all those men maimed and killed, they forget that the purpose of war involves the constant risk of maiming and killing. Halsey was behaving in his own aggressive fashion, and by destroying the enemy force in the north he made sure it would not have to be done on another day. The *Gambier Bay* and the other ships of "Taffy Three" (the name of the command under Rear Admiral Clifton Sprague) were operated in the best tradition of the American naval service, and did the job they were supposed to do but had never before been called upon to perform.

CHAPTER THIRTEEN

The Battle for the Philippines

The Sho 1 operation had ended in total defeat for the Japanese. Their fleet no longer existed as such, and their air force in the Philippines was in tatters. The only significant new threat to the airmen after October 24 was something quite new, and very terrible and terrifying: the kamikaze attack by a handful of aircraft or only a single aircraft at a time; small, but deadly because of the determination of the Japanese pilots to die and sell their lives at as high a price as possible.

The kamikaze attack proved a threat that the U.S. Navy never did overcome; a special headquarters set up in Boston failed to solve the problem, and the airmen's solution—to knock out all the Japanese aircraft that came within flying distance of the naval operations, but hitting them at the source or airfield—was more successful but could never be totally so. (The Japanese capacity to produce aircraft was still remarkably high even at the date of the surrender aboard the battleship *Missouri*.) Fortunately for Japanese and Americans, the war ended before the suicide weapon was put into general use, as was planned.

But on October 25, the day that the airmen of the *Essex* were so busy destroying Admiral Ozawa's northern decoy force of carriers, one kamikaze got through the combat air patrol above the escort carriers in Leyte Gulf and dived on the deck of the *St. Lo*. The result was the sinking of this carrier by the single-handed effort of one man, with one bomb built into his aircraft. Fortunately for the American navy, the Japanese supply line for aircraft was not able to recover quickly enough to meet the demands of Admiral Onishi, the new commander of Japanes naval air forces in the Philippines, and so the Japanese kamikaze attacks were relatively few. To the airmen of the *Essex* they were mostly a matter of hearsay.

The conventional war in the Philippines still required the full concentration of the carrier pilots. On October 26, the *Essex* fueled. The next day, a dozen *Essex* fighters were sent on a fighter sweep over the Manila area to Coron Bay, to discover the state of Japanese air defenses. They ran into enemy aircraft.

The searches were made by three divisional teams of four planes each. The planes they encountered were all down low, around 2,000 feet, which suggested they were busy on administrative or observation affairs. (The Japanese often used twin-engined transports, the exact copy of the Betty twin-engined bomber, for these purposes.)

Lieutenant Morris led three other planes out on search of a pie-shaped wedge, a section 300 miles out from the carrier, from 250 degrees to 260 degrees. They flew out the 250-degree line, across the short side of the triangle at the 300-mile mark, and then back along the 260-degree line. They discovered six aircraft on the ground at Legaspi Airfield and strafed them. They also found a cargo ship off Burias Island, which they attacked with rockets and machine gun fire. Not far away they encountered a pair of destroyers, which they also attacked. Equally important, they brought back information for the air strike that was to follow.

Lieutenant Twelves led the next search group, which followed the 260-degree line out and the 270-degree line back. They found a number of cargo ships and naval vessels in Manila Bay, remainders of the enormous battle that had raged for the past two days. Then they ran into enemy aircraft. Lieutenant Deming encountered a Fran, a Nakajima navy bomber that was headed for several naval vessels not far from Cavite. He shot down the Fran, which took no evasive action.

Lieutenant Twelves went down low to strafe a cargo ship, and then saw a twin-engined Betty bomber and shot it down. The Betty exploded 500 feet above the water, and the empennage fell off first. Ensign Self discovered a Kate, a Nakajima torpedo plane, which was carrying a torpedo. Where it was going and what it was doing out here over Manila Bay, where there were no enemy ships, was a mystery that would not be solved because Self shot down the Kate, and it nosed over and carried its torpedo to the bottom of the bay.

On the way back to the *Essex,* this team also passed over Legaspi Airfield and stopped to strafe, probably working over the same planes that Morris's group had shot up.

Lieutenant White led the 270-degree-280-degree search. The first thing his division encountered was a PT boat west of Cautanduanos Island. They went down to look. The PT boat was supposed to have a big white star on the deck, but this one did not. It did have what appeared to be stars on the hull, port and starboard, so White gave the boat the benefit of the doubt and left it alone. This was a bit difficult since the PT boat fired at the aircraft orbiting around it with a pair of .50 calibre guns. But no one was hurt.

The F6Fs then encountered a pair of Betties at about 1,500 feet, and Ensign D.H. Gonya shot one down and Ensign J.H. Duffy shot down the other. On the way back to the *Essex,* one plane (coming back early because of engine trouble) saw a submarine crash dive, and radioed the *Essex* for instructions. The submarine was on the edge of the "safe" zone where American submarines were operating. The answer was delayed for a few minutes, and by the time the F6F was ordered to attack, the submarine was well down below the surface. The pilot dropped a bomb, but had no hope that it did anything more than kill a few fish.

Because the search that day was a long one, the admiral sent up four F6Fs to act as a "communications relay"; the idea being that the searchers' radio might not carry back to the base, so the relay teams could keep the *Essex* informed as to developments. Lieutenant Crittenden took his wingman out 100 miles, relayed communications and returned to the *Essex* without incident.

But Lieutenant (jg) T.N. Thompson and Lieutenant (jg) K.B. West had quite a different experience. They went out 200 miles to do the relays, and had just gotten on station, when West spotted a flock of "bogeys," at least thirty fighters and bombers. The odds were not good: a pair of F6Fs against at least a dozen enemy fighters. But Thompson and West's only reaction was to shout "Hey Rube" (the old circus cry for help that had been adopted by the American airmen), then to jettison their belly tanks and head toward the enemy formation, dropping their bombs as they went.

As was usual with the Japanese, even before coming to the target, the bombers and torpedo bombers were below, with the Zero fighters above them. Thompson chose the leader of the Zeros, climbed and attacked head-on, flamed the Zero and it crashed. He then continued on to attack the leader's wingman and saw smoke coming from the Zero's engine as it turned away.

By this time, Thompson had climbed up through the Zero formation and now turned back down to attack a formation of three enemy fighters. He saw the smoke start on one plane's engine after a long burst, but there was no time for "dogfighting." He used his speed to get back up and on the way met another Zero coming down. Once more he chose the head-on fight, and fired; the Zero burst into flame and the pilot bailed out.

At that point Thompson was beset by half a dozen Zeros and the action went so fast that he had no time to look around. It was fire, zoom, make sure no one was on his tail, gain altitude, make another pass, and find another target.

All this while Ensign West was flying Thompson's wing to protect him. That did not mean he had no chance to fire his guns. He saw a Zero coming, opened up, and the Zero began smoking and pulled away. On the next run he shot at a Zero, and the pilot bailed out. As he pulled up from that encounter he nearly ran into another Zero; he fired, and the Zero began to smoke and disappeared. One Zero then flew right between Thompson and West, and West fired at the plane as it went away. He did not see what happened to the Japanese plane.

All this furious activity by the Americans broke up the Japanese raid. Down below, the dive bombers, watching their escorts go down in flames one after the other, jettisoned their bombs and torpedoes and reversed course. While the pair were congratulating themselves, a Zero appeared out of the clouds, made a pass at West, and its bullets smashed an oil line and the windshield fuzzed up from the splatter and then became virtually black. West called Thompson and told him the problem, and they disengaged and headed back to the *Essex,* Thompson circling the damaged plane and warding off the attacks of half a dozen "rats" that followed them. One Kawasaki army fighter got on West's tail, but he turned on the water injection and sped away, and after a few minutes the Japanese fighters stopped following the American pair.

West made it all the way back, although he had to land on the *Lexington* while Thompson went back to the *Essex*. Just two *Essex* fighters had broken up a major air attack by the enemy on the carriers. The action had come so fast that they really had no idea of the number of planes damaged or shot down. Thompson claimed two Zeros destroyed and West claimed one, but that was the least of it. Their swift and really heroic action might have saved a ship that day.

The Japanese confusion was almost total, partly because Imperial General Headquarters chose that time (urged by stark necessity) to order combined army and navy air force operations in the Philippines. So on October 26 and 27, before the commands began to pull themselves together, almost everything that happened to the Japanese was disastrous. Actually, had they been able to pull themselves together on those two days, they might have struck some really serious blows against the American invasion, because Admiral Halsey was too far away to give support to the landings, and, for administrative reasons, the army air force was having difficulty getting planes into the Tacloban Airfield. Admiral Sherman's carriers, including the *Essex,* and Admiral Davison's carrier group were ordered to make the effort, but as Admiral Halsey radioed General MacArthur, "The pilots are exhausted and the carriers are low in provisions, bombs, and torpedoes. . . ."

On October 28, the *Essex* started back for Ulithi to pick up some of those needed supplies, some new aircraft, and to give the air crews a little respite from a grueling campaign. But if anyone believed they would get much of a rest, he was mistaken. They were recalled on October 30.

On the evening of November 1 came word that the Japanese were launching a new set of attacks at Leyte and that a force of four battleships, three cruisers, and three light cruisers was out, and might attack the transports off the Leyte beaches. Admiral Onishi had gotten his kamikaze forces together. Five suicide squadrons had been organized on October 27: the Chuyu (Loyalty and Bravery), Giretsu (Nobility of Soul), Seichu (Sincere Loyalty), Shisei (Devotion), and Yamato (Historic Japan). Immediately they began moving, and their attacks began.

While the *Essex* and the rest of her group were off in Ulithi, other carriers began to get hurt. On October 29, the *Intrepid* was hit by a kamikaze, with sixteen casualties. On October 30, the *Franklin* was hit, with thirty-three planes destroyed and seventy casualties. That same day, the *Belleau Wood* was hit by a suicide plane, with twelve planes lost and 146 casualties. On November 1, the destroyer *Claxton* unwillingly took a kamikaze aboard, and so did the destroyer *Ammen* and the destroyer *Abner Read* (which sank).

It was apparent that the Japanese were regrouping for another effort, with many planes being staged in through the pipeline and troops being landed on the western shore of Leyte at Ormoc Bay. That old hunting ground of the *Essex*, Bacolod air complex, had become a major base for the defensive effort. Halsey's reaction was to marshal his carrier forces again, leaving Bogan's force at Ulithi because of its battered carriers, and order a series of air strikes to once again knock out the Japanese air power in the Leyte region. The *Essex* was fueled on November 3, and the next day began a high speed run toward the central Philippines to start work on Luzon once more. On the way, the task group's cruiser *Reno* caught a torpedo and had to retire to Ulithi. In less than ten days, Admiral Sherman's task group had lost the use of two ships, the sunk *Princeton* and the damaged cruiser.

The *Essex's* day began on November 5, 1944, with a fighter sweep over the Manila area, so that Admiral Sherman could have a good idea of what to expect. The sweep involved fifty-two F6Fs from the *Essex,* the *Ticonderoga,* the *Langley,* and the *Lexington.* Lieutenant Commander Rigg led the whole group.

At Nichols Field, they saw a number of Japanese aircraft down on the deck and took after them. Lieutenant Overton saw two planes below him and attacked. They were army fighters, Nakajima-made, called by the Americans Oscars. One of them, the lower, was being chased by two F6Fs but they could not turn with the Japanese plane, and it came up toward Overton, who got in range, fired, and shot down the Oscar. It flamed briefly, then the wind blew out the fire, and it crashed into the ground and exploded.

Lieutenant Bare encountered a lone Kawasaki army bomber (called a Lily) just after he finished a strafing run on Nichols Field. He made several passes, while the bomber's pilot tried to get away. Finally the Lily crashed.

As soon as the fighters had finished their sweep, the air strike came in, with Commander McCampbell again functioning as target coordinator for the eighty-eight planes of the four carriers. The fighters had accomplished the objective set out for them: no Japanese aircraft disturbed the air strike, and this new set of fighters strafed and fired their rockets, and the bombers dropped their bombs on hangars, buildings, runways, and parked aircraft. They came away, having plastered the field very well and destroyed many planes.

Even though there were not many Japanese aircraft around Manila that morning, Commander McCampbell managed to find some. Over Subic Bay he encountered an Aichi bomber (Val) which came down from the clouds to attack. The bomber stayed low and managed to evade most of McCampbell's fire for a time, but then he got on its tail and one burst stopped the engine. The bomber made a water landing, but sank immediately, and there seemed to be no survivors.

Not long after this encounter, McCampbell saw a pair of Zero fighters, dead ahead, on an opposite course. McCampbell and his wingman, Lieutenant Rushing, had the advantage of altitude, so they rolled over and came down on the tails of the Zeros and just kept firing at both of them. McCampbell had his troubles. Four of his gun barrels burned out, and at the end he destroyed the Japanese plane with bullets from his port outboard gun, the only one still firing. Rushing was having some of the same trouble: after he shot down his Zero he had only two guns left. They saw another eight or nine Zeros in the area, but since they had very little weaponry, they did not go after them, and the Zeros left them alone.

McCampbell was hanging around the area, waiting for the second strike to come in. When it came—seventy-three planes from the four carrier force—it was a repeat of the first mission, with more tons of steel and explosive piled into the Nichols air base installations. But the *Essex* fighters had a little unusual excitement. After the air strike, the second division of four planes was suddenly jumped by half a dozen Japanese army fighters. But when the four American planes turned as one, and came at them, and shot down two of the Japanese fighters on the first pass, the enemy planes dispersed. These army aviators simply did not have the experience or the command of fighter technique to stay with the Americans.

Lieutenant Strane, back from his destroyer trip, shot down one Oscar, and Lieutenant Duffy shot down one Nick, the Kawasaki heavy army fighter. This day the torpedo planes did a lot of damage to Japanese parked aircraft. Lieutenants Bentz, Goodwin, and Deputy went down the east-west runway and dropped their bombs in a neat row alongside a dozen twin-engined planes. Lieutenants Crumley and Chaffe bombed a large concentration of planes at the south end of the field and strafed more.

After Commander McCampbell reported ruefully that his guns were practically out and that there were Zeros floating around the Manila area, the carrier sent up another air sweep, led by Lieutenant Commander Duncan. He started with seven planes, but the canopy of one fighter would not close, so the pilot had to return to the *Essex*. Then another pilot ran out of oxygen, and he had to turn back. At about this time, Duncan was finding the Japanese fighters over the Clark Field area. Almost immediately, one enemy plane blew the canopy sides out of another F6F, and that pilot had to go home. The other four fighters mixed it up with the Japanese.

Duncan saw two Nakajima army fighters (Tojos). They attacked first, making a high-side run, but over-ran, and Duncan turned to meet the leader. The Tojos pulled out and split, one making a chandelle turn to the right, and the other turning to the left and then coming at Duncan and his wingman, head-on. Duncan got in a short burst on the first one, but then a Zero came into the fight and made a run on his plane from the port quarter, pulled out and turned right. Duncan then saw his wingman, Lieutenant Bertschi, finish off one Tojo. Duncan got in several shots at the Zero, which burst into flame and exploded. "The usual flamer," said the jaded fighter pilot.

Lieutenant Twelves was scouting Clark Field, after the Helldivers had bombed, when his division was jumped by a pair of Tojos. Twelves turned into them, and then two more Tojos came down out of the clouds to join the fight. They had scarcely appeared when four Zeros came in. Twelves got a deflection shot on one Zero, and it smoked, burned, and crashed. Twelves was watching it fall when he felt his F6F being hit and saw tracers going over his wings. He had not been looking: his wingman's engine had acted up and he had fallen back and a band of five Zeros was after Twelves. He shot at one, it went up to 3,000 feet above him and dived on him. He turned into it and maintained the relative position, firing. The Zero fell away in flames, but Twelves in turning got into a spin and spun three times before getting out.

The Zero's wingman was now coming in so Twelves switched over to water injection for power and hit his flap switch. The F6F with flaps down performed beautifully with a Zero, he found. On one turn, Twelves pulled in too tight and went into a snap-roll, which may have confused the Zero pilot, whose fire was coming too close for comfort. The Zero went into a slow roll to get back in position, Twelves went for the deck with his engine wide open, and the F6F did what it always did so beautifully—sped down and away from the pursuing Zero.

Twelves's wingman, Ensign Self, had trouble with his plane all through the mission. He could get only about two-thirds power. He encountered four Tonys (army Kawasaki fighters), and they were after blood, perhaps sensing that this F6F did not have the power they usually saw. But he shot down one and, remembering every maneuver he had ever learned, managed to stunt and jink his way through the others and out to safety in a low cumulus cloud. He stayed in the cloud for a few minutes, and when he came out, the Japanese fighters were gone. He went home.

Ensign Bertschi was flying on Duncan's wing when his instinct told him to look up, and he saw several Tojos coming down on them at great speed. Bertschi and Duncan got in some bursts, then Duncan went after his Zero, and Bertschi went after a Tojo and shot one down. Bertschi rejoined Duncan, and they fought off several other attacks by groups of Japanese fighters. It was his very first mission.

So the pilots of Fighting Fifteen came home that day, to apologize for not having followed standard operating procedure, which was never, never to break away from the two-plane-section defensive posture. But all things considered, they had not done too badly, and most important, they all got home again. But the condition of the aircraft that had caused three planes to abort and one (Ensign Self's) to be what Lieutenant Commander Duncan called a "flying dud," something that could not be taken lightly. Obviously, the *Essex* needed a rest, and time to put the aircraft back together and to get new ones to replace the "duds" that had seen more than their share of combat. But the *Essex* was not to have a respite just yet.

On the air strikes, the pilots had noticed a larger number of ships in Manila Bay than usual, and when that word reached Admiral Sherman he ordered an attack on the shipping. So at 11:00 on the morning of November 5, ninety-eight fighters, dive bombers, and torpedo planes set out for Manila. Their targets were two destroyers and a cruiser. A dozen fighters led the way, and, when the strike was threatened by four Zeros, a division of fighters frightened them off. The fighters then went down to strafe the cruiser and the two destroyers, and to drop their bombs and fire their rockets. They did not claim any bomb hits (although they had several near misses), but did make several nice flame splashes on the destroyers with rockets.

Lieutenant Brodhead took the Helldivers in on this mission. They were assigned to strike the cruisers, and did, making three hits with 1,000-pound bombs out of seven dropped.

But the spectacular job this time was done by the torpedo bombers. Six of them came in. Lieutenant Commander Lambert's torpedo missed just astern of the ship, which was turning like a snake as they attacked. The Japanese captain was skillful, and he managed to evade four of the six "fish," but two of them got the cruiser, and one enormous explosion sent fire, smoke, and debris high into the air. The cruiser (she was the heavy cruiser *Nachi*) went dead in the water and settled down by the stern. She was sinking as they left the scene.

After a busy morning and lunch, Commander McCampbell was off again leading another seventy-two plane strike against Japanese shipping in Manila Bay. He took off at 1:00 to go in and coordinate the attacks from the different carriers. Lieutenant Commander Rigg's fighters and those of the *Lexington* and the *Ticonderoga* watched over the bombers and protected them from any air attack (there was none). Lieutenant John D. Bridgers was the mission commander of the Helldivers. They were assigned to a light cruiser, but could not find it beneath the clouds so they attacked a destroyer that was just moving through the Manila Harbor breakwater into Manila Bay. The destroyer began to take violent evasive action, which was fairly successful; although the seven bombers came down and dropped, there were no direct hits. But there were near misses and damage to the Japanese ship.

The *Essex* torpedo planes were told to attack the light cruiser that Commander McCampbell had seen between Cavite and the Manila breakwater. Only one pilot found this cruiser and went in. He was Lieutenant Cosgrove. As he approached, the anti-aircraft fire was intense, particularly so since he was the only attacker, and a burst killed his gunner, L.E. Dean. He had no way of telling, then, what happened to his torpedo, but when he returned to the *Essex* his fellow pilots cheered him with the thought that, even if it had missed the cruiser, it would have hit something—it was like shooting fish in a barrel, so crowded was the Japanese anchorage that day.

The other *Essex* torpedo planes found cargo ships for their torpedoes, but only Ensign P.J. Ward saw his torpedo hit; it sent up a geyser of water against the side of a big cargo ship.

Lieutenant Crittenden of the fighter squadron shot down one snoopy Judy who got in too close at the wrong time. Then the airmen of the *Essex* went home to the carrier. Crittenden and seven others had been "scrambled" in a hurry as an emergency combat air patrol because of reports that a Japanese air strike was coming in. It was true, Crittenden's Judy was part of it. Another plane splashed into the water not far from the *Essex*, and the Task Force flagship, the *Lexington*, was hit in the island structure by a Zero rigged up as a suicide plane.

Four of these suicide planes slipped through the combat air patrols and got inside the carrier screen. Three of them were shot down by anti-aircraft fire, but the fourth went straight into the island of the flagship, the *Lexington*, causing 187 casualties. Fires broke out, but the damage control teams worked energetically and no basic control weapons (such as the water injection system) were hit, so the fires were put out and the carrier was operating again within twenty minutes.

Another plane managed to get inside the *Essex* group's perimeter, but it was shot down by anti-aircraft gunners and splashed in the water not far from the carrier.

That night, the *Essex* sent out its night fighter patrol, armed with 250-pound bombs. Lieutenant J.C. Hogue and Ensign K.M. Roberts were catapulted from the flight deck. It was actually the early morning hours of darkness: 2:30 a.m. The purpose of this mission was to throw a monkey wrench into Japanese pre-dawn flight operations in the Manila area. The night fighting F6Fs had to be very careful; they were almost as likely to be shot down by their own forces as by the enemy.

They flew to the north tip of Polillo Island and then turned toward Manila. When they took off they turned on the radio signal (IFF) that identified them as American aircraft. When they were seventy-five miles out and clearly away from the U.S. forces, they turned the signals off. Virtually the entire flight was managed by radar navigation; Polillo Island came up quite clearly on the radar, but when they reached the

Manila area, the lights of the city and even the lights of radio tower showed them their position.

Lieutenant Hogue dropped his bomb on the runway at Nichols Field, and then the two planes strafed. During the strafing they saw a plane taxi across the field toward the runway that ran north and south. Ensign Roberts dropped his bomb, and they strafed the area, but they could not see much because of the deep shadows. They moved over to Neilson Field and strafed there, too; they saw about twenty twin-engined bombers parked near the runway. Lieutenant Hogue came back in for several strafing runs and hit many of the bombers. His plane was picked up by about ten searchlights, which stayed right on him until he dropped suddenly to 100 feet above the ground. They lost the F6F then; they focused straight up, and then they all went out, one by one.

The two night fighters met over Laguna de Bay and started for the base. As they did so, they saw lights going on at Manaluyong Airfield about five miles northeast of Neilson, and a white light moving along the runway. That would seem to indicate an aircraft taking off. Ensign Roberts made the attack. He swooped down just after the plane cleared the runway and made a turn to the left. He got on the tail and above, and fired a burst. Immediately the twin-engined Japanese aircraft (he never determined what sort) exploded, and he flew through the explosion, which caused considerable damage to both wings and the ailerons and elevator surfaces. The Japanese plane fell to the ground and started a grass fire that was still burning as they moved out of the area.

The two night fighters got separated and returned to the *Essex* individually (which was not regarded as standard procedure). On the way in they passed the outgoing fighter sweep, with Lieutenant Commander Duncan in the lead. Forty-eight F6Fs from the four carriers of Admiral Sherman's group were going back to the Manila area to hit those planes again. They found a pair of twin-engined Betty bombers just getting ready to take off, and they burned very quickly. Duncan's four-plane division also attacked the only aircraft they saw leaving the ground just then, a Fran—or Nakajima bomber. Lieutenant Commander Duncan took a shot, the Fran groundlooped and crashed, and no one got out.

At 6:10, the day's first air strike also left the *Essex,* with Commander McCampbell flying out in front as target coordinator. It was a dreadful day for attack, the clouds hung low and below the clouds the haze was thick, so visibility over the target was low. The target was Manila Bay shipping, and to attack the planes had to find holes in the cloud cover and then come through. The trouble was that the anti-aircraft gunners were keeping their eyes on the holes, and firing at anything that came through. Lieutenant Overton led the fighters in, and they claimed to have caused serious damage to a patrol boat in the middle of the harbor.

Lieutenant Bridgers led the nine *Essex* Helldivers. They had to use the glide bombing technique because the visibility was so poor, and even then they did not see what happened below with much clarity.

Lieutenant R.D. Cosgrove led the torpedo bombers, which were carrying bombs. They, too, used the glide bombing run. Lieutenant Goodwin claimed hits on one transport anchored just outside the breakwater, and said it was burning as he left the area. Other pilots claimed near misses on various ships.

But the Japanese war history, which is not known for partiality to the Japanese side in the matter of losses, says that no damage at all was done to the ships that day, and with the heavy overcast, none of the *Essex* pilots could really tell.

They did know one thing: Lieutenant William Rising's Helldiver was hit by anti-aircraft fire as he came in. He managed to continue flying across the harbor, skirt the Bataan Peninsula, and then turn west. Lieutenant Overton went down to accompany him and stayed with Rising until he was forced to make a water landing twenty-six miles off Sampoloc Point. The spot was marked, the rescue submarine was notified, and later in the day two Helldivers from the *Essex* made a special trip to the spot and found Rising and his gunner, John Ward Montgomery, sitting in their life raft, waving up at them. They dropped extra life rafts and supplies, and before they left the area had the comforting word that the rescue submarine was only twenty-one minutes away from the pair.

For obvious reasons Manila was not a good target that day so the next strike ordered by Admiral Sherman was on the shipping in Port Silanguin, Luzon, which was far enough away from the typhoon disturbances to give reasonable visibility. Commander McCampbell was target director again, under his eye seventy-eight planes moved to attack. The fighters strafed the cargo ships and smaller vessels. The bombers were able to dive this time through the thin cumulus cloud cover. The torpedo planes, again carrying bombs, used the glide approach. They claimed to have sunk at least two vessels and probably one other, and to have done serious damage to a number of others.

One more fighter sweep over Manila that day was to hit Clark Field, and Lieutenant Overton who led the flight claimed that at least a dozen Betty bombers were set afire. They were brand new planes, just ferried in from Japan, discernible as such by their lack of camouflage and prominence of shiny chrome. But for the most part, the strafing was difficult because the Japanese had begun to move their planes away from the air installations, even into the open fields, and to camouflage whole areas with netting. A division of the fighters went down to take a check on Rising and Montgomery in their raft. They were still floating around, but when the fighters raised the lifeguard submarine, the skipper reported that he was just fifteen minutes from rescue. The fighters were growing low on gas, so they went back to the *Essex*, believing the two pilots would be rescued.

Ensign W.B. Riffle did not make it, he ran out of gas a mile from the destroyer screen and had to ditch. He was picked up by a destroyer within a few minutes. Another of the fighters just back aboard was surveyed by the air officer, who looked at the engine, wings, and hydraulic system, all shot up by anti-aircraft fire, and ordered Bureau of Aeronautics aircraft number 58403 pushed over the side.

While the airmen had been over Luzon much of the day, the *Essex* had been at action stations a good part of the time because of the large number of "bogies" floating around the task group. Nor had the men of the *Essex* gotten much sleep in the last two days; on the night of November 5, while the night fighters were keeping up

Japanese airmen at Nichols Field, several night fighters and night bombers from the Japanese bases snooped around the task group, seeking an opening. The men of the *Essex* were at general quarters most of the night, so by the end of November 6, it was a weary carrier crew, as well as a weary air group, that knocked off for fueling and a break in the action. Admiral Sherman ordered retirement from the battle zone that night, and the next day in comparatively safe waters, the *Essex* fueled.

Sherman's group was certainly due for a blow, but they were not to have it yet. The army was still having difficulty in getting its land-based air program into action from Philippine fields, and so the carriers were stand-by for several days longer. The *Essex* was in "strategic support," which meant she had to be ready for action on very short notice, and on November 10 the notice came: the Japanese seemed to be reinforcing the Visayas. On the morning of November 11, a convoy of four large troop ships was sighted rounding Apale Point, on Leyte, bound for Ormoc and less than an hour away from there. The troop ships were supported by several destroyers.

The convoy was discovered by the early morning search, four teams of F6Fs, sweeping the Sibuyan, Visayan, and Camotes Seas.

Lieutenant Carr was not far from Ormoc Bay when he suddenly looked down and there were the transports and five destroyers, and one destroyer escort. As the American fighters appeared, the Japanese destroyers were formed in an ellipse around the transports, but as they saw the enemy, they moved outboard, putting up a smokescreen that was supposed to blow over the transports and conceal them from the air. Lieutenant Carr radioed the base and then kept in touch with the convoy as it moved. Five Zeros appeared, but they remained well off and did not try to attack.

Lieutenant Deming's search team did not find the convoy on its run, but did shoot up some small craft, and then went in to take a look at Legaspi Airfield. There Deming's fighter was so badly shot up by anti-aircraft guns that he had to make a water landing at Albay Gulf, where he was picked up by a native canoe. The men in the canoe and in others with it looked up and waved, and it seemed most likely that Deming had been rescued by friendly Filipinos. That was the pattern and had been since the early days of the invasion.

The last team was that of Lieutenant J.J. Collins and Lieutenant (jg) Thompson. Over northwest Leyte they encountered three unpainted aircraft. They were above and quite far out, and Collins looked hard; they looked like P-47 army fighters, and the leader was waggling his wings at them, which was supposed to be a signal of "friendlies." But as Collins looked the planes over, he caught sign of the red "meatballs" on the wings of the aircraft (none on the fuselage or tail), and just as the planes dropped their wingtanks he recognized them as Oscars (Nakajima army fighters).

The Oscars pulled up high and turned left, trying to gain altitude on the American fighters. But the best characteristic of the F6F was then used by Collins and Thompson: they dropped their belly tanks, shifted into full low propeller pitch, and turned on the water injection and low blower, to get the utmost power for climbing. Then they climbed to meet the Japanese fighters. Collins turned to the left and pulled up into the leading Oscar which tried to dive past him. He waited until it filled his gunsights—it was turning hard with him—and opened fire at 1,500 feet, with a full deflection shot, and then revised to a sixty-degree deflection shot. The tracers splashed into the Oscar's wing roots, and the Oscar spun into the water, followed closely by Thompson's Oscar, which left a great column of smoke in the air.

Earlier in the Philippines campaign, Commander McCampbell and other American pilots had been surprised to find the Japanese so lacking in aggression, particularly the army pilots. That certainly could not be said this day. Three Oscars dove down and caught Collins and Thompson from behind; the first Collins knew of it was when his F6F began bucking from the impact of shells. He looked around and saw an Oscar only 100 feet away, firing at him. He was lucky to have the seat armor at that moment. He pulled to the right and Thompson pulled to the left, and the Oscar zoomed away, just as another Oscar came in on a high-side run on Collins. He saw this one, turned into it, and the Oscar tried to dive under him. Collins rolled over and followed it down, shooting. The Oscar went into flames and crashed. Thompson was right next to Collins, and they were weaving, when another Oscar came in, and Collins got a deflection shot that made the engine smoke, and the Japanese fighter pulled away.

But back in the weave position, Collins noticed that Thompson's plane was smoking, and it started to nose over. Collins followed it, as the plane went down, down, down, still smoking from the port wing root. Another Oscar started a run on Collins, which he evaded, and still another ran in on Thompson. Collins pulled over, shot a burst, saw the tracers splash on the fuselage of the Oscar and the Oscar pulled away. Thompson's plane had started down from 8,500 feet; by the time it hit 3,000 feet the plane was almost vertical, and it continued in this position until it splashed with an enormous impact and sank.

Collins had followed; he looked in his rear view mirror and saw a pair of Oscars after him, one coming from the port and the other from the starboard. Back to water injection and heading for a cloud several miles away, he watched the Oscars. They were about 2,000 feet behind, traveling as he was at 320 knots, and not losing ground. But Collins made his cloud, ducked in, turned sharply into another cloud and came out the top to find his Oscars gone. He headed back to the *Essex*.

That morning, the second combat air patrol had some action as well. At 12:30 the third combat air patrol went aloft, and Lieutenant (jg) R.N. Stime, Jr., looked for enemy planes. "Looked" is not quite the word; the looking was done by the radar operators, who then gave the position, and the fighter director vectored the combat air patrol to intercept.

On this day, Stime was warned of a bogey at 6,000 feet coming in. It was a Judy, a Japanese dive bomber, and it was fast! The F6Fs chased, but the Judy kept gaining, until the pilot made the mistake of jinking, which slowed him down, and the F6Fs overtook him. All four of them made passes, and they all connected. When Stime got in close he could see that the Judy was full of holes, and the tail gunner's hatch was open, but there was no gunner at the gun. He had been either wounded or killed at some point in the action. The F6Fs continued to chase and fire, and eventually the Judy made a long flat glide and crashed in the water.

After the morning search, Commander McCampbell took the biggest bomber strike force the carrier group had yet launched out to hit the Japanese transports before they could land their troops at Ormoc. That landing represented something that had been building for days: the Japanese decision to fight the decisive battle of the Philippine archipelago at Leyte instead of at Luzon as originally planned in the Sho 1 operation. Everyone concerned knew the importance of stopping the Japanese reinforcements from reaching shore. So Admiral Sherman put together forty dive bombers and thirty-two torpedo bombers, with forty fighters also loaded with bombs.

This was far from the first convoy bringing troops to Ormoc. The landings had begun on October 23 and had continued every day or two since that time. A whole division of the Kwantung army from Manchuria (Japan's most celebrated troops) had already been landed on November 1. After that landing, the interdictions by American planes became more effective and no whole convoy got through, but this one on the 11th was very close to doing so. If these thousands of troops could get through, then the battle situation on Leyte would certainly change for the worse for the Americans.

Convoy Number Two, as it was called by the Japanese, consisted of six transports escorted by five destroyers—the *Shimakaze,* the *Hamanami,* the *Wakatsuki,* the *Naganami,* and the *Asashimo*—and the 30th Protective Force, a minesweeper unit.

On the night of November 10, the convoy had been sailing along on its route from Manila, trying to make up time because it was already long overdue. But that night the convoy slowed down under orders from the convoy commander. At 3:10 in the morning, the convoy was moving slowly when someone reported "fish" alongside the ship. They were just off Masbate Island.

Almost immediately thereafter the convoy was attacked by four American PT boats, but luckily for it all the torpedoes missed. There was one narrow escape: the *Shimakaze's* lookouts spotted a torpedo coming directly at one ship as the minesweepers were working. The warning gave the transport time to turn. One minesweeper was lost that night, but the rest turned around after the attack and left.

The convoy, otherwise, got safely through. But behind it came Convoy Number Three, pushing. At daybreak on November 11, Convoy Number Two was off the northwest point of Leyte Island, and it continued to head south. So far Convoy Number Two had been extremely lucky; on November 10 at about 10:45, a number of U.S. Army attack planes had flown over, but they were obviously on some other mission and did not stop to investigate or bother the convoy.

On the morning of the 11th, the convoy was moving at only 7.5 knots. The convoy commander estimated that they would arrive at Ormoc anchorage at noon, and from dawn on slowed or speeded up to keep that schedule. But at 8:30 that morning, the fireworks began. The convoy had been snooped by the *Essex* search and others. The first attack came from army planes, the Japanese reported. The *Essex* strike took off at 8:42 and reached the convoy at 10:30.

When Commander McCampbell and his planes arrived, the convoy was just rounding Apale Point into Ormoc Bay. In fact, Captain Oshima Ichitaro, aboard the destroyer *Asashimo,* could see the Ormoc anchorage ahead of them as the American planes swooped down. The convoy increased speed, and scattered, and began to put up a smoke screen. That was one of the jobs of the destroyers.

Commander McCampbell estimated that the Japanese were not five miles from the safety of anchorage—safety from storms, at least, if not from American aircraft. But there was no safety for Convoy Number Two. Below, McCampbell saw four large transports. He did not know it, but they were carrying provisions for a whole army division for three months, ammunition enough for an extended battle, and 6,000 troop reinforcements.

Commander McCampbell and the other three planes of his division orbited at 14,000 feet, while he directed the planes in the battle below. While McCampbell was circling, a Japanese army fighter—Oscar—appeared; McCampbell gave chase and caught up in about three minutes. Then he opened fire, and his first burst started the Oscar's engine smoking. The pilot twisted and turned and rolled, trying to get away, but McCampbell stuck right behind him and got in another burst. The Oscar tried harder to escape, but McCampbell got in more shots and this time either killed or wounded the pilot, so that the Oscar flew into the ground and exploded.

Meanwhile, a dozen fighters from the *Essex*, led by Lieutenant Commander Rigg, had escorted the bombers safely to the target, and looking around, and seeing no enemy aircraft, they went down to strafe and drop their 500-pound bombs. They concentrated on three of the four transports, attacking in formation by divisions. At the same time, the dive bombers were attacking, too, and the fighters made careful moves to await the dive bombers' first strikes. Then they went in.

The dive bombers sank one of the transports almost immediately. It happened so fast it was hard to believe. Commander McCampbell had assigned this leading transport to the Helldivers of the *Essex*, and Commander Mini, the strike leader, told his first division to go ahead from 15,000 feet. The second division was to follow, but there was no need. The first division sank the ship. Hurriedly, Commander McCampbell diverted the rest of the *Essex* dive bombers to the other transports, and they began the attack. They got four hits on the second transport and three hits on the third. But it was costly; the Japanese anti-aircraft gunners aboard the ships were well-trained, and their fire was devastating.

Lieutenant (jg) J.S. Foote's bomber caught fire in the bomb bay from the anti-aircraft shell explosions. He pulled out and seemed to gain altitude for about three seconds. But he must have been hit himself, for he nosed over and the plane headed for the water. Just before the plane crashed, when it was about thirty feet above the water, Gunner Schmidt jumped out and landed on his back. But then no one saw him again; the air was too full of action.

Ensign J.E. Avery must have been killed by anti-aircraft fire in his dive because his plane went straight in, with no attempt made to pull out. It splashed and burned.

Ensign M.G. Livesay released his bomb at 2,500 feet and seemed to be pulling out at 2,000 feet when his plane was visibly struck by anti-aircraft fire. It lurched, and went over on the port wing, and straight through the smoke screen, to land in the destroyer formation. There were no heads in the water.

Lieutenant (jg) D.R. Hall was hit during the attack, but still made a successful water landing south of the target area. He was rescued by natives in a canoe, and later picked up (along with his crewman) by a flying boat.

During the dive, Lieutenant J.W. Barnitz's plane was hit by anti-aircraft fire, and his gunner told him that he had been wounded. Barnitz recovered from the dive, and then headed directly for Tacloban Airfield, which had been captured by the Americans in the first hours of the Leyte campaign; he landed, dropped off the gunner for immediate medical attention, and then flew back to the carrier.

Lieutenant (jg) R.G. Brice's Helldiver was badly shot up, but Brice managed to fly it back to the carrier disposition, and made a water landing near the *Essex*. He and his gunner were picked up by a destroyer and returned to the ship.

By taking the brunt of the anti-aircraft fire, the Helldivers must have saved the fighters and the torpedo bombers, because they came off very easily. Lieutenant Commander Lambert, the leader of the torpedo bombers, took them in on the usual glide pattern. Once again they were carrying bombs, not torpedoes. By the time they arrived on the scene, the first transport was sinking so they attacked the other three. They secured hits on numbers two and three and near misses on the fourth transport.

Then, fighters, dive bombers, and torpedo bombers all headed for the rendezvous point, where the first planes to arrive would circle until the rest came in, and then the whole contingent would go back to the base. But as the rendezvous began, so did Japanese air action. Lieutenant (jg) R.E. Foltz had just finished the important task of photographing the targets after the attack, for interpretation by the intelligence officers, when the word came that the rendezvous circle was alive with "rats"—Japanese fighters.

Foltz and his wingman sped from the scene of the convoy attack to the rendezvous point, and almost there, Foltz saw an Oscar at 8,000 feet. He pulled up and got a shot, and the Oscar began to smoke, but at that moment he felt his plane shudder; another Oscar was attacking him. The two planes came at one another head-on, then Foltz pulled up, and as he passed over the Oscar he saw it smoking. It did not burn, but went into the water trailing smoke.

Ensign Frazelle, who was covering the photographic plane, stayed with Foltz until he saw another Oscar come after the photo plane. He took after it, the Oscar ducked into a cloud, and Frazelle went to the top and lurked. When the Oscar came out, Frazelle got on its tail before the pilot could see him. He began firing and fired steadily until the Oscar flipped over and dove into the sea from 2,000 feet, and crashed with an enormous splash.

Lieutenant Milton also tangled with the Japanese army fighters in the area. He shot down one. Lieutenant Nall ran into a pair of them and shot down one. Lieutenant Berree was retiring from his bombing run in the F6F when he saw Nall's other Oscar and shot it down.

Ensign Smith was having trouble with his F6F during the bombing run. The heater wouldn't work, and the windshield fogged up. He opened the hood to clear it as he came out of his bombing run, and there, over his shoulder, was an Oscar. In fact, as he looked he saw a sky full of Oscars. One of them peeled off and began a "beautiful" (Smith's word) run on Smith. He could either run or turn into the enemy, and he did the latter, firing steadily as the Japanese plane marched right into his gun pattern. Another Oscar turned in front of Smith and he tried a very long deflection shot using an enormous amount of ammunition. To his surprise, the Oscar rolled over on its back and went into the water like and arrow.

Ensign Lemley found an Oscar for himself and followed it, shooting steadily, until the plane crashed.

So the mission ended for the airmen of the *Essex*. When they returned to the carrier and the reports were made out, for the first time in their battle history one section of the action report was filled:

VII. PERSONNEL CASUALTIES . . .

a No.	b Squadron	c Name and Rank or rating	d Cause	e Condition or Status
1	VB-15	Lt. John Storrs Foote A-V (N) USNR	enemy AA	Killed in action
1	VB-15	Norman Woodrow Schmidt ARM2c USNR	"	"
2	VB-15	Ens. John Avery, A-V (N) USNR	"	"
2	VB-15	Alfred Theodore Graham, Jr. ARM3c USNR	"	"
3	VB-15	Ens. Melvin Gray Livesay, A-V (N) USNR	"	"
3	VB-15	Charles Ernest Swihart ARM2c USNR	"	"
*4	VB-15	Lt. (jg) David Rogers Hall A-V (N) USNR	"	Water landing, believed friendly hands
*4	VB-15	Oscar Coleman Adams, ARM3c USNR	"	*Subsequently rescued by AV
5	VB-15	Lt. (jg) Robert Greenleaf Brice A-V (N) USNR	"	Rescued by DD uninjured
5	VB-15	Louis James Penza ARM2c USNR	"	"
6	VB-15	Herbert Neal Stienkemeyer ARM3c USNR	"	wounded leg and hand, not serious
10	VF-15	Ens. R.W.N. Erickson USNR	"	Rescued uninjured by DD

This casualty report was most unsettling, particularly to the enlisted men of VB-15, the Helldiver squadron, whose major complaint had always been that they were at the mercy of their pilot and if he goofed, they died. That feeling is more understandable when one examines that casualty report and sees that all the casualties that day were USNR—United States Naval Reserve—which meant "hostilities only" sailors and airmen, who had interrupted the threads of their civilian life to go to war against an enemy who had attacked the United States.

The weight of the list represents the weight of the service by the autumn of 1944: the vast majority of young men in uniform then were civilians-gone-to-war. The regulars had taken their hard knocks; Commander Brewer, for example, was the second to fall. But the regulars had to expect possible death as the price of their careers in the service; some of the volunteers, particularly the enlisted men, were not sanguine about the prospects.

A rebellion began on the flight deck, so to speak. The gunners of VB-15—or a number of them—decided they would not fly again under these dangerous conditions. When the matter was brought to Commander Mini's attention, he was not sure what should be done—this sort of rebellion was a court-martial offense and could be punished by death (cowardice in the face of the enemy). Commander Mini consulted with Commander McCampbell, who did not want his men's blood, but a solution.

"Tell them they are not going to fly any more, then." he said. "Take away their flight papers." (That also meant the end of flight pay for those concerned—a ten percent bonus.)

So Commander Mini announced that even if the gunners did not fly, the Helldivers would fly with empty back seats, but they would fly and bomb and fight the enemy. The announcement silenced the rebellion.

As for Japanese Ormoc Convoy Number Two, its situation became desperate when the first flight of American bombers appeared at 8:30 on the morning of November 11. No one had remembered that it was international Armistice Day, the holiday celebrating the end of the 1914-1918 "War to End all Wars." Thousands of Japanese men and boys were dying in the water that morning.

By Japanese count, the convoy was attacked by 260 aircraft. By American count, 347 carrier planes were involved from three groups of Admiral Halsey's Third Fleet. The Japanese can be pardoned for erring in their estimate, for they were much too busy down there to have much time to count.

The first ship to come under attack was the destroyer *Shimakaze,* the flagship of the little fleet. Then the ships went down one after the other: all four transports, with their thousands of pounds of supplies and their thousands of troops. Of the troops aboard, only 2,000 managed to get ashore or be saved. The destroyer *Hamanami* came under fire but managed to evade bombs for a time, but the four transports were soon gone, and then the *Naganami,* the *Shimakaze,* and the *Wakatsuki.* The smoke screen, which was to prevent all this, blew harmlessly away across the land.

One of the few survivors of the naval vessels was Captain Oshima of the *Hamanami,* which somehow managed to thread its way through the rain of bombs and rockets until one bomber dropped squarely on the bow.

Captain Oshima had been worried about an air attack all morning, and especially after the convoy entered the narrow waters between Ponson Island and Ormoc. When it started, he had been able to maneuver through the destruction, until a near-miss jammed the ship's rudder. After that, the *Hamanami* was a slowly-moving duck as far as the bombers were concerned. It was only moments until another bomber dropped a 500-pound bomb squarely on the forward turret, destroying it and knocking out all the anti-aircraft guns forward. Next came a bomb on the bridge, which smashed through "officer's country" and the wardroom, killing many of the officers at their posts. Captain Oshima was so battered by the shock that he was half senseless, although he had no blood wounds. When he next looked at his watch, he saw that it had stopped at 11:45, the moment of the bomb impact.

From then on, the time was simply a gray void for Captain Oshima, and he remembers only that somehow the destroyer *Asashimo* managed to bring her bow alongside the sinking ship, and that he got aboard, as did a handful of others. The *Asashimo* then managed to evade the remaining aircraft and get out into the open sea to head for Manila.

But Convoy Number Two was a dead loss, and in the official records in Tokyo the Imperial General Staff made the notation: killed in action.

On November 12, the *Essex* fueled, along with other ships of the Sherman task group. Admiral Halsey was eager to leave the waters of the Philippines to the army air forces and head for Japan. The reasoning was sound, as postwar evaluation of Japanese air strength showed, but the situation in the Philippines was not nearly as settled and positive as General MacArthur indicated in his communiqués. The fact was that the Japanese air pipeline was working very well, and, as the American airmen had noticed in recent weeks, the quality of Japanese fighter pilots—particularly army pilots—had improved considerably since the days of the invasions of Palau and Leyte. What was left of the first team was being thrown into the Philippines.

General MacArthur insisted that he must have the services of the Third Fleet to pound the enemy. For some reason, the army air force's ability to bring aircraft and services up to Leyte just did not exist. A handful of fighters came in, and the Japanese records are filled with reports of raids by B-24s on Luzon and other targets, but they did not seem to be as effective as the close, pinpoint bombing of the carrier planes.

All these arguments were made to Admiral Halsey, and he had to agree, much as he hated having the task force carriers used as troop support. That, he had always said, was the job of the escort carriers; the job of the task force was to cripple the enemy before he could strike.

On November 11, as his aviators were knocking out the Ormoc convoy, Admiral Halsey agreed that the Third Fleet should remain longer in Philippine waters, and so informed Admiral Nimitz. The answer would not be to take the carriers out of service, rest them, and then strike Japan. The answer would be to change carrier air groups in mid-passage and continue the fight off Leyte and Luzon. It would not be long before the airmen of the *Essex* would be going home.

But on November 13, they were back at the attack. The first priority was to be shipping that could reinforce the Leyte defenses, and much of that shipping came to Leyte from Japan by way of Manila Bay. So the *Essex's* first strike on the morning of November 13 was to be against ships and dock facilities in that area.

Commander McCampbell led the way, as was usual these days, with his fighter division. He would act as coordinator and director of the strike of the *Essex,* the *Ticonderoga,* and the *Langley.* At 8:00 in the morning, the strike began with the fighters going down alongside the bombers, since there was no air opposition that day. The *Essex* group was the first to attack the shipping.

The Helldivers peeled off from 15,000 feet and dropped to 2,500 feet to release their bombs. Commander Mini got a hit on a 10,000-ton cargo ship, and so did Lieutenant (jg) T.A. Woods and Lieutenant (jg) L.E. Nelson. They sank the ship. Lieutenants (jg) W.P. Kelley and R.L Turner did the same to another 10,000-ton freighter, and it burned and sank. Lieutenant J.W. Barnitz and Lieutenant (jg) F.S. Matthews bombed a 6,000-ton freighter and saw it sinking also. Other planes of the *Essex* damaged and burned and sank another half dozen vessels. The torpedo planes bombed the old Dollar Line Pier, set it afire from end to end, and sank a large cargo ship that was tied up there.

The only plane casualty was the TBF of Lieutenant (jg) Otto R. Bleech, which was badly hit by anti-aircraft fire. The oil system was damaged, and Bleech reported his oil pressure dropping sharply. There was nothing to be done but make a water landing in Manila Bay, which was anywhere but the best place to be that day. But down they went, the three men of the TBF, and Bleech made an excellent water landing in the northern part of the bay. At least that gave them a chance to fall into friendly hands. They climbed out of the sinking airplane, and into their three-man raft.

Almost immediately, a number of sailboats in the harbor began to head toward the yellow raft. The fighter pilots saw this and flew down to strafe, warning the sailboats away. Lieutenant (jg) R.E. Foltz spotted a Tony (Kawasaki army fighter) and gave chase. He overhauled the Japanese plane and shot it down. But then the planes of the *Essex* went back to the carrier, not knowing what had happened to Lieutenant Bleech, Gunner T.M. Barber, and Radio Operator W.J. Gormley. On the report, no one wanted to list them as missing in action, so it was simply said that they were last seen in a rubber boat with sailboats approaching.

Before this air strike returned to the carrier, Admiral Sherman sent out a fighter sweep of twenty-four planes, eight of them from the *Essex,* to see what was happening around the Clark air base complex outside Manila. They found a few aircraft parked on Mabalacat Airfield and strafed them, and they came down they saw that the Japanese had been busy camouflaging their aircraft dispersal areas. Only two of the planes they strafed burned, which meant that the Japanese were degassing their planes, or that some of them were decoys, which proved to be true.

At noon, Lieutenant Commander Lambert led a seventy-six plane strike from the three carriers, the *Essex,* the *Ticonderoga* and the *Langley,* against Manila Bay shipping a second time. Once again the dive bombers took the worst beating. The anti-aircraft guns concentrated on them, it seemed. They attacked two large merchant ships, one cruiser, and two destroyers. They did sink the light cruiser *Kiso* and did considerable damage to a pair of destroyers, but, in attacking one of them, Lieutenant Noyes's plane was shot down and went straight into the water, burning. Noyes and Gunner P.H. Sheehan were killed.

Lieutenant (jg) W.L. Moore and Gunner T.R. Forrest made a water landing after the plane's rudder jammed on the way home, knowing it would have been nearly impossible to land safely on the carrier. They were picked up by a destroyer.

In the afternoon, another fighter sweep in the Clark base area confirmed the belief that the Japanese were constantly bringing in new aircraft along the island chain. The *Essex* and the *Ticonderoga* fighters strafed Bamban Airfield, where a few days—even hours—ago there was nothing, and saw at least twenty parked aircraft. Some were dummies, but more planes were concealed around the revetments and even off the field. They could only get one to burn, and that one might well have been a dummy.

The real air action that day for the fighters was that of the combat air patrol. Beginning at 7:30 in the morning, the Japanese began trying to get at Admiral Sherman's carriers. Lieutenant J.C.C. Symmes shot down a Watanabe seaplane (Jake) on the edge of the American ships formation. Later in the day Lieutenant Carr's group shot down another plane, a Nakajima reconnaissance plane (Myrt). Late in the afternoon, just before dark, three more Japanese planes were shot down; none of them had gotten anywhere near the carriers.

At the end of November 13, the airmen of the carriers had every right to feel proud of a job well done, and to the Japanese the whole day had turned out to be another in a series of nightmares. Summing up the events of the past three days, the Japanese high command saw nothing but disaster to report. The cruiser *Kiso* was sunk, along with half a dozen destroyers. The whole aviation complex south of Manila had been attacked repeatedly, and the air action was so powerful that half a dozen kamikaze planes that had taken off from the Clark Field complex turned back and landed without making any air strikes.

The damage to ships and dock facilities in Manila Bay was enormous and disturbing to the Japanese. The destroyers *Akebono*, *Akishimo*, *Kiyoshima*, and *Hatsuhara* had all been bombed and strafed, and all but the *Akishimo* had sunk. The *Akishimo's* damage was so great, though, that the Japanese wrote her off as well. They also wrote off the seven transports, four of 10,000 tons, and all the precious war cargo they had been carrying, most of which was destined for the Leyte front.

In fact, at the end of November 13, the high command declared a crisis in transportation in the Philippines.

On November 14 the Americans were back again over Manila Bay in force. Commander McCampbell was strike coordinator for ninety-two planes from the *Essex*, the *Ticonderoga* and the *Langley*, an attack force that left the carriers just after dawn. It was a hazy day, and many air groups were attacking at the same time, so it was hard to see the damage. That, and the fact that there were already so many sunk or sinking ships in Manila Bay, made the strike seem less effective than that of the previous day.

Commander McCampbell engaged a number of Japanese army fighters (Oscars) that day, but did not get involved in protracted combat with any of them since it was his job to direct the whole strike. Only at the end of the attack did he go after one seriously, and he shot it down in flames. Ten Helldivers made the dive bombing attack, and nine came through with very little damage, but Lieutenant (jg) Raymond L. Turner's plane was hit in its dive and went right on into the sea, killing Turner and Gunner Simon Dorosh.

The second air strike that day was even less spectacular. The ship to which the dive bombers were assigned was already sitting on the bottom of Manila Bay, its decks half awash, and it was hard to see what further damage the bombers did, since the ship did not burn. The other targets were buildings at Cavite and oil tanks along the docks. Once again, so many aircraft from so many groups were attacking at once that it was impossible for the pilots to tell whose bomb did what. But at least this time the antiaircraft fire was negligible, which was a nice way to end a tour of combat duty.

For that is what the airmen of the *Essex* did that day. The whole task force steamed off to the east, but Admiral Sherman's task group continued to Ulithi. The war would go on, and Task Force 38 and the Third Fleet of which it was so vital a part would not stop smashing the Japanese, but Admiral Sherman's group was due for a break at the big naval base, and Carrier Air Group Fifteen was due for a real blow. Indeed, the men were going home for leave and reassignment. They left the *Essex* on November 18 and transferred to the *Bunker Hill,* which was heading for Pearl Harbor and Bremerton, Washington. Just before the *Bunker Hill* left Ulithi, Lieutenant Van Altena, who had been shot down off Formosa, rejoined the squadron.

There were a few anxious hours when a Japanese submarine which had slipped in past the harbor defenses torpedoed a tanker next to the *Bunker Hill.* All day long on November 20, destroyers and escorts ranged the harbor dropping depth charges.

Then, on November 20, the ship sailed, and the airmen of Carrier Air Group Fifteen were on the high seas, heading home, when the *Essex* took her first kamikaze aboard on November 25, at the cost of fifteen casualties. But by this time Commander McCampbell and his men had left the war behind for awhile, and their thoughts had turned toward home.

The war and all its troubles now belonged to the airmen of Carrier Air Group Four.

EPILOGUE

Commander McCampbell went on to a distinguished career, or perhaps I should say a more distinguished career, in the Navy. He was awarded the Congressional Medal of Honor for his actions on October 24, when he shot down nine Japanese fighters of that great attack force that came to destroy the American carriers off the Philippines. Eventually he commanded his own carrier, the *Bonhomme Richard,* and finally, as a captain, he retired from the service to live in Florida.

There were many medals and many distinguished careers for the men of the original Air Group Fifteen, and they cannot all be detailed here, though all are worthy.

Most remarkable about the history of Carrier Air Group Fifteen during this brief period (May-November, 1944) is the amount of damage the airmen did to the Japanese war effort, and the relatively minor destruction and casualties inflicted on the American side. Not one bombing pilot of the dive bomber squadron or torpedo squadron was lost due to enemy aircraft, because of the jealous shepherding of the fighters of Fighting Fifteen. During the "Marianas Turkey Shoot" on June 19, 1944, the aviators of the *Essex* shot down sixty-seven Japanese planes and were credited with another "half" an airplane, sharing the kill with a pilot from another carrier. They also damaged more and laid claim to a dozen of them.

The *Essex* planes sank or damaged 560,000 tons of enemy shipping. That is the equivalent of fifty-six Liberty ships, which were the standard 10,000-ton American cargo vessels that carried the war against Japan. The fighters also protected their own ship so that she never received a scratch while they were aboard, although not quite as much could be said for the task group as a whole, which lost the *Princeton* to a Japanese bomb and saw the *Reno* go out of action (from a submarine torpedo) and the *Lexington* take a kamikaze aboard that did serious damage to the island.

The fighter squadron claimed between 600 and 700 planes destroyed, half of them in the air. Among the fighter pilots, twenty-six qualified as "aces," which meant they shot down, in the air, at least five enemy aircraft; several of them—McCampbell, Berree, Duncan, Carr, Pigman, Rigg, Rushing, Self, Singer, Strane, and Twelves—shot down many, many more.

The fighter squadron also claimed to have sunk nine warships, ranging from a destroyer to a PT boat, to have damaged six warships so badly that they probably sank, and to have inflicted serious damage on another twenty-six enemy warships, ranging from a battleship to a PT boat again, and including three carriers and the strange half battleship-half carrier *Ise*. The squadron lost seven pilots in operational accidents, six killed in action, thirteen missing in action, and had ten men wounded in action.

The Helldiver squadron took the worst beating in terms of casualties, with seventeen pilots and fifteen crewmen killed or missing in action. (The discrepancy between pilots and crewmen lost occurred because two pilots were killed flying F6Fs after they were converted into fighter-bomber pilots.)

The dive bomber squadron claimed to have sunk or damaged seventeen warships, definitely to have sunk one carrier in the battle of Engano Point with eight bomb hits, and to have sunk twenty-one cargo vessels and damaged another fifty.

The torpedo squadron's results were harder to assess, since much of the time this squadron's targets were shore installations, whose destruction was imperative, but whose tallying did not lend itself to neat columns of figures. There were few attacks with torpedoes because the operations of the *Essex* did not offer many torpedo targets, but, as noted, against the one big convoy the torpedo pilots did perform as best they knew how.

Altogether Carrier Air Group Fifteen chalked up a remarkable record during those six months of combat; and if one multiplies that record by nine (the number of fleet carriers in Task Force 38), and then adds about half as much again for the eight light carriers, and tops it all off with the strong performance of eighteen escort carriers, the result gives an idea of the enormous striking power of the naval carrier forces at this point in the Pacific war.

It was small wonder that the Japanese felt completely overwhelmed. From the Marianas operation on until the end of the war, the carriers played a major offensive role in the victory that was finally won. By August, 1945, before the dropping of the atomic bomb, Japanese defense installations in Formosa and in most of the outer islands were in shambles. Japanese shipping, courtesy of the carriers and the American submarines, was almost non-existent. The airmen of the *Essex* and of all the other carriers had every right to be proud.

INDEX

INDEX